11+ Non-Verbal Reasoning

For GL Assessment

When it comes to 11+ preparation, nothing beats practice — and this CGP book is packed with the best practice you'll find, all at the perfect level for ages 10-11.

It starts with questions that focus on one concept at a time, so children can really get to grips with each crucial skill. Once they're confident, there's a selection of mixed-topic Assessment Tests to help them get used to the style of the real 11+ papers.

We've also included fully explained answers at the back of the book. Everything you need!

How to access your free Online Edition

This book includes a free Online Edition to read on your PC, Mac or tablet. You'll just need to go to **cgpbooks.co.uk/extras** and enter this code:

0544 9850 5775 4214

By the way, this code only works for one person. If somebody else has used this book before you, they might have already claimed the Online Edition.

Practice Book – Ages 10-11

with Assessment Tests

How to use this Practice Book

This book is divided into three parts — Spotting Patterns, Spatial Reasoning* and Assessment Tests. There are also answers and detailed explanations at the back of the book.

*Not all GL Assessment Non-Verbal Reasoning tests will include Spatial Reasoning questions — it depends on the region in which your child is sitting the test. If you are in a region that does not test Spatial Reasoning, then you can ignore the questions on p.14-21, as well as Assessment Test 6 (p.82-93).
For more information on test content in different regions, please visit cgpbooks.co.uk/11plus.

Spotting Patterns

- Each section contains practice questions focusing on one of the main concepts your child will need to understand for the Non-Verbal Reasoning test.
- These pages can help your child build up the different skills they'll need for the real test.
- Your child can use the smiley face tick boxes in this section and in the Spatial Reasoning section to evaluate how confident they feel with each topic.

Spatial Reasoning

- This part concentrates on the skills your child will need to tackle the Spatial Reasoning questions that are tested in some regions.

Assessment tests

- The third part of the book contains six assessment tests, each with a mix of question types. They take a similar form to the real test.
- You can print multiple-choice answer sheets so your child can practise the tests as if they're sitting the real thing — visit cgpbooks.co.uk/11plus/answer-sheets or scan the QR code.
- Use the printable answer sheets if you want your child to do each test more than once.
- If you want to give your child timed practice, give them a time limit of 30 minutes for each test, and ask them to work as quickly and carefully as they can.
- Tests 1-5 get progressively harder, so don't be surprised if your child finds the later ones more tricky.
- Your child should aim for a mark of around 85% (48 questions correct) in each test. If they score less than this, use their results to work out the areas they need more practice on.
- If they haven't managed to finish the test in time, they need to work on increasing their speed, whereas if they have made a lot of mistakes, they need to work more carefully.
- Keep track of your child's scores using the progress chart at the back of the book.

Answer Sheets

Published by CGP

Editors:
Chris Burton, Ceara Hayden, Kirstie McHale, Anthony Muller and Luke von Kotze

With thanks to Rebecca Tate and Judy Hornigold for the proofreading.
With thanks to the moderators of ElevenPlusExams.co.uk for their input.

ISBN: 978 1 78908 163 3
Printed by Elanders Ltd, Newcastle upon Tyne
Clipart from Corel®

Based on the classic CGP style created by Richard Parsons

Text, design, layout and original illustrations © Coordination Group Publications Ltd. (CGP) 2019
All rights reserved.

Photocopying this book is not permitted, even if you have a CLA licence.
Extra copies are available from CGP with next day delivery • 0800 1712 712 • www.cgpbooks.co.uk

Contents

Tick off the check box for each topic as you go along.

Spotting Patterns

Spatial Reasoning

Assessment Tests

Shapes

Most questions will be based around shapes, so you need to get to know them.

Warm Up

1. How many **sides** does each shape have?

a. b. c. d. e. f.

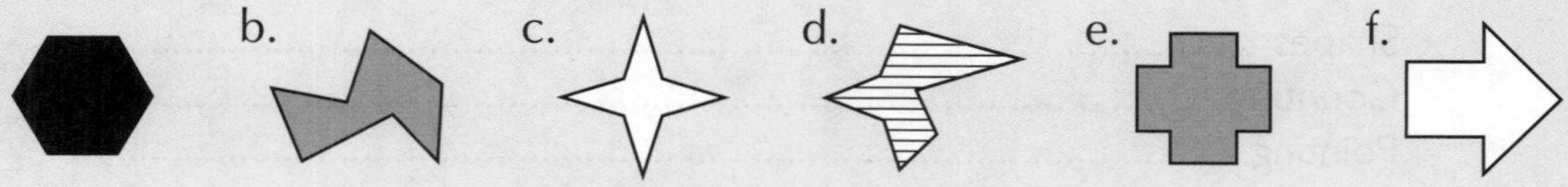

___ ___ ___ ___ ___ ___

2. How many **lines of symmetry** does each shape have?

a. b. c. d. e. f. g.

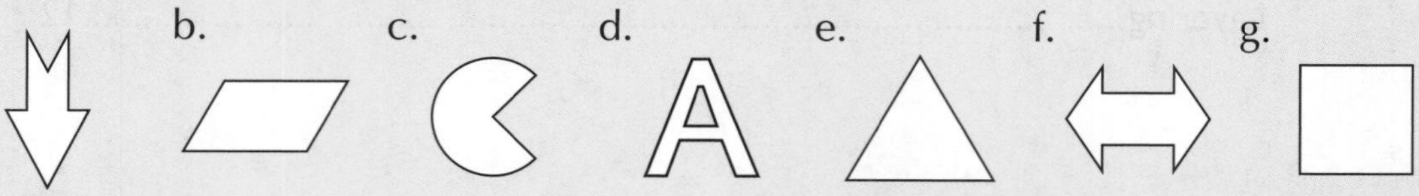

___ ___ ___ ___ ___ ___ ___

Odd One Out

Look at the five figures below. Find which figure is most unlike the others.

Example:

a b c d e (C)

C is the only figure with an inner shape that isn't identical to its outer shape (apart from size and shading).

3.

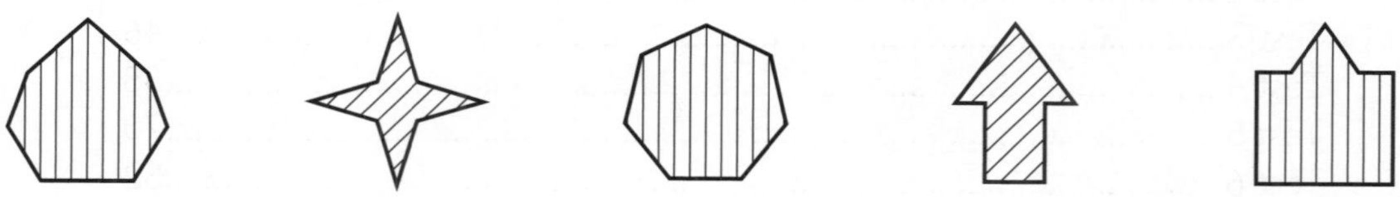

a b c d e (___)

4.

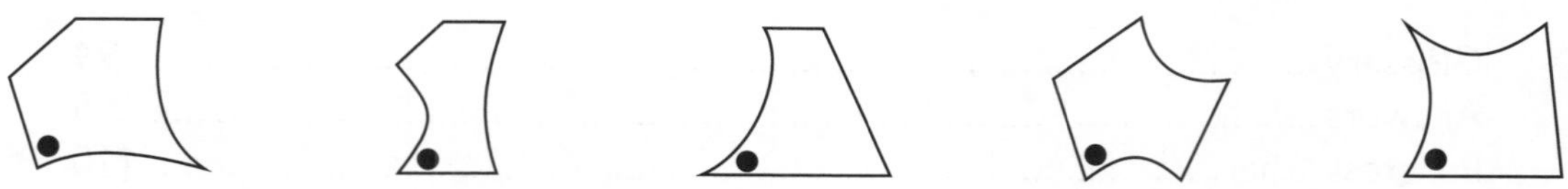

a b c d e (___)

5.

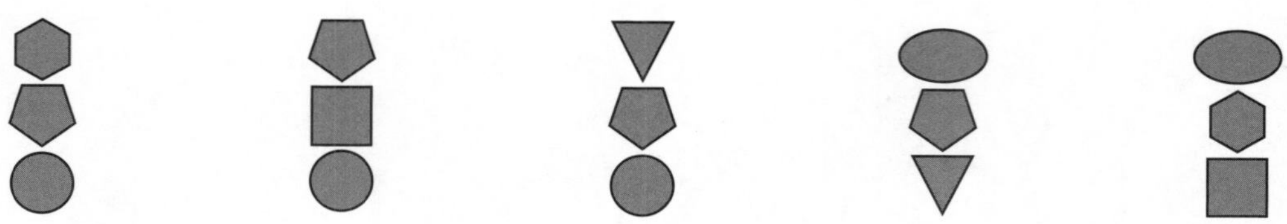

a b c d e (___)

Counting

If in doubt, count everything — shapes, sides or lines. It might give you a clue to the answer.

Warm Up

1. How many **points** do each of the stars below have?

a. b. c. d. e. f. g.

____ ____ ____ ____ ____ ____ ____

2. How many of these shapes have an **odd number** of dots?

Number of shapes with an **odd** number of dots: ____

Horizontal Code

In the boxes on the left are shapes with code letters. The top letters have a different meaning from the bottom ones. Work out how the letters go with the shapes and then find the code for the new shape from the five codes on the right.

Example:

a b c d e (d)

G means one grey section. K means eight sections in total.

3.

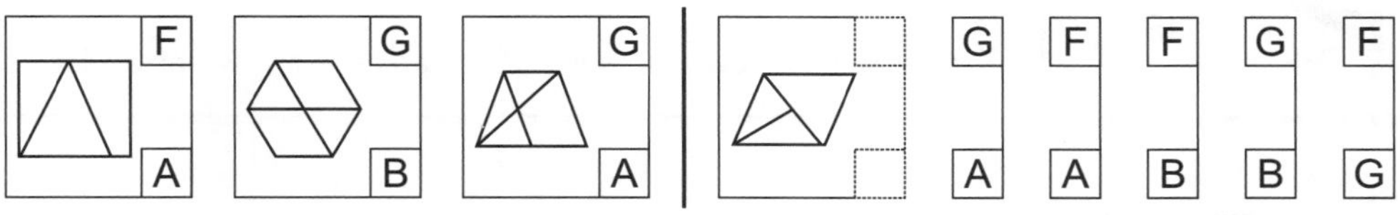

a b c d e (____)

4.

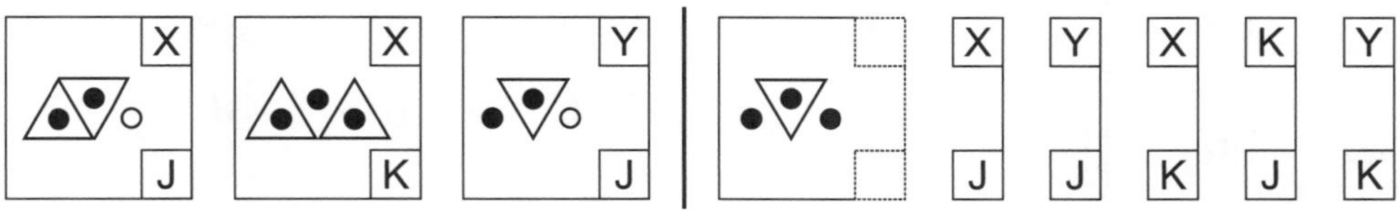

a b c d e (____)

5.

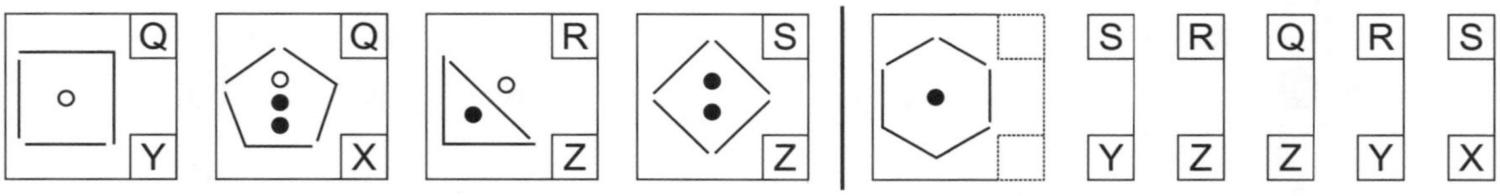

a b c d e (____)

Pointing

You should always check what an arrow is pointing at, and in which direction it's pointing.

Warm Up

1. How many of these arrows are pointing **clockwise** in each figure?

a. b. c. d. e. f. g.

a. ____ b. ____ c. ____ d. ____ e. ____ f. ____ g. ____

2. In each figure are there more arrows pointing **left** than **right**?

a. b. c. d. e. f. g.

a. ____ b. ____ c. ____ d. ____ e. ____ f. ____ g. ____

3. Which **direction** are most of the arrows pointing?
Which type of **shape** has the most arrows pointing at it?

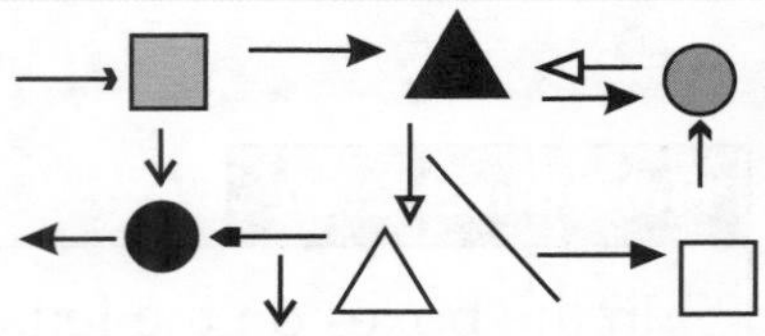

Most common **direction**: ________

Type of shape: ________

Vertical Code

On the left are shapes with code letters that describe them. You need to work out what the code letters mean. There is then a shape on its own next to a choice of five codes. Work out which code describes this shape.

Example:

 JR

 KR

 JS

JS	KS	JR	KR	JR	
a	**b**	**c**	**d**	**e**	(b)

K means the arrow points left. S means the arrow has a black shape.

4.

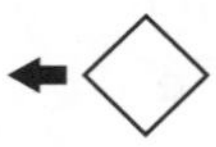 TP

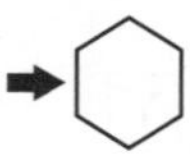 SP

 SR

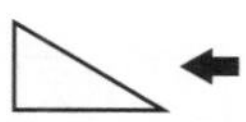

TR	SP	VP	SR	TP	
a	**b**	**c**	**d**	**e**	(____)

5.

 JX

 KX

 KY

JX	JK	KY	KX	JY	
a	**b**	**c**	**d**	**e**	(____)

6.

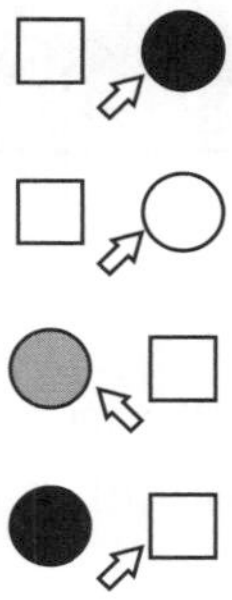

BG

BH

BF

CH

BG	CG	CH	BH	CF	
a	**b**	**c**	**d**	**e**	(____)

7.

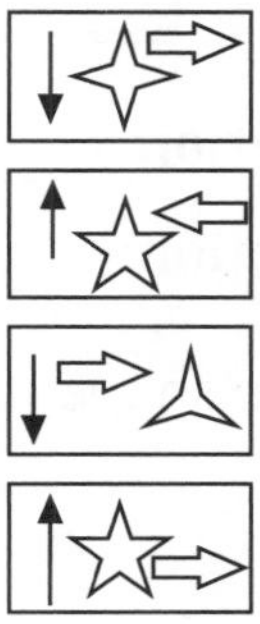

JM

KN

JM

KM

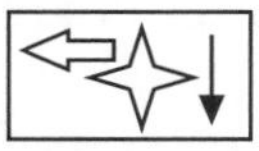

KN	JM	JN	JK	KM	
a	**b**	**c**	**d**	**e**	(____)

Find the Figure Like the First Two

Find the figure on the right that is most like the two figures on the left.

Example:

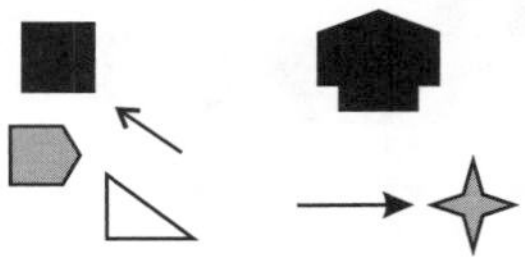

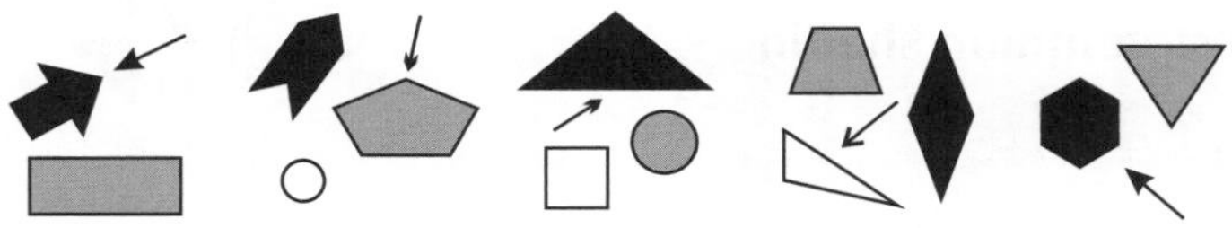

a **b** **c** **d** **e** (*e*)

All figures must have an arrow pointing at an even-sided shape.

8.

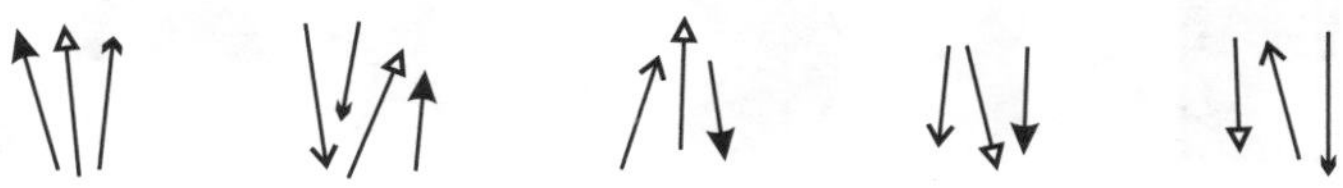

a **b** **c** **d** **e** (____)

9.

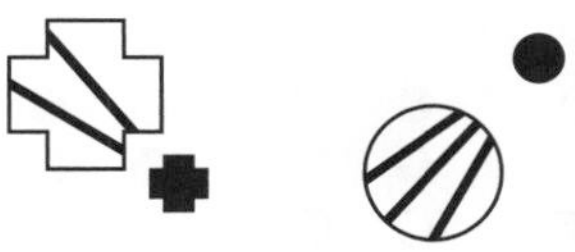

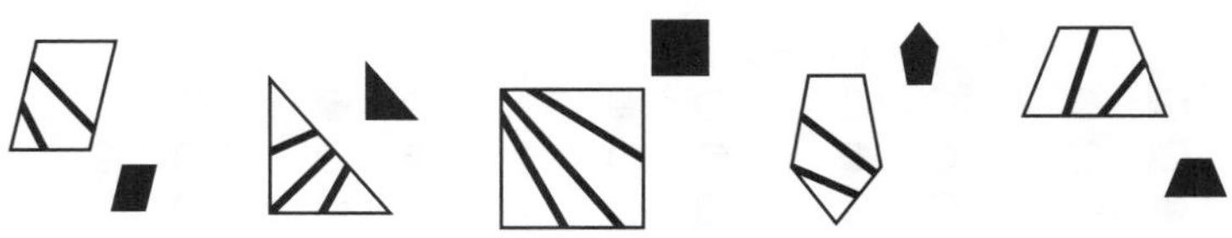

a **b** **c** **d** **e** (____)

10.

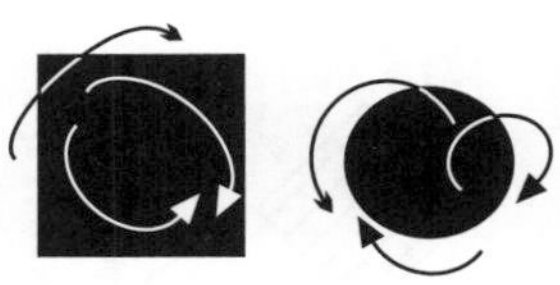

a **b** **c** **d** **e** (____)

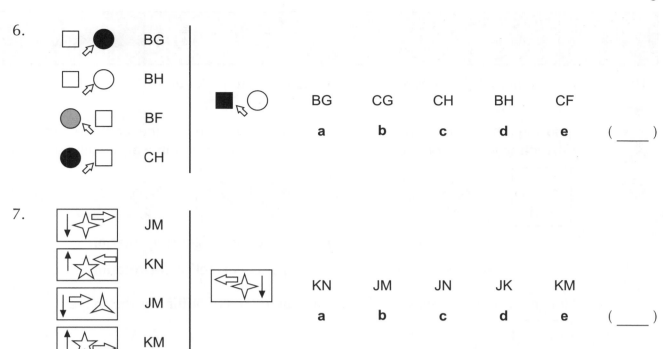

Shading and Line Types

There are lots of different shadings and line types you need to look out for.

Warm Up

1. **Ignoring** rotation, how many arrows are hatched the **same** as the left hand arrow?
Correcting for rotation, how many arrows are hatched the **same** as the left hand arrow?

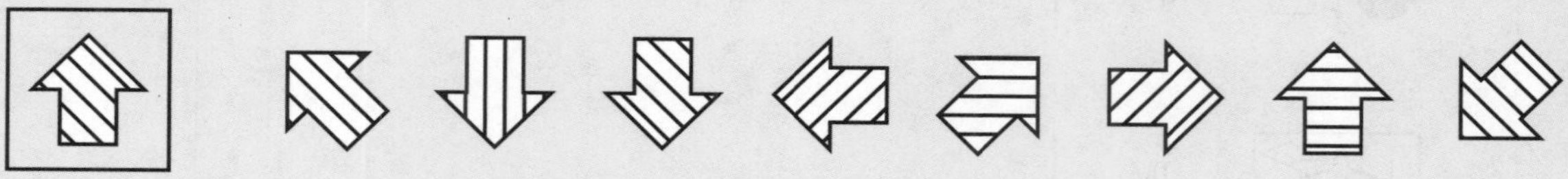

Number of arrows hatched the **same**, **ignoring rotation**: ____

Number of arrows hatched the **same**, **correcting for rotation**: ____

2. How many of the shapes below have the **same type** of **outline** as the shape on the left?

Number of **shapes** with the **same outline**: ____

3. What is the most **common shading** shared by the shapes below — black, white, grey, spotted or hatched?

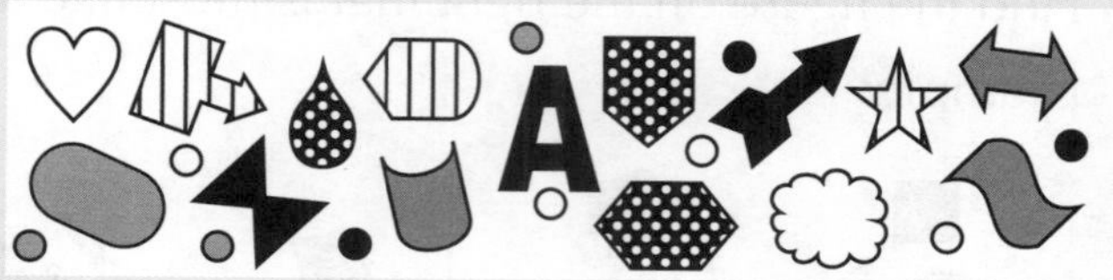

Most **common shading**: ________

Find the Figure Like the First Three

Find the figure on the right that is most like the three figures on the left.

Example:

a b c d e (d)

Three quarters of the shape must be shaded black.

4.

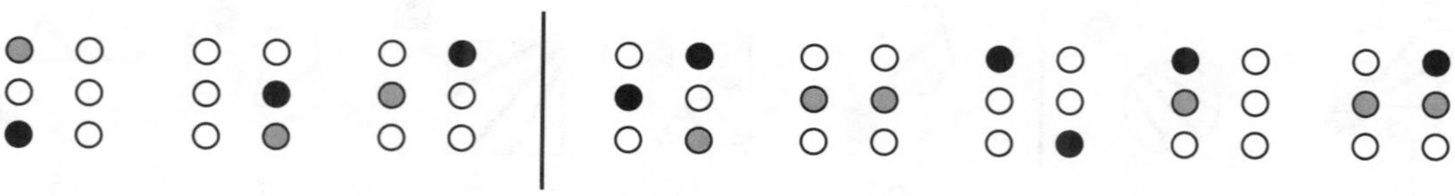

a b c d e (____)

5.

a b c d e (____)

6.

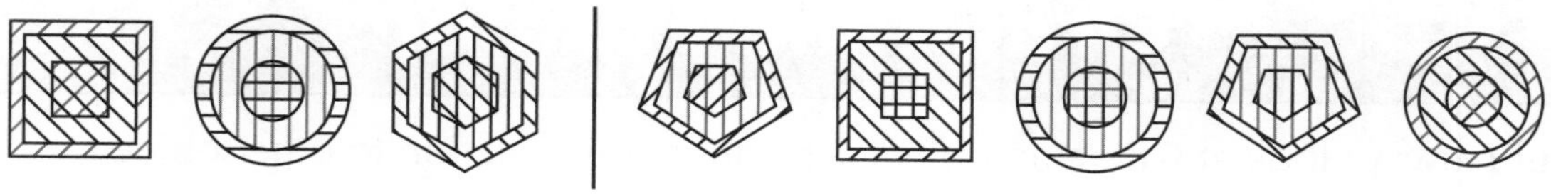

a b c d e (____)

7.

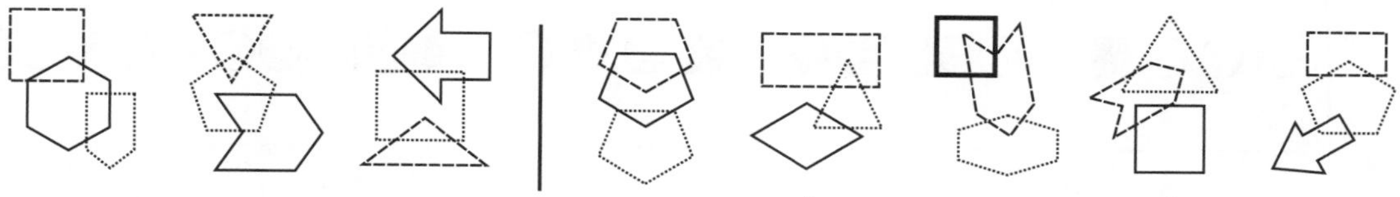

a b c d e (____)

Horizontal Code

In the boxes on the left are shapes with code letters. The top letters have a different meaning from the bottom ones. Work out how the letters go with the shapes and then find the code for the new shape from the five codes on the right.

Example:

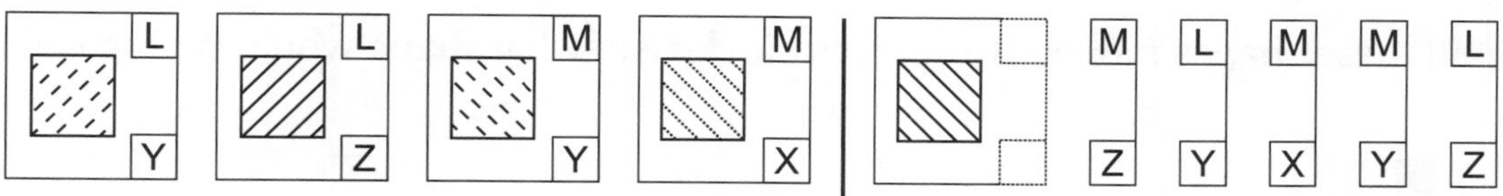

a b c d e (a)

M means hatching going diagonally down to the right. Z means solid-line hatching.

8.

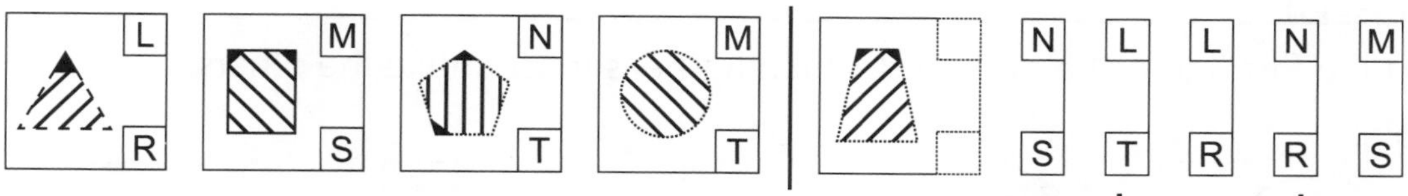

a b c d e (____)

9.

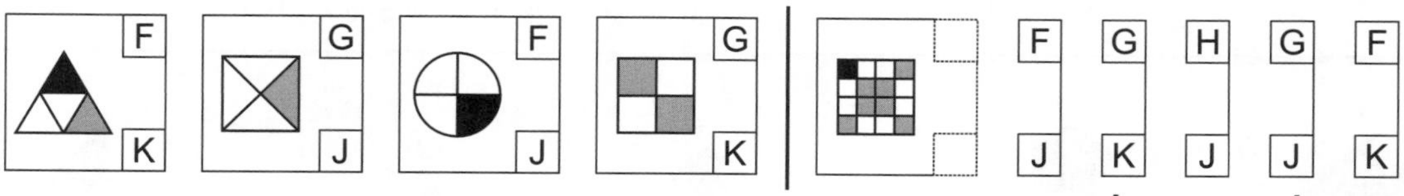

a b c d e (____)

10.

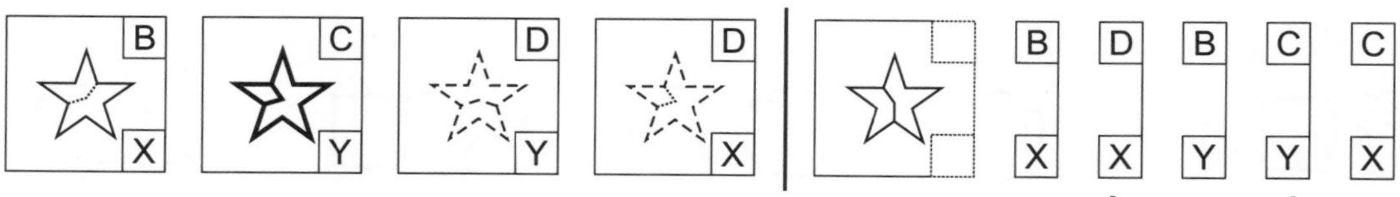

a b c d e (____)

Order and Position

You should always look at where an object is positioned in relation to other objects.

Warm Up

1. If each figure's shadings moved **right two places**, what **colour** would the square be?

a. b. c. d. e.

________ ________ ________ ________ ________

2. i) What **shape** is **two places anticlockwise** from the X in each of the figures below?

ii) What **colour** is the shape **one place clockwise** from the X in each of the figures?

a. b. c. d. e. f.

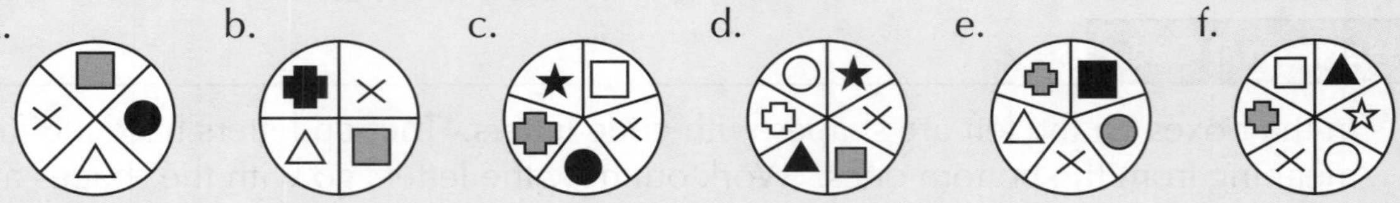

i) ________ ________ ________ ________ ________ ________

ii) ________ ________ ________ ________ ________ ________

3. If all these **shapes** moved **two places clockwise**, what **shape** would be **top right**?

a. b. c. d. e.

________ ________ ________ ________ ________

Odd One Out

Look at the five figures below. Find which figure is most unlike the others.

Example:

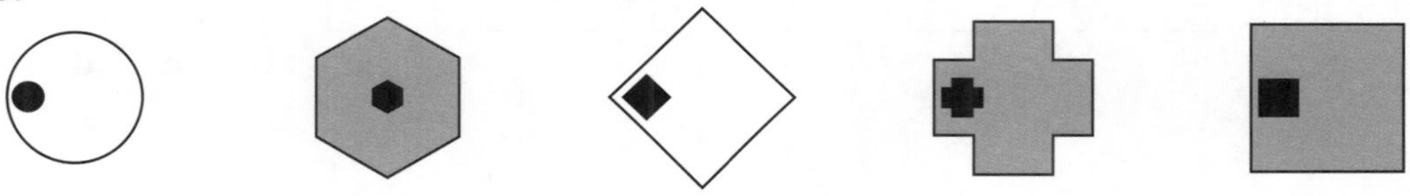

a b c d e (b)

All the other figures have the black inner shape on the left hand side.

4.

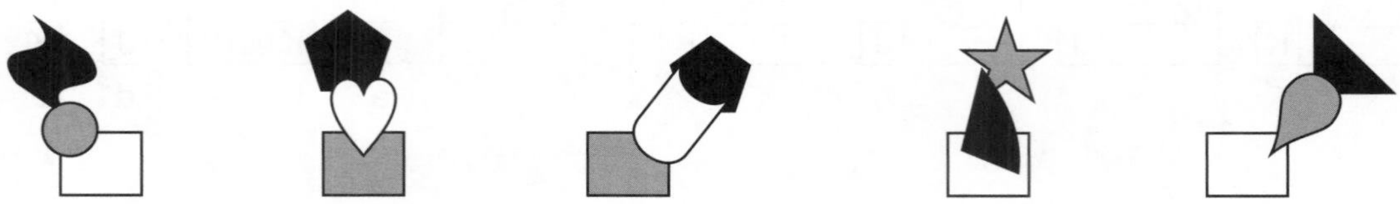

a b c d e (____)

5.

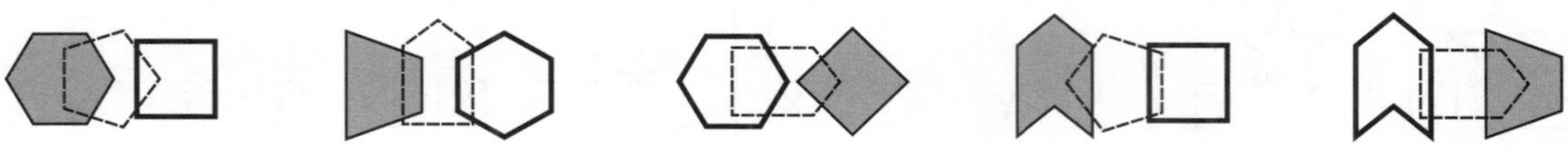

a b c d e (____)

6.

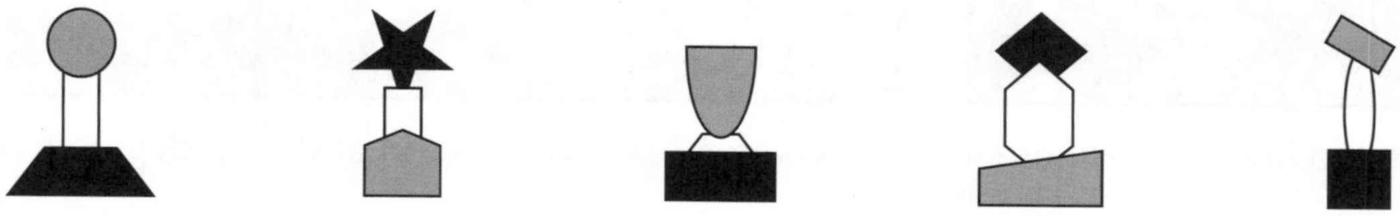

a b c d e (____)

7.

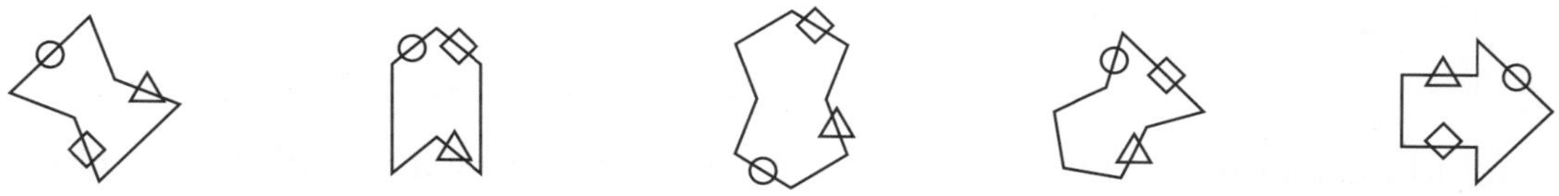

a b c d e (____)

Complete the Series

In the question below, the five squares on the left are arranged in order. One of the squares is missing. Work out which of the five squares on the right should go in its place.

Example:

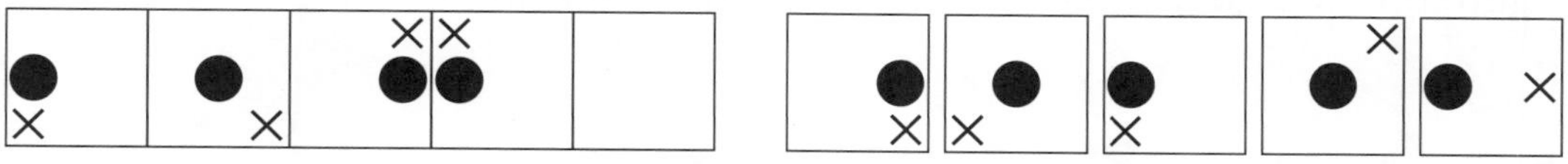

a b c d e (b)

The X moves one corner anticlockwise round the four corners. The circle moves one place to the right.

8.

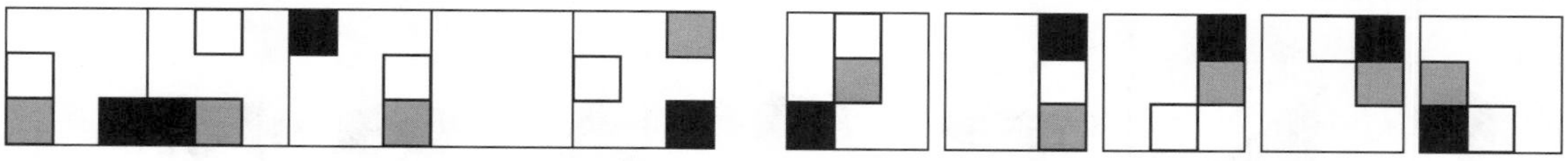

a b c d e (____)

9.

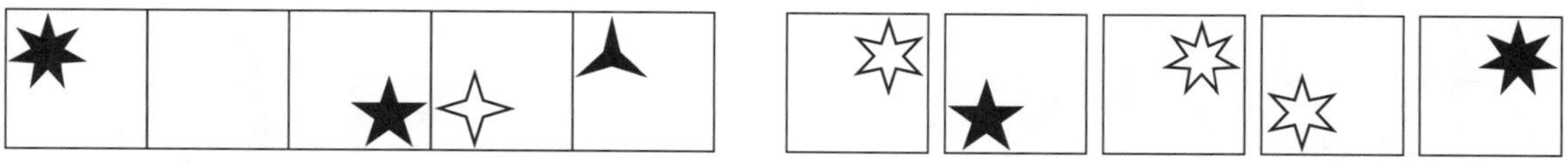

a b c d e (____)

10.

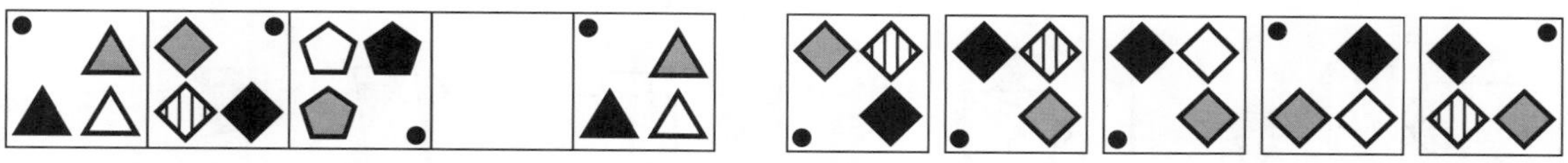

a b c d e (____)

Rotation

You will need to know the difference between a 45 degree rotation and a 90 degree rotation.

Warm Up

1. How many of these shapes are **identical** to the left hand shape apart from **rotation**?

Number of **identical shapes**: ____

2. Including shading, how many right hand shapes below are a 90 degree **clockwise** rotation of the left hand shape?

Number of **clockwise** rotations: ____

Find the Figure Like the First Two

Find the figure on the right that is most like the two figures on the left.

Example:

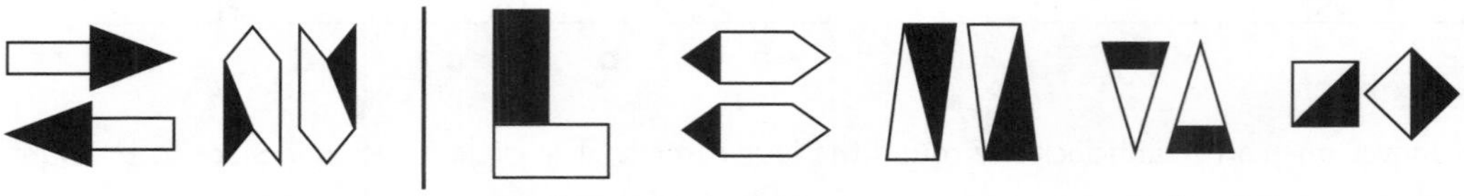

a b c d e (d)

In all figures, one shape must be a 180 degree rotation of the other shape.

3.

a b c d e (____)

4.

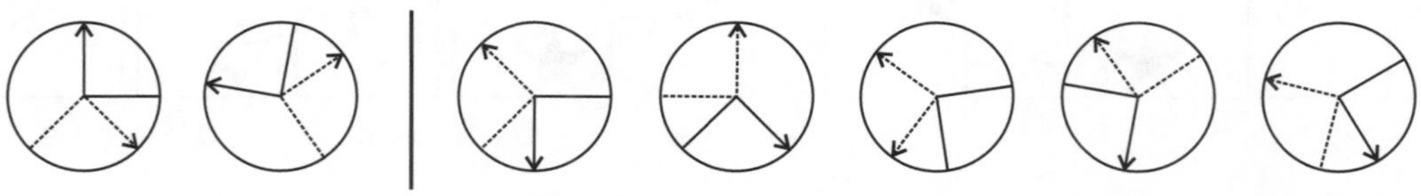

a b c d e (____)

5.

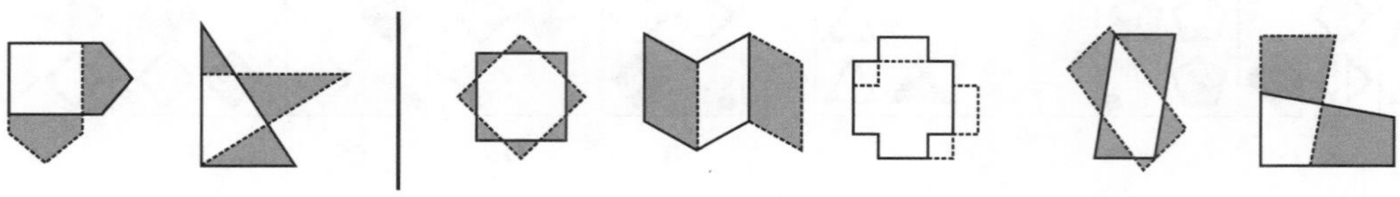

a b c d e (____)

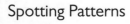

Reflection

Reflection and rotation are very similar so you should make sure you don't get them confused.

Warm Up

1. In each figure, is the right hand shape a **reflection** or **rotation** of the left hand shape?

a. b. c. d. e. f.

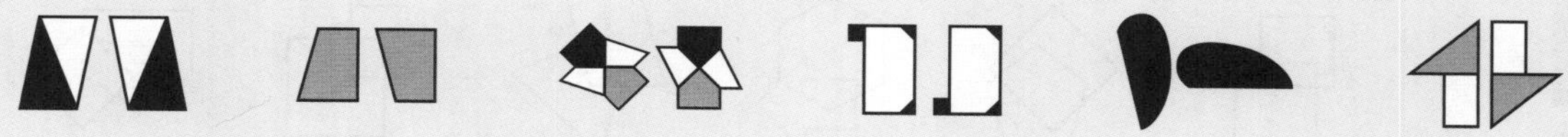

a. ________ b. ________ c. ________ d. ________ e. ________ f. ________

2. Will each figure still look the same and have the same rotation after being **reflected**?

a. b. c. d. e. f.

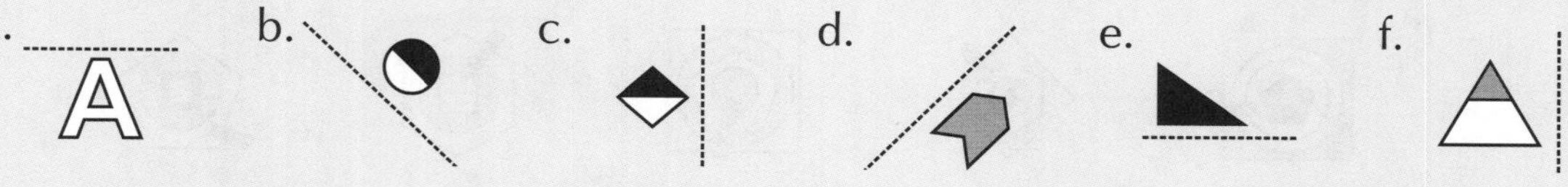

a. ____ b. ____ c. ____ d. ____ e. ____ f. ____

Complete the Pair

The first figure below is changed in some way to become the second. Choose the figure on the right that relates to the third figure in the same way that the second relates to the first.

Example:

a b c d e (d)

The figure reflects across.

3.

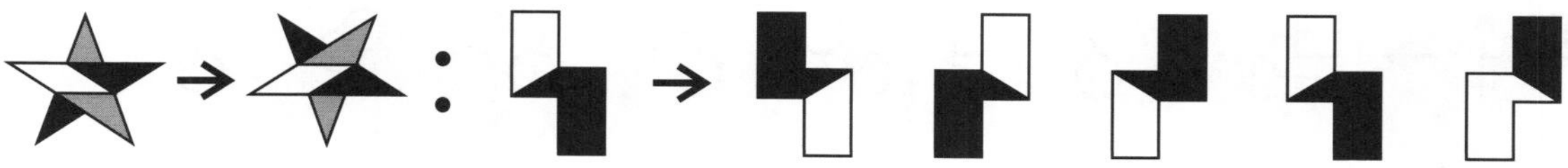

a b c d e (____)

4.

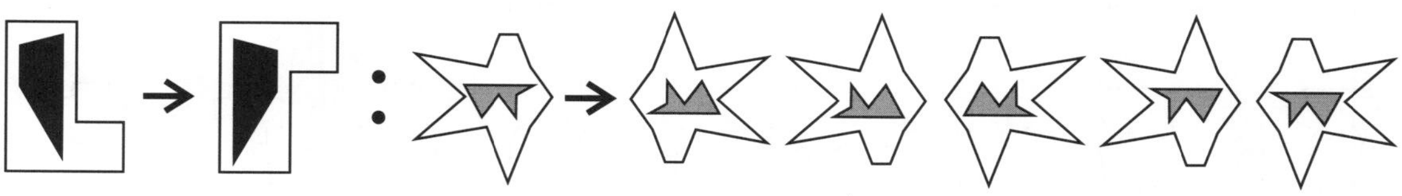

a b c d e (____)

5.

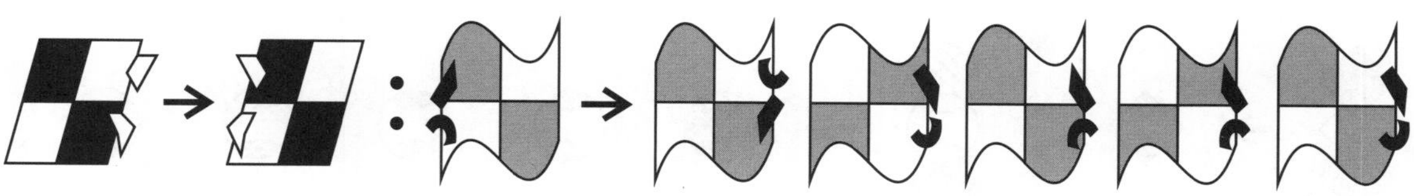

a b c d e (____)

Layering

Layering is about the position of shapes in front of or behind other shapes.

Warm Up

1. How many **sides** does the **inner shape** have in each of these **overlapping shapes?**

a. b. c. d. e. f. g.

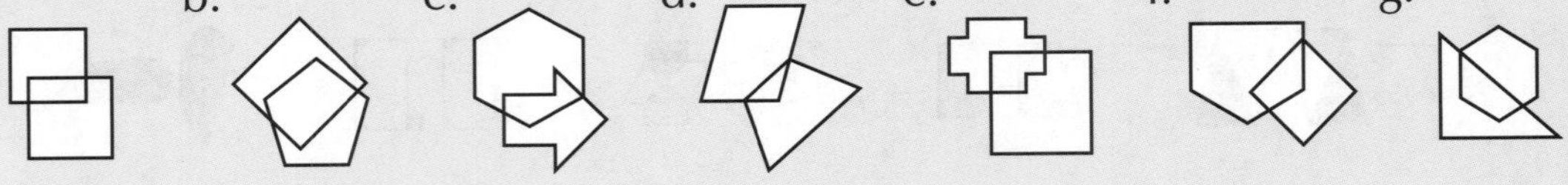

2. How many **shapes** does the black rectangle overlap?

a. b. c. d. e. f.

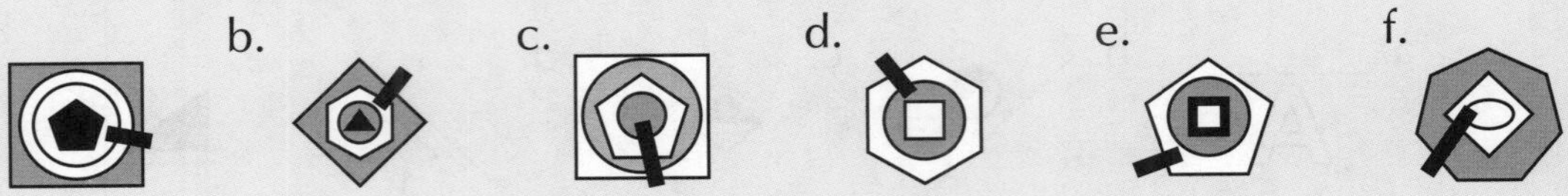

3. Could the shape on the left be the **same shape** (S) that is underneath the other shapes, or must it be **different** (D)?

a. b. c. d. e. f.

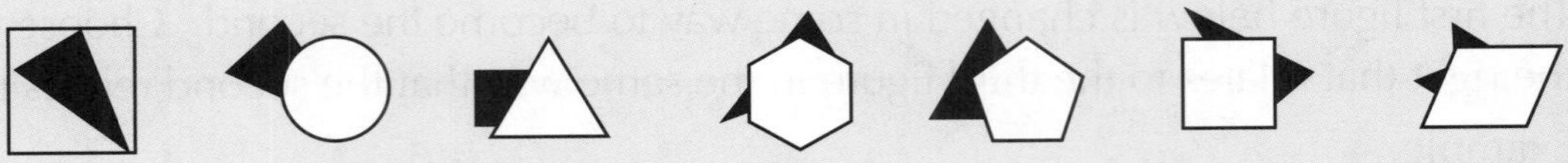

Complete the Pair

The first figure below is changed in some way to become the second. Choose the figure on the right that relates to the third figure in the same way that the second relates to the first.

Example:

a b c d e (e)

The front shape moves to the back, and the back shape moves to the front.

4.

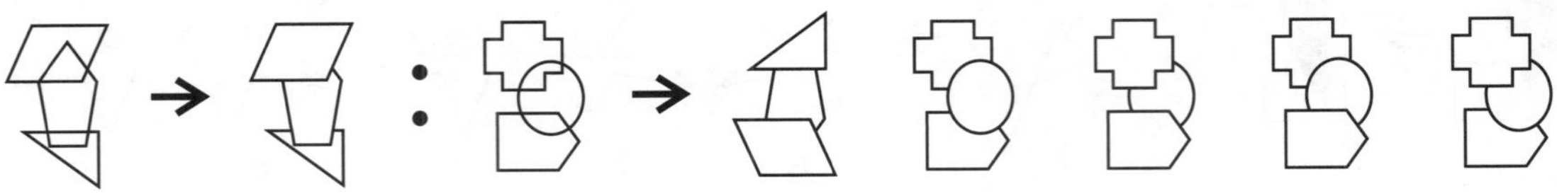

a b c d e (____)

5.

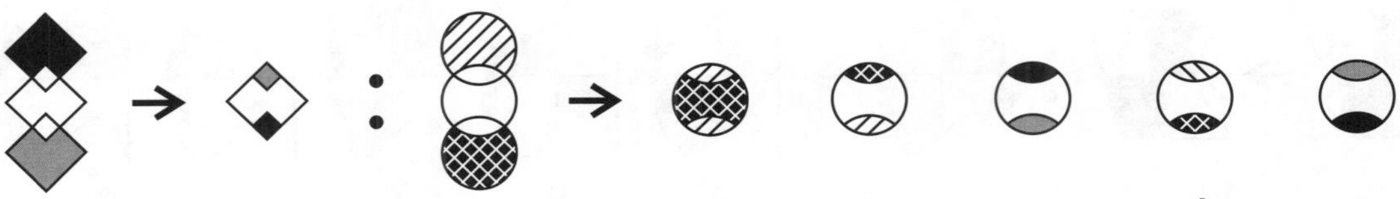

a b c d e (____)

6. 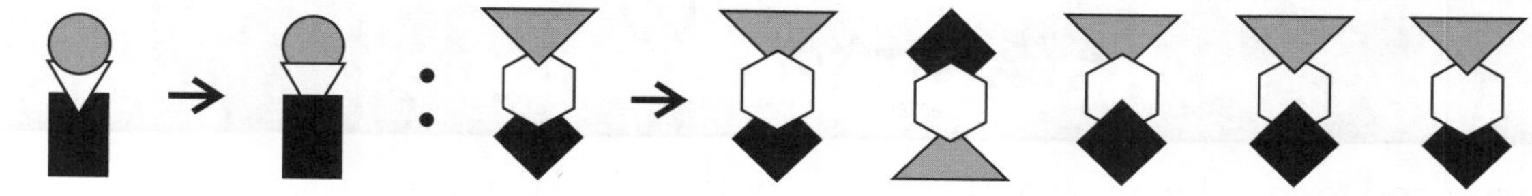

a	b	c	d	e	(____)

7. 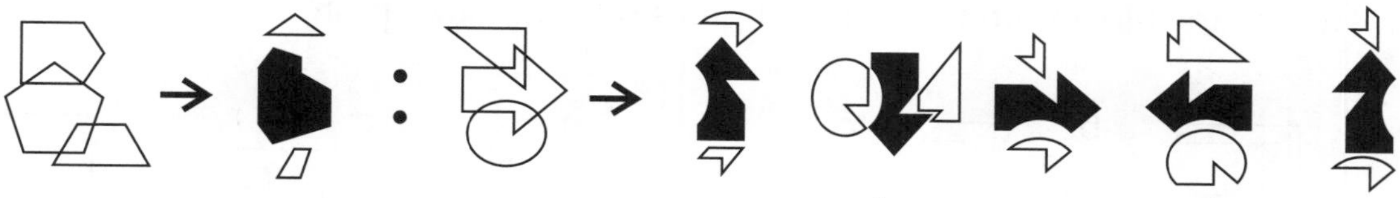

a	b	c	d	e	(____)

Vertical Code

On the left are shapes with code letters that describe them. You need to work out what the code letters mean. There is then a shape on its own next to a choice of five codes. Work out which code describes this shape.

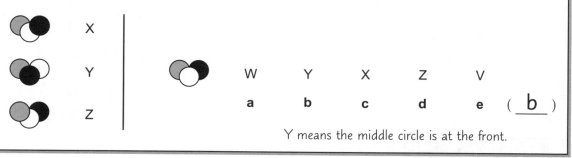

Example: 

X

Y

Z

W	Y	X	Z	V	
a	b	c	d	e	(b)

Y means the middle circle is at the front.

8. 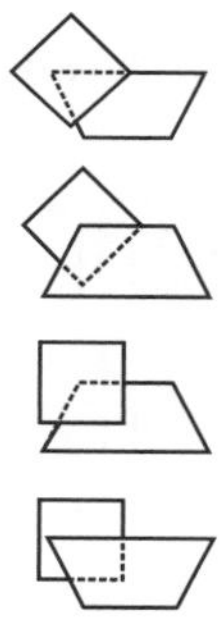

TW

SV

SW

SV

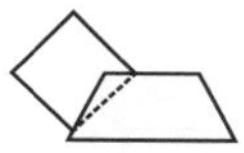

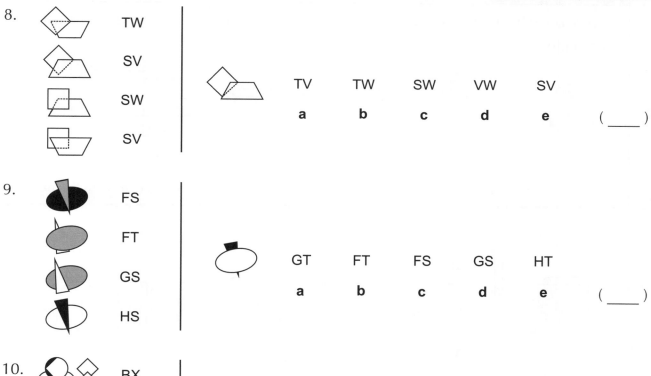

TV	TW	SW	VW	SV	
a	b	c	d	e	(____)

9. 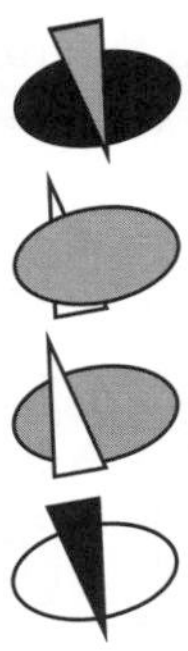

FS

FT

GS

HS

GT	FT	FS	GS	HT	
a	b	c	d	e	(____)

10. 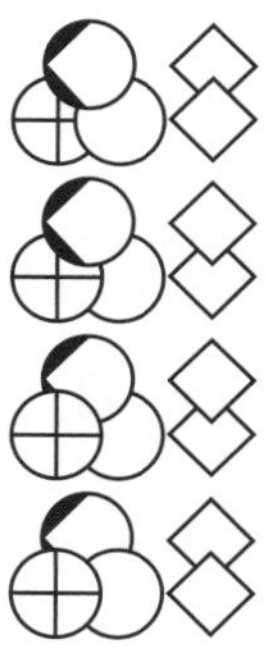

BX

BY

AY

CX

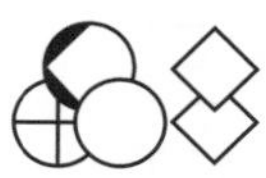

BY	AY	AX	CY	CX	
a	b	c	d	e	(____)

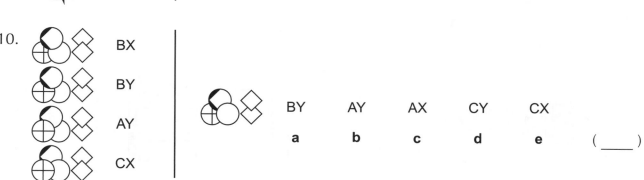

Rotating 3D Shapes

You might need to imagine what a 3D shape would look like if it was rotated.

Warm Up

1. How many blocks are each of the figures below made up of?

a. 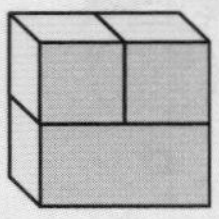
b. 
c. 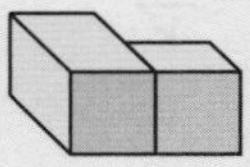
d. 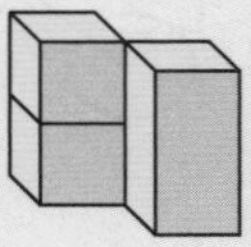
e. 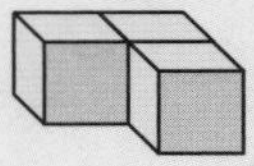
f. 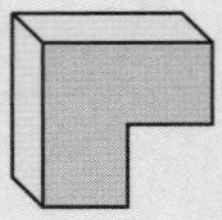

_____ _____ _____ _____ _____ _____

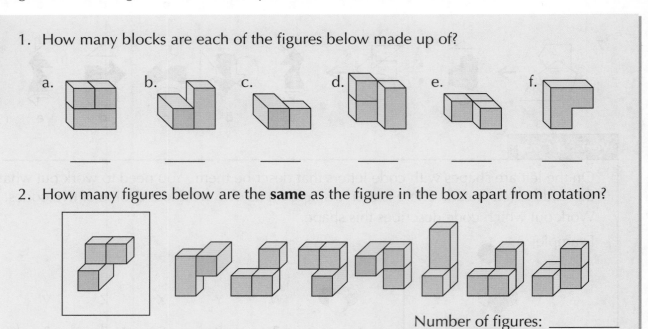

2. How many figures below are the **same** as the figure in the box apart from rotation?

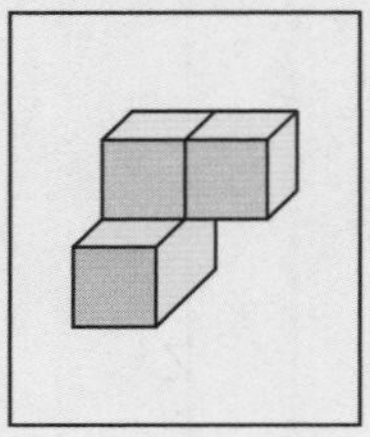

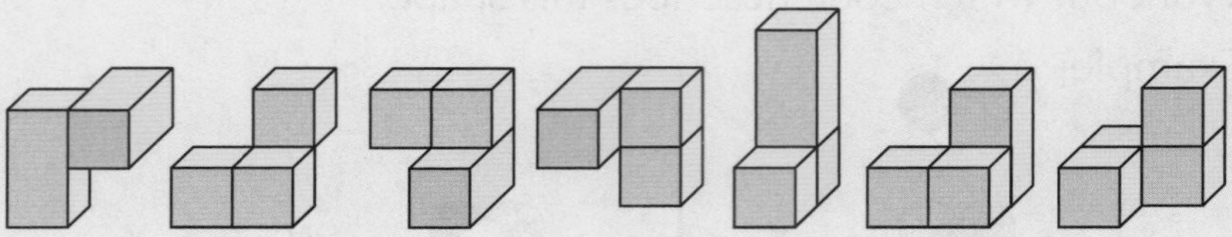

Number of figures: _________

3D Building Blocks

Work out which set of blocks can be put together to make the 3D figure on the left.

Example:

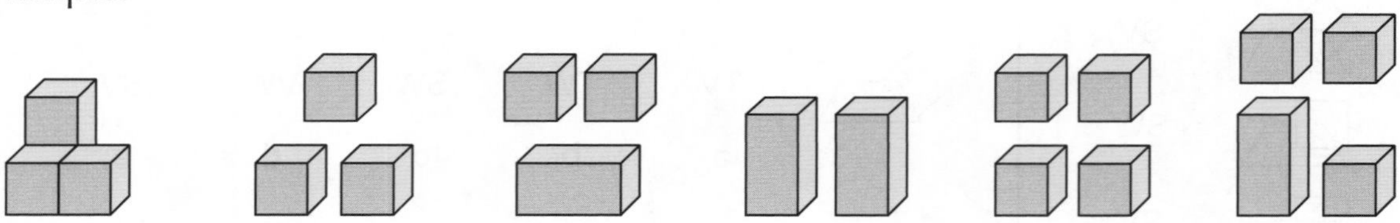

a b c d e (b)

The block at the bottom rotates 90 degrees in the plane of the page and the two cubes move to the front.

3.

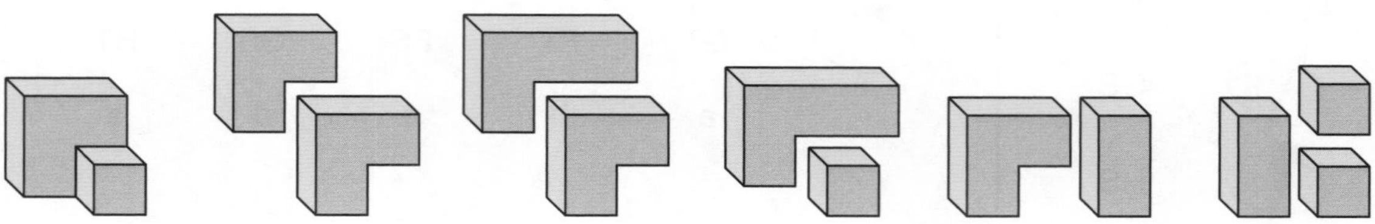

a b c d e (____)

4.

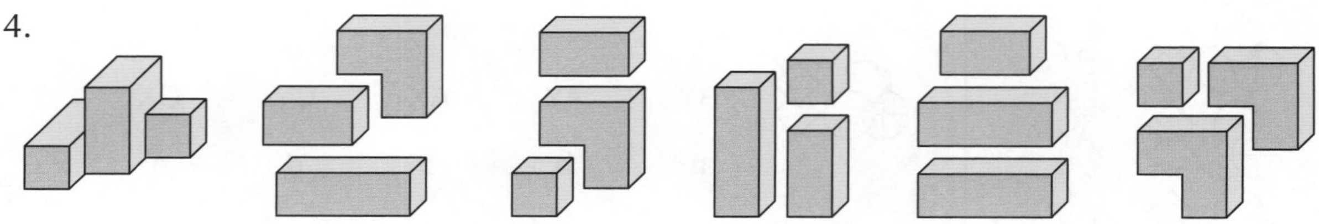

a b c d e (____)

5.

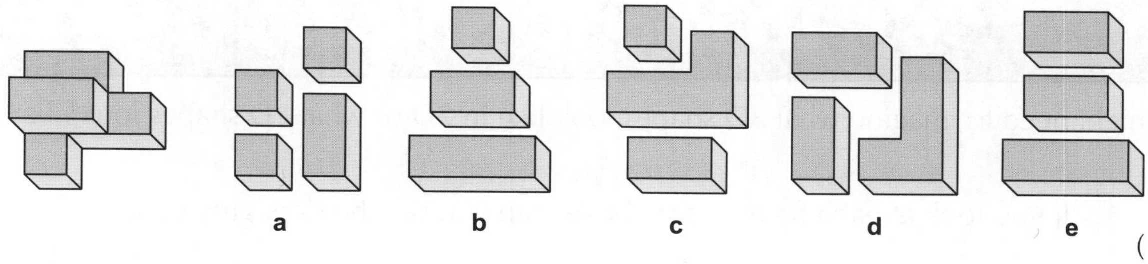

(____)

3D Rotation

Work out which 3D figure in the grey box has been rotated to make the new 3D figure.

Example:

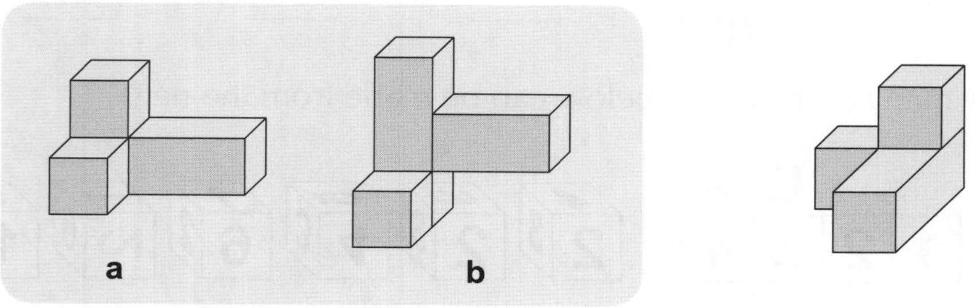

(a)

Figure A has been rotated 90 degrees right-to-left.

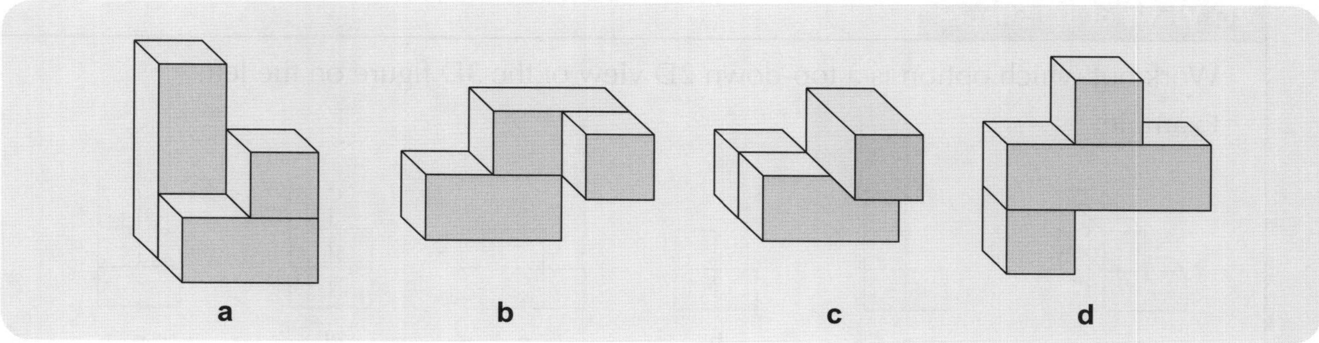

6.

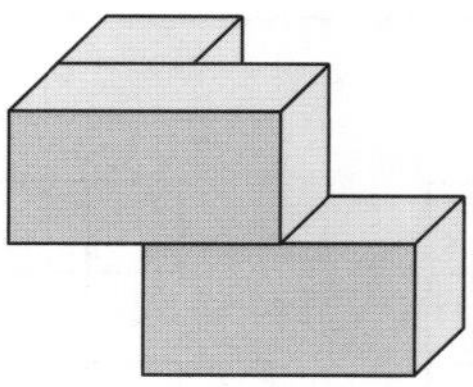

(____)

7.

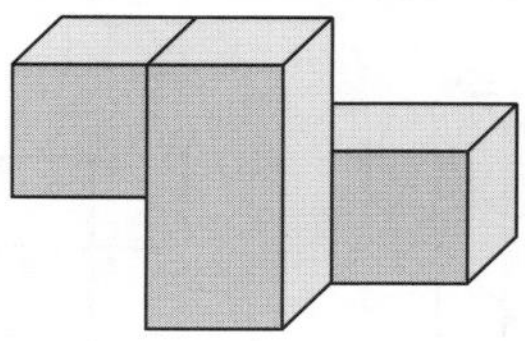

(____)

8.

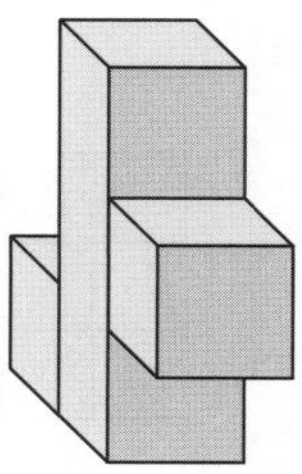

(____)

9.

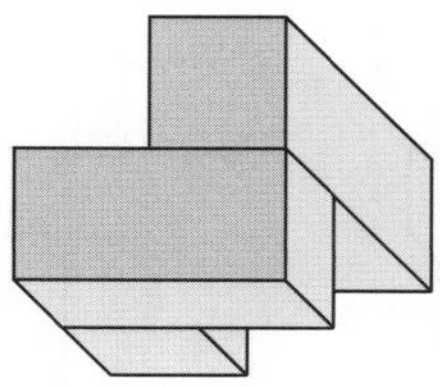

(____)

2D and 3D Shapes

You might need to imagine what 3D shapes look like in 2D or what 2D shapes look like in 3D.

Warm Up

1. If you look at each figure from above, can you see the dark grey cube?

a. 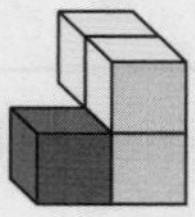 ______

b. 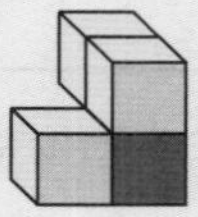 ______

c. 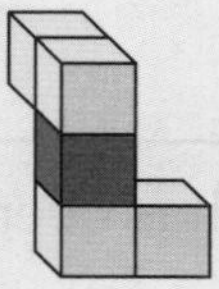 ______

d. 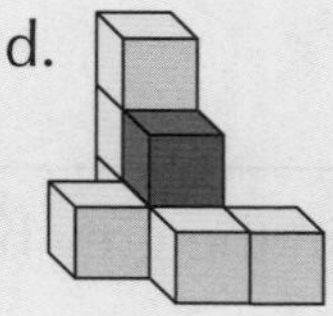 ______

e. 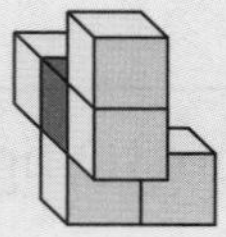 ______

f. 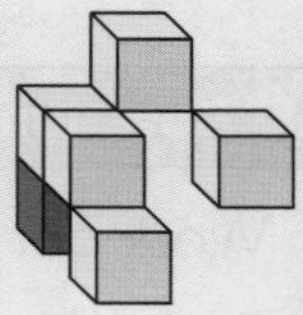 ______

2. How many of the cubes below can be made from the net?

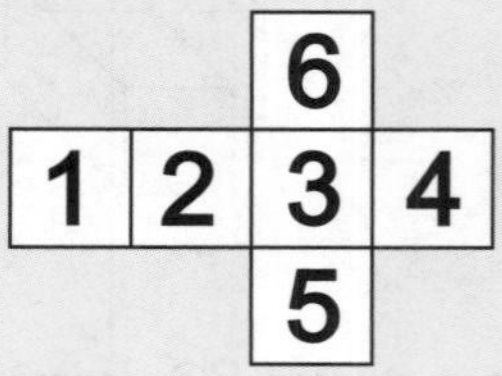

Number of cubes made from the net: ______

2D Views of 3D Shapes

Work out which option is a top-down 2D view of the 3D figure on the left.

Example:

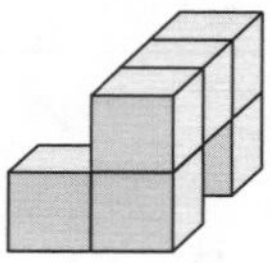

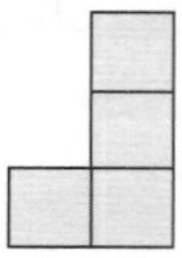
a

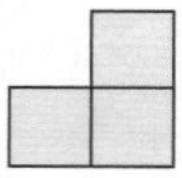
b

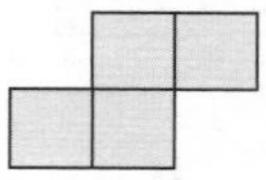
c

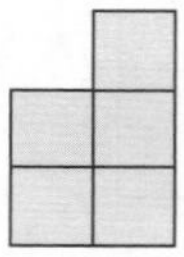
d

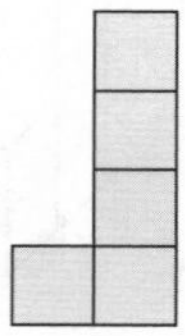
e

(a)

There are four blocks visible from above, which rules out options B, D and E. There is a line of three blocks on the right-hand side of the shape, which rules out option C.

3. 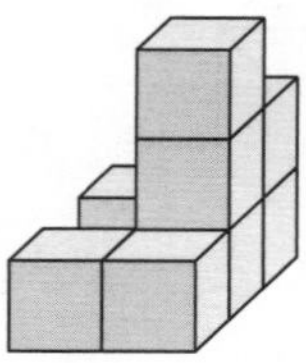

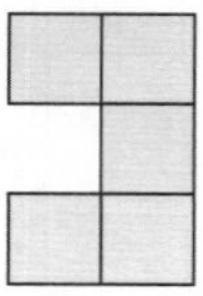
a

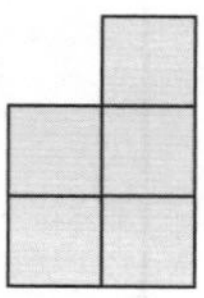
b

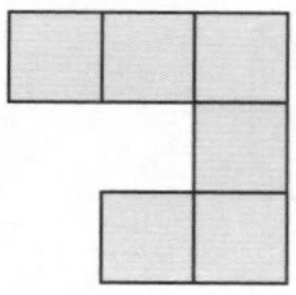
c

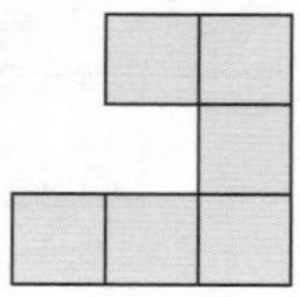
d

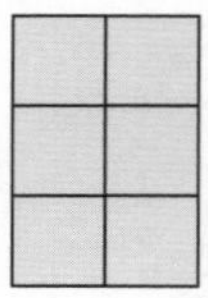
e

(____)

4. 

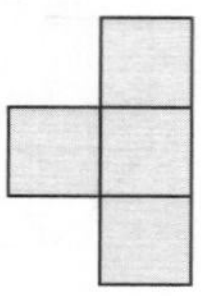
a

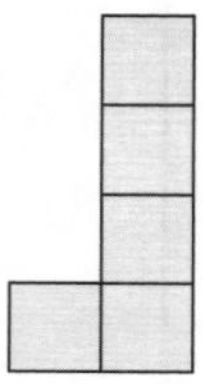
b

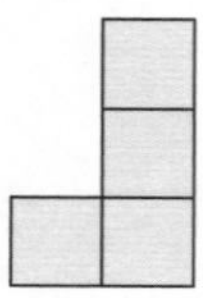
c

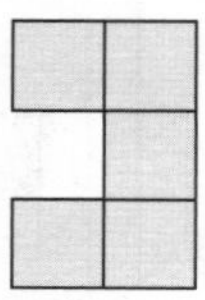
d

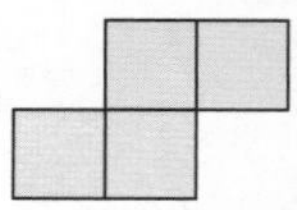
e

(____)

5.

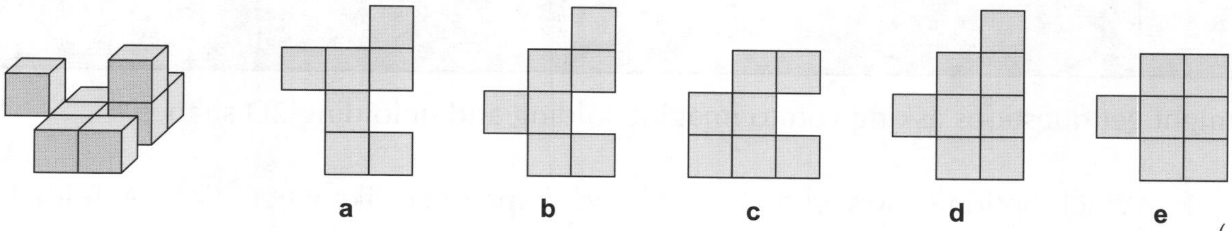

(____)

Cubes and Nets

Work out which of the five cubes can be made from the net.

Example:

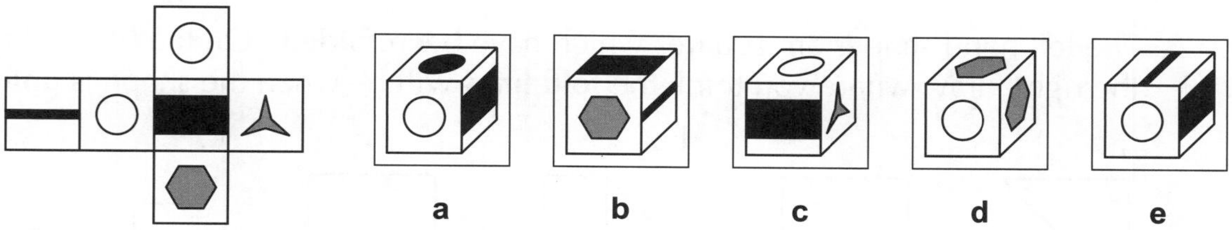

(C)

There is no black circle, which rules out option A. The thick black line and the thin black line must be on opposite sides, which rules out options B and E. There is only one grey hexagon, which rules out option D.

6.

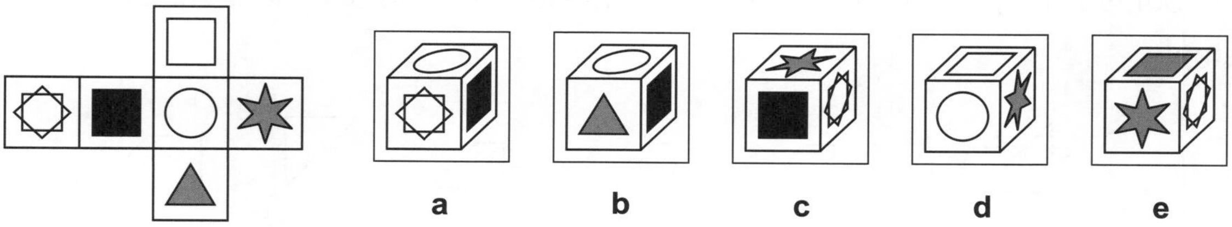

(____)

7.

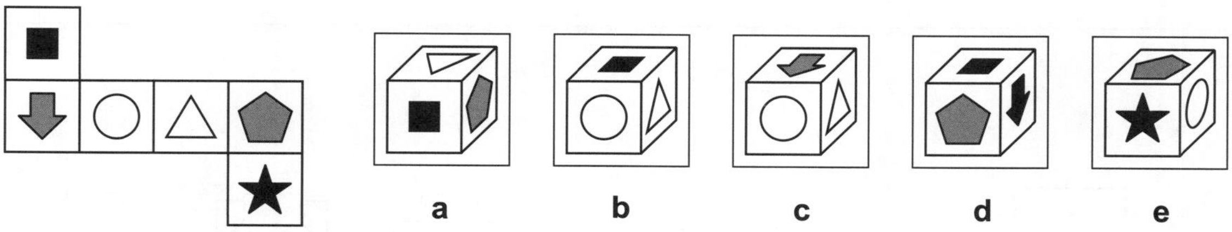

(____)

8.

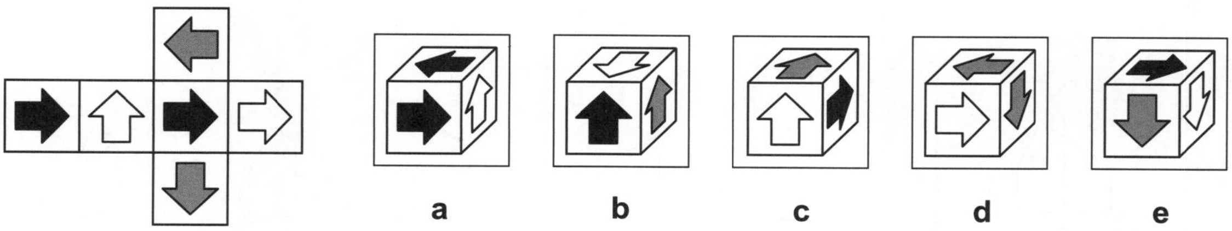

(____)

Folding

You might get questions asking you to imagine folding and unfolding 2D shapes.

Warm Up

1. Which option shows what the left hand shape looks like when it's been **folded once**?

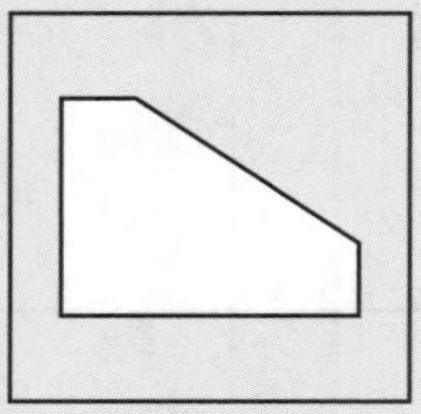

a. b. c. d.

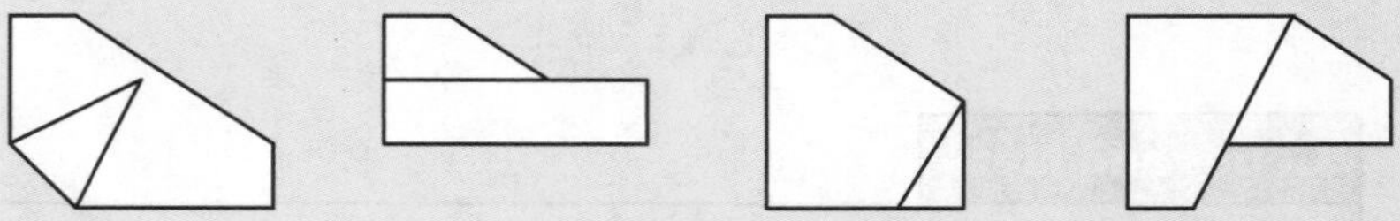

Option: _____

2. The left hand shapes are squares which have been **folded**. On the blank shapes on the right, draw where you think the **fold lines** will be when the shape is **unfolded**.

a. b. c.

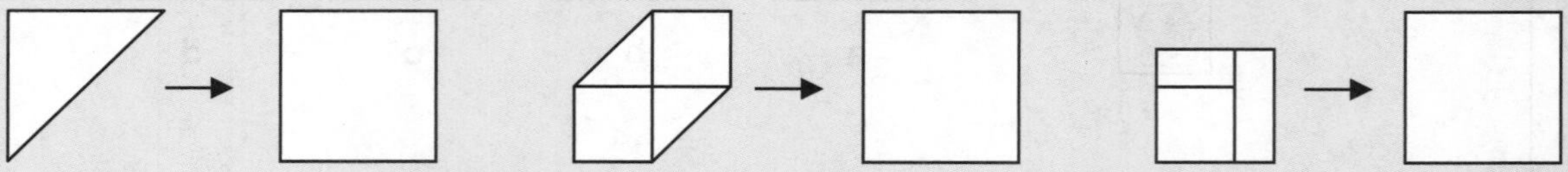

Fold Along the Line

Work out which option shows the figure on the left when folded along the dotted line.

Example:

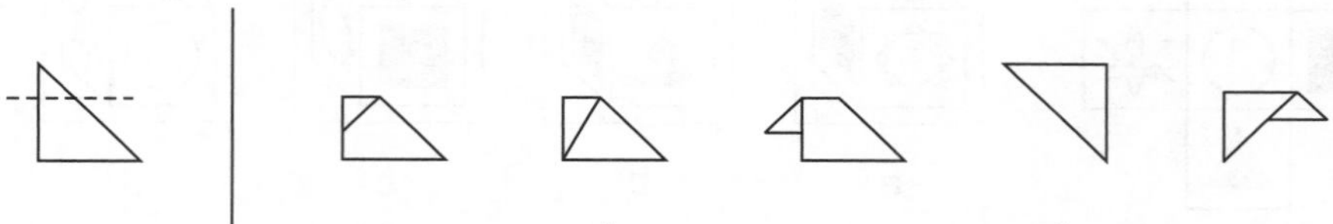

a b c d e (a)

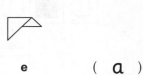

In options B and C, the part of the figure that has been folded is the wrong shape. Option D has been rotated and not folded. In option E, the fold line has moved.

3.

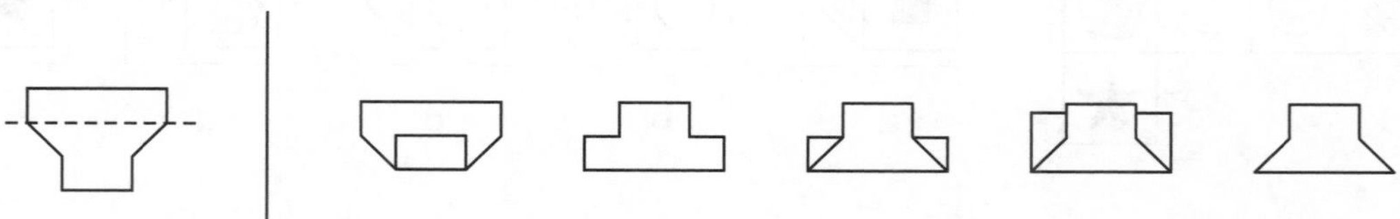

a b c d e (____)

4.

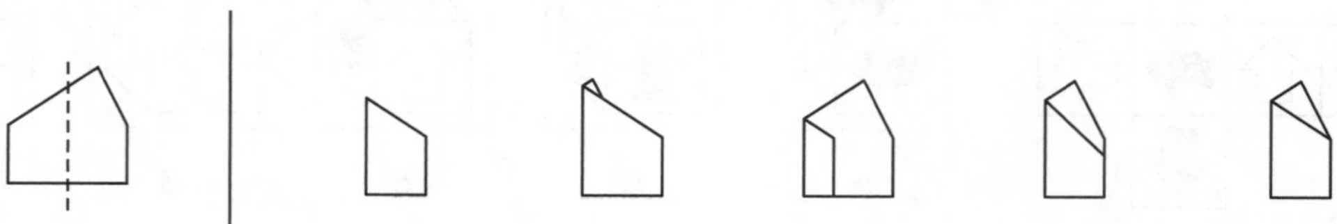

a b c d e (____)

5.

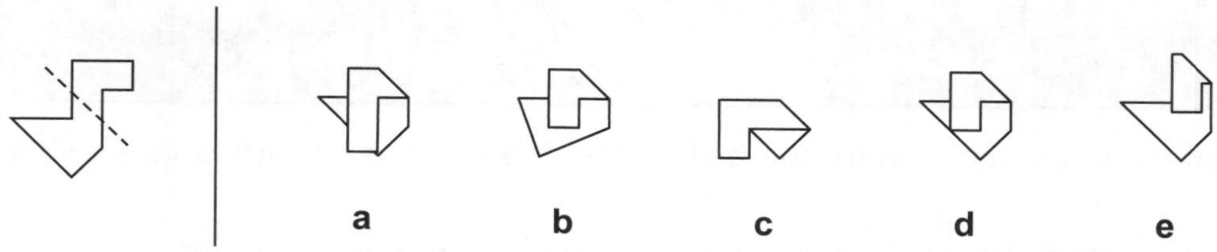

(____)

Fold and Punch

A square is folded and then a hole is punched, as shown on the left.
Work out which option shows the square when unfolded.

Example:

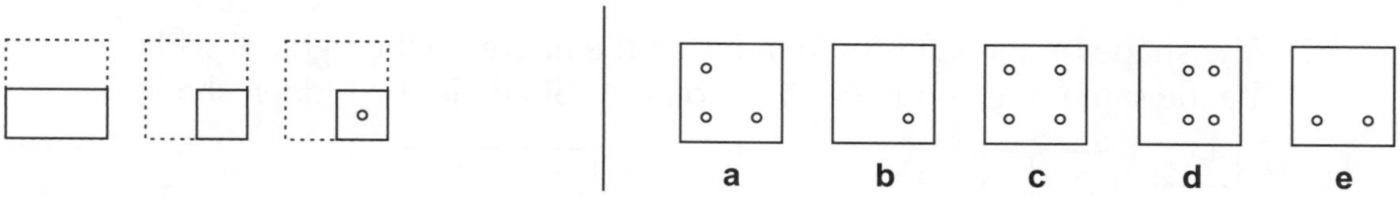

(C)

Unfold the figure, one fold at a time: 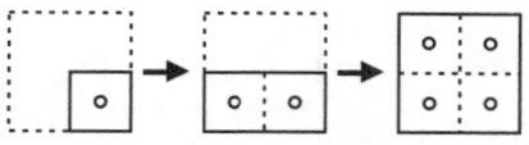

6.

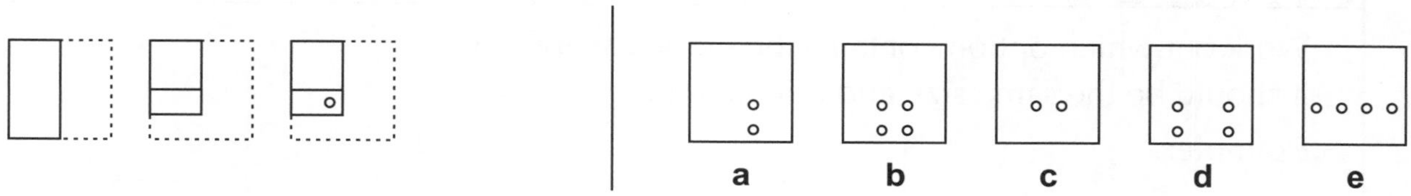

(____)

7.

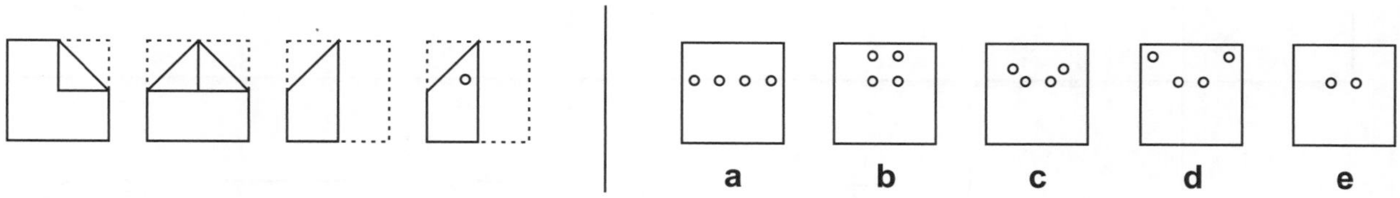

(____)

8.

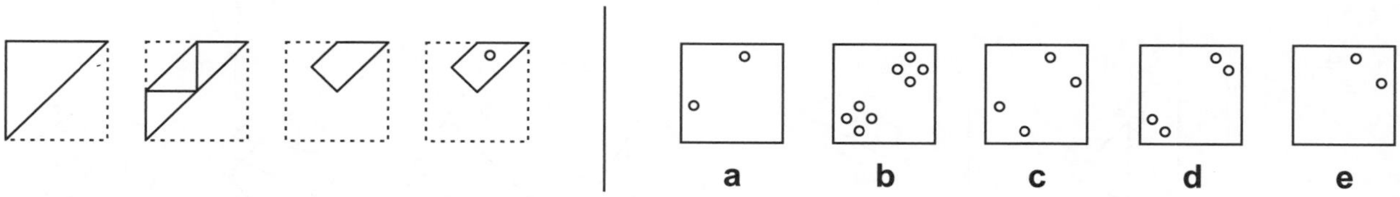

(____)

Hidden Shape

Some questions might ask you to find a shape which is hidden inside a larger shape.

Warm Up

1. How **many times** does the shape on the left appear in the figure on the right? It will be the same size and it won't be rotated.

a.

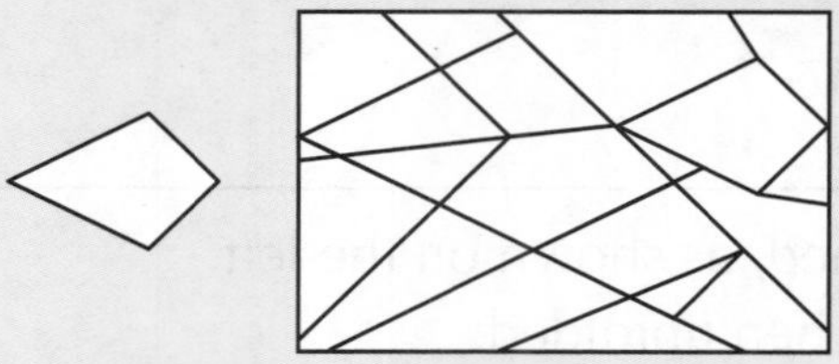

Number of times: _____

b.

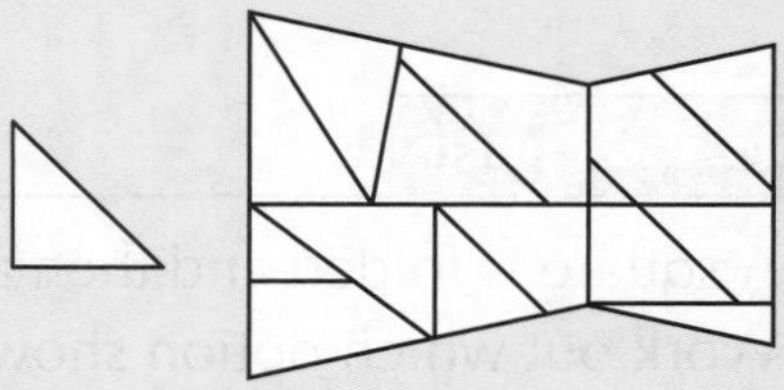

Number of times: _____

2. The shape on the left is hidden inside the figure on the right. It will be the same size and it won't be rotated. **Shade in** the hidden shape.

a.

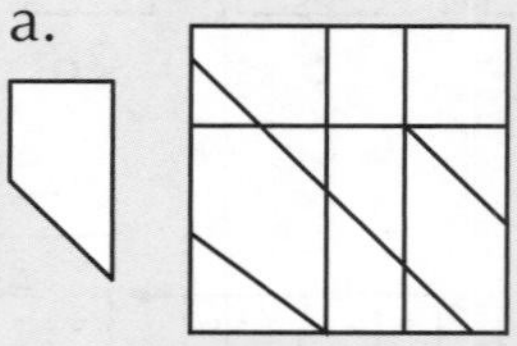

b.

c.

Hidden Shape

Work out which option contains the hidden shape shown.
It should be the same size and orientation.

Example:

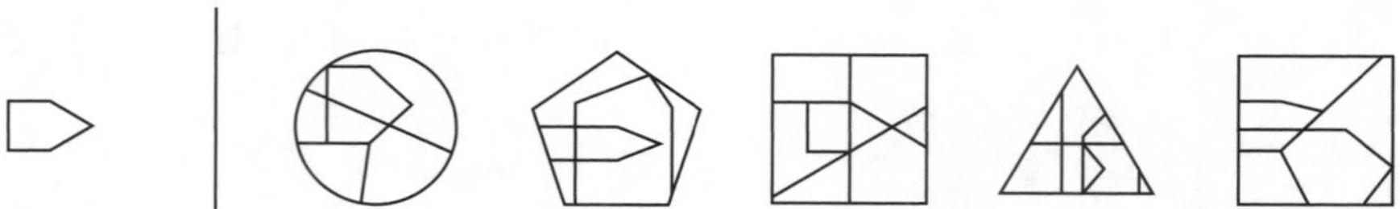

a b c d e (C)

The hidden shape is here:

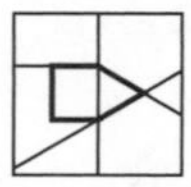

3.

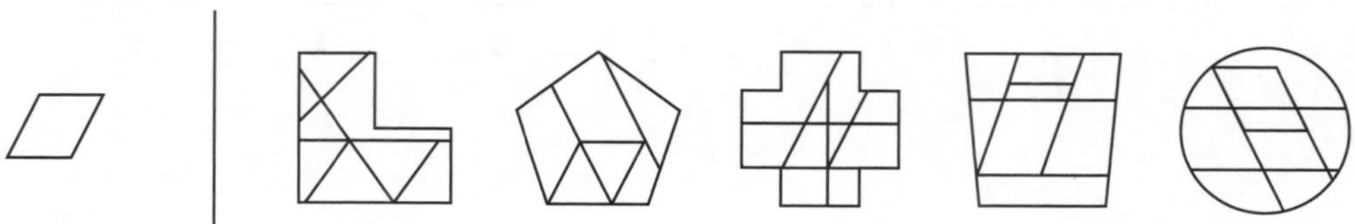

a b c d e

(____)

4.

a b c d e

(____)

Connecting Shapes

You might get questions asking you to join a set of shapes together in your head.

Warm Up

1. The three shapes on the left are **joined** to make the figure on the right. This is done by connecting sides which have the **same letter**. One shape has been joined **incorrectly**. Circle the **incorrect join** on the right hand figure.

a.

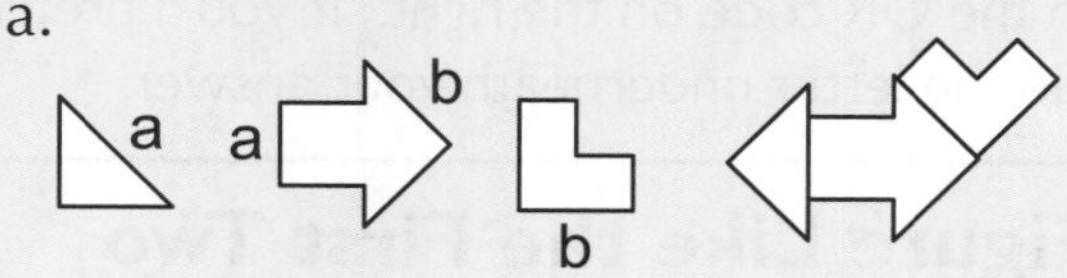

b.

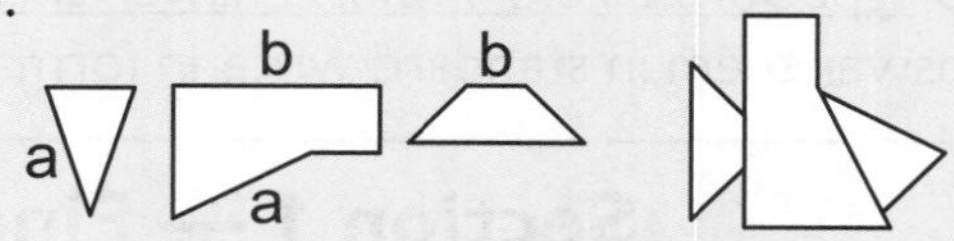

2. One of the shapes on the left needs to be joined to the figure in the box so that the sides with the same letter are connected. **Draw** the shape in the right place in the box.

a.

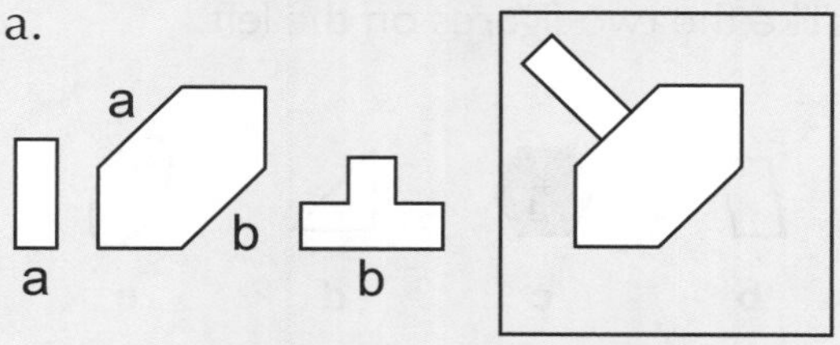

b.

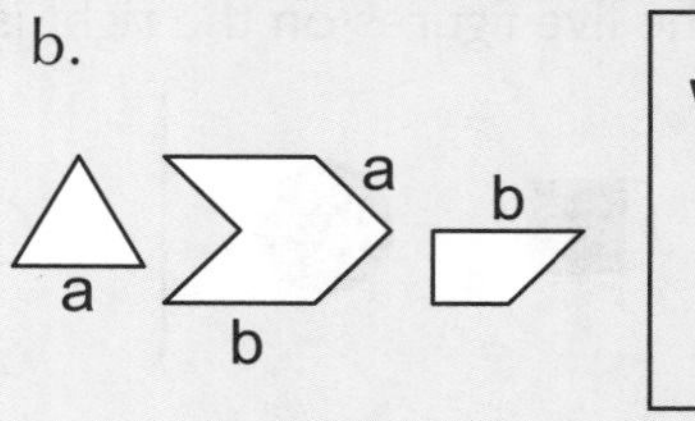

Connecting Shapes

Work out which option shows how the three shapes will look when they are joined by matching the sides with the same letter.

Example:

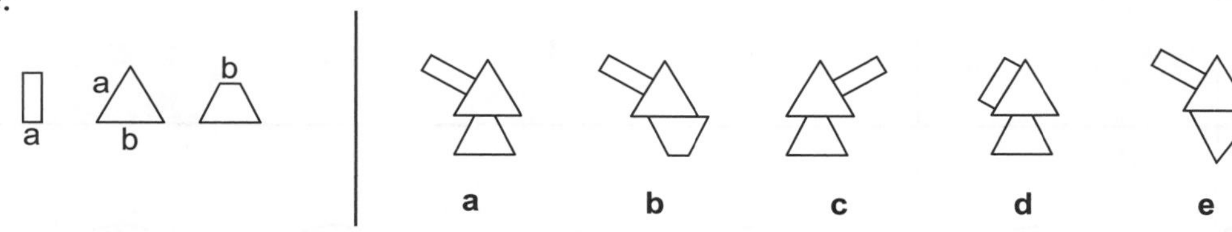

(a)

Options B and E are ruled out because the wrong side of the trapezium is connected to the triangle.
Option C is ruled out because the rectangle is connected to the wrong side of the triangle.
Option D is ruled out because the wrong side of the rectangle is connected to the triangle.

3.

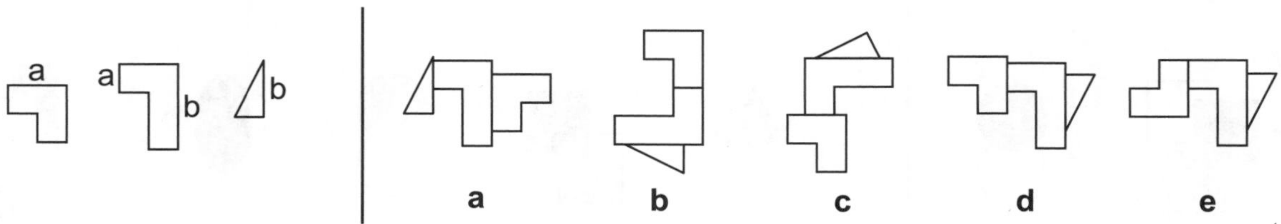

(____)

4.

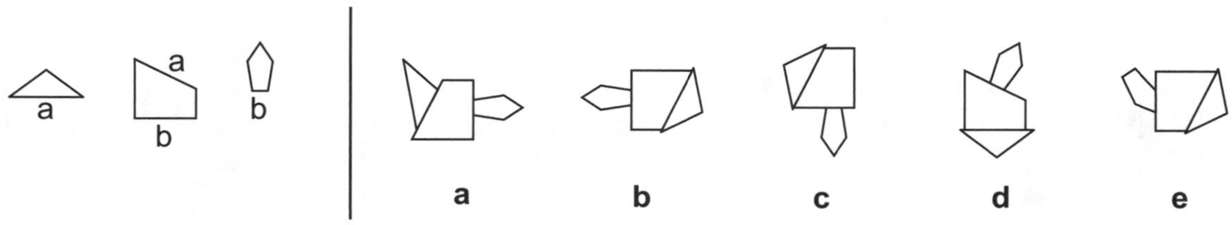

(____)

Assessment Test 1

This book contains six assessment tests, which get harder as you work through them to help you improve your NVR skills.

Allow around 30 minutes to do each test and work as quickly and as carefully as you can.

If you want to attempt each test more than once, you will need to print **multiple-choice answer sheets** for these questions from our website — go to cgpbooks.co.uk/11plus/answer-sheets or scan the QR code on the right. If you'd prefer to answer them in standard write-in format, just circle the letter underneath your answer.

Answer Sheets

Section 1 — Find the Figure Like the First Two

For each question below there are two figures that are like each other in some way. Find which of the five figures on the right is most like the two figures on the left.

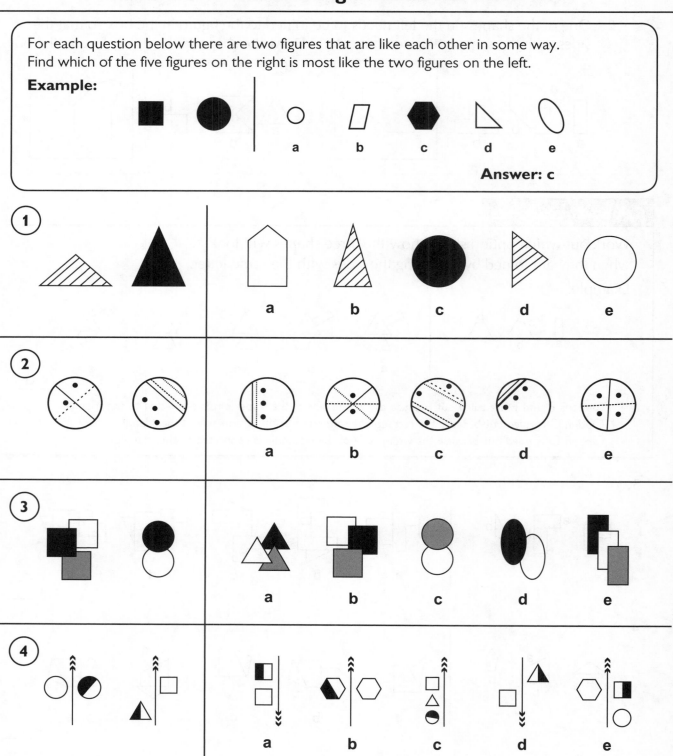

Example:

a b c d e

Answer: c

(1)

a b c d e

(2)

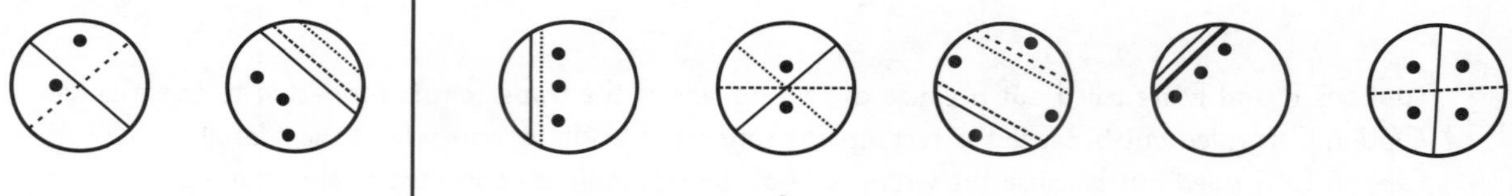

a b c d e

(3)

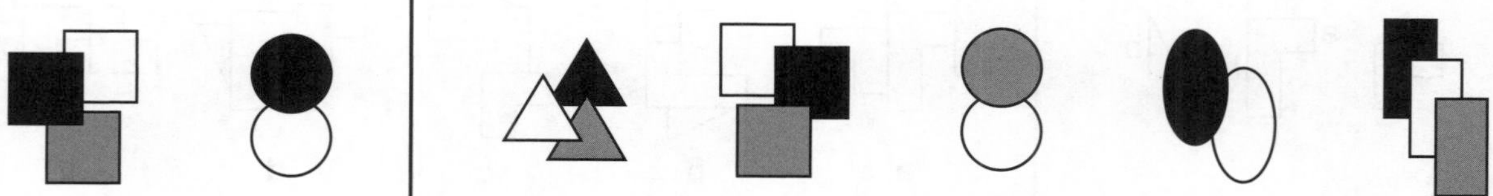

a b c d e

(4)

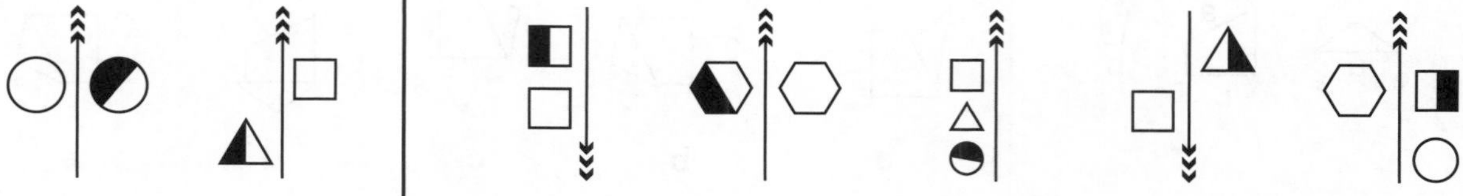

a b c d e

5

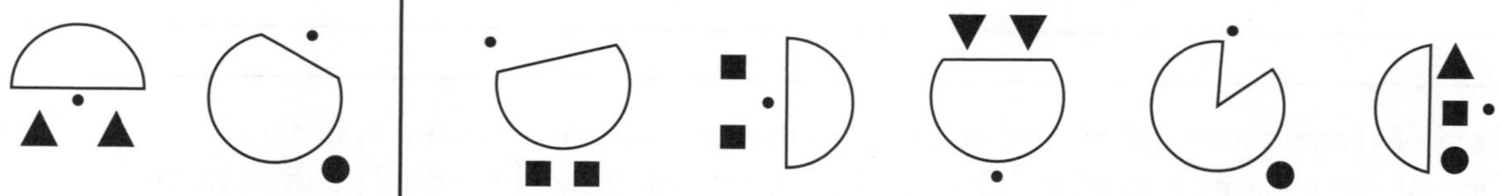

a b c d e

6

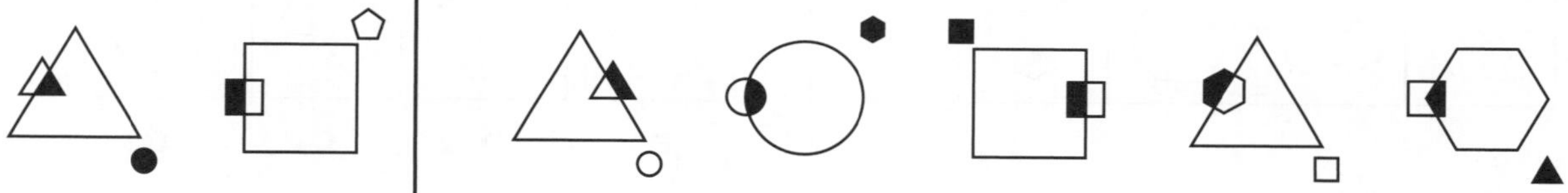

a b c d e

7

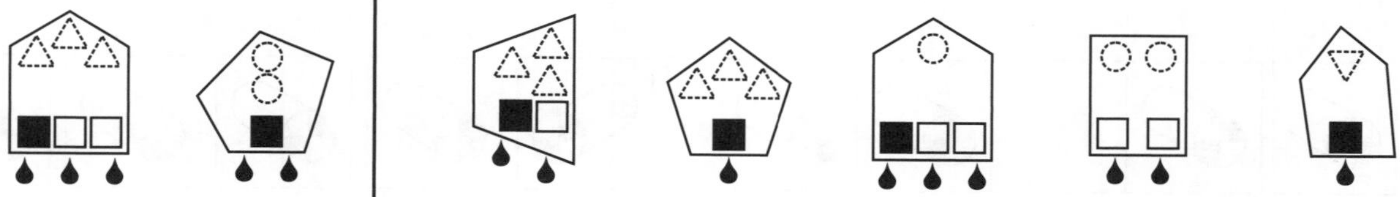

a b c d e

8

a b c d e

9

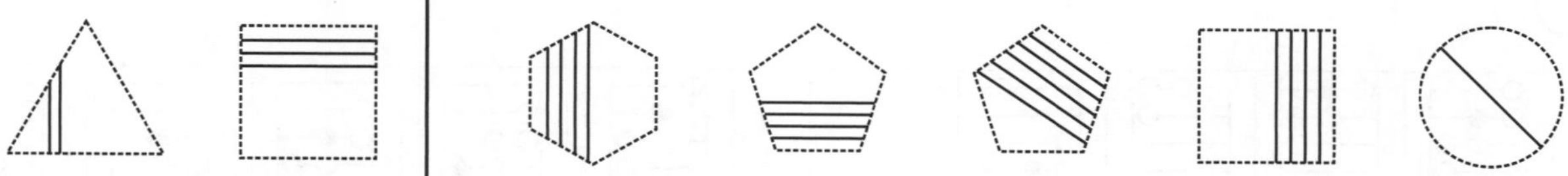

a b c d e

10

a b c d e

/ 10

Carry on to the next question → →

Section 2 — Complete the Series

Each of these questions has five squares on the left that are arranged in order.
One of the squares is missing. One of the squares on the right should go in its place.
Find which one of the five squares on the right should go in place of the empty square.

Example:

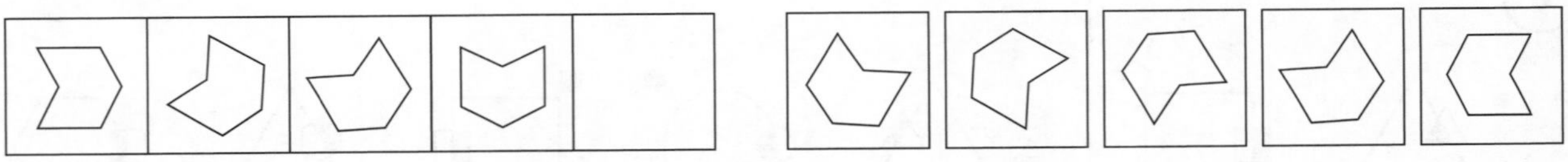

a b c d e

Answer: a

1

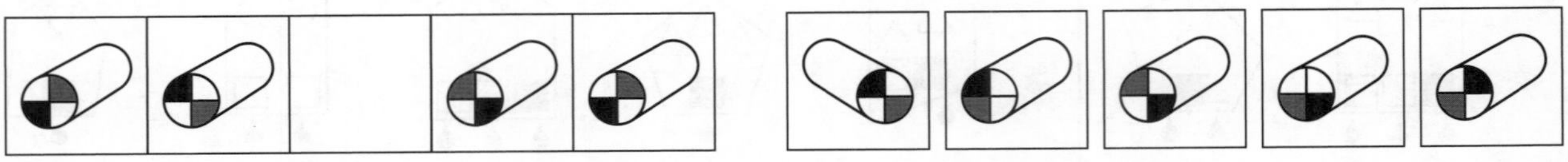

a b c d e

2

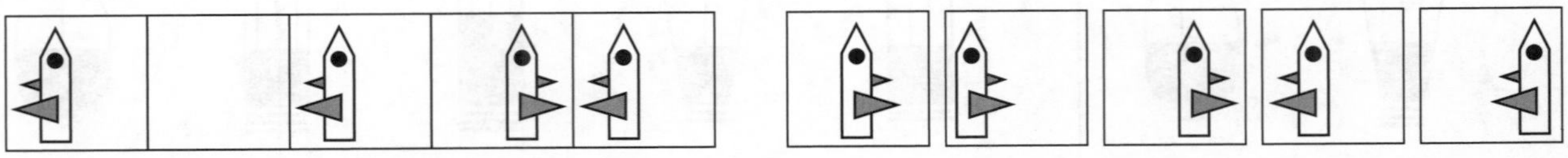

a b c d e

3

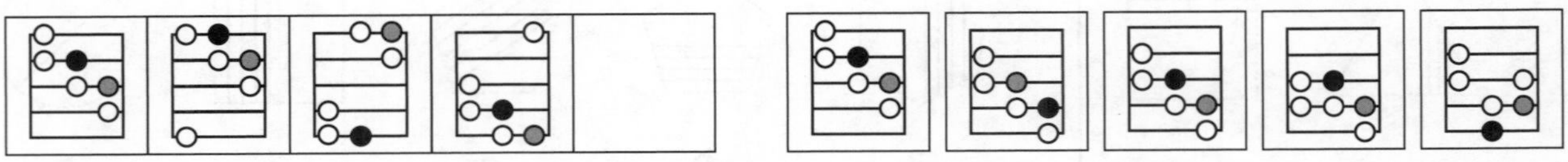

a b c d e

4

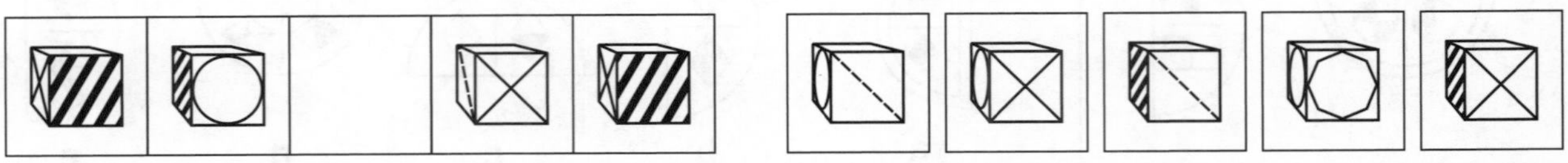

a b c d e

5

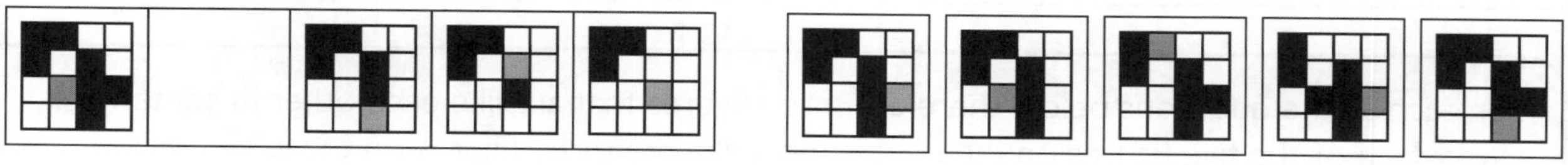

a b c d e

6

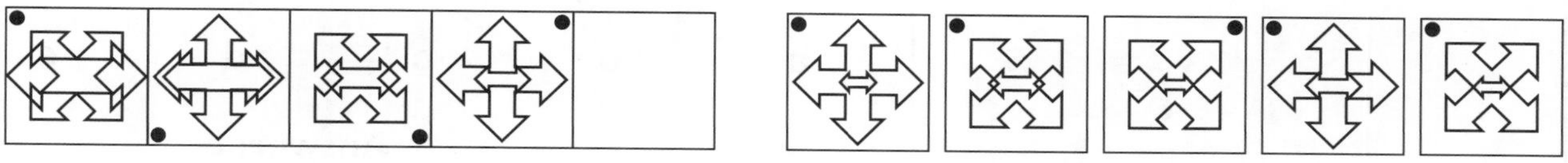

a b c d e

7

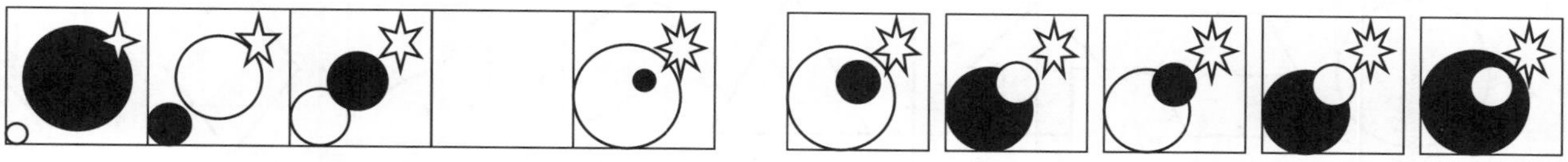

a b c d e

8

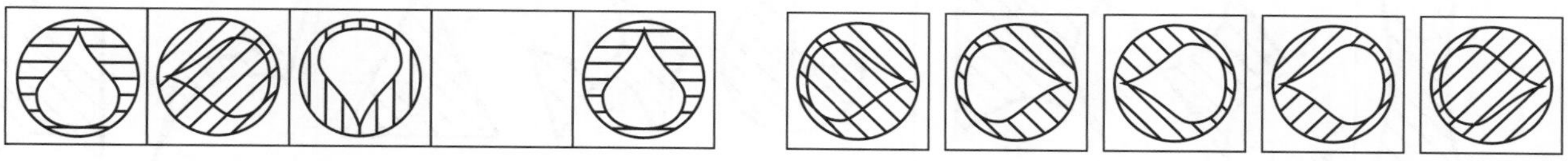

a b c d e

9

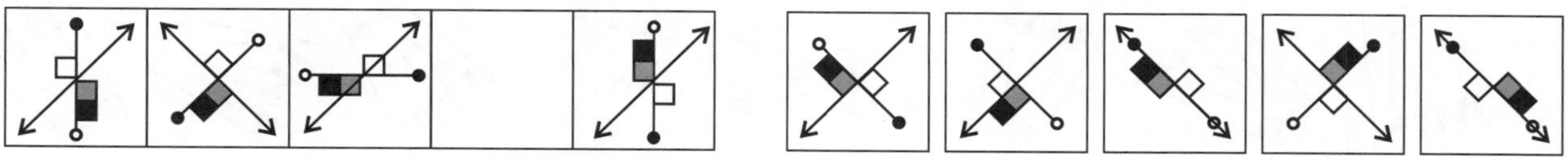

a b c d e

10

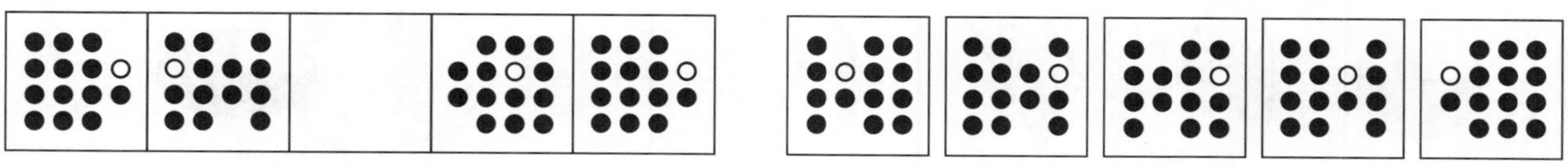

a b c d e

/ 10

Carry on to the next question →→

Section 3 — Find the Figure like the First Three

For each of the questions below there are three figures that are like each other in some way.
Find which of the five figures on the right is most like the three figures on the left.

Example:

a b c d e

Answer: c

(1)

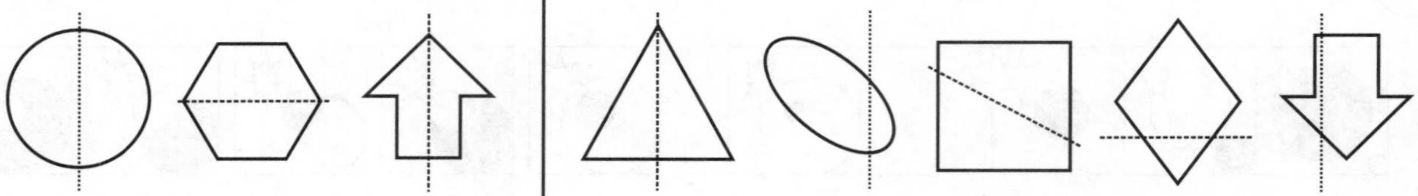

a b c d e

(2)

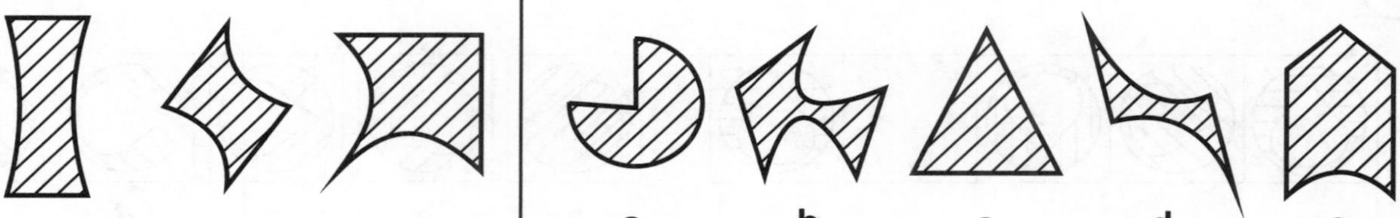

a b c d e

(3)

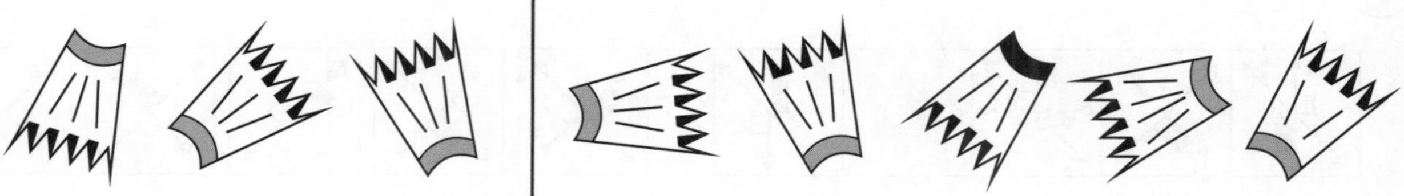

a b c d e

(4)

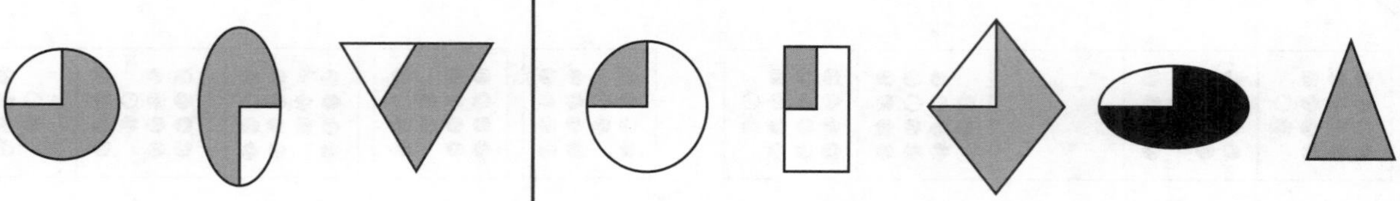

a b c d e

5

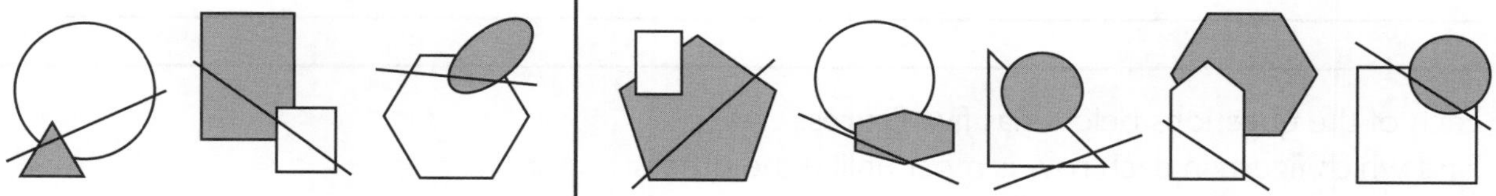

a b c d e

6

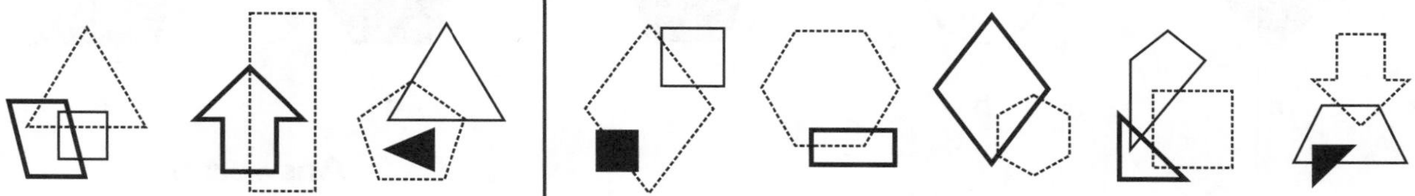

a b c d e

7

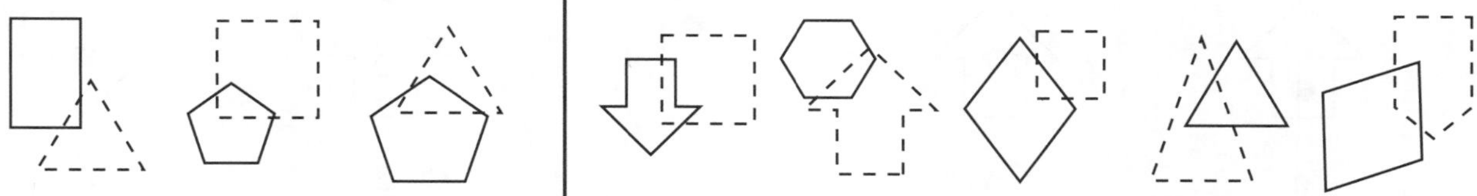

a b c d e

8

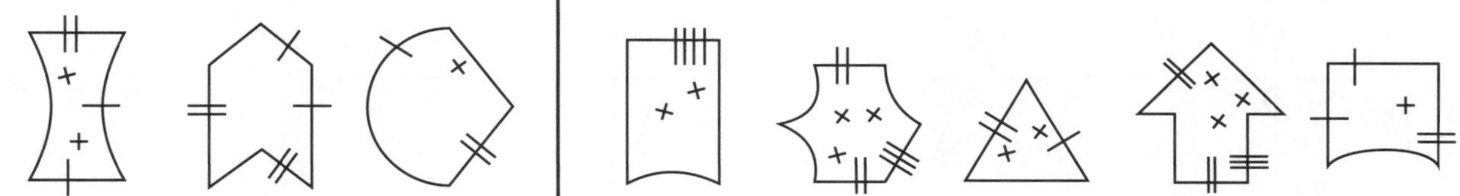

a b c d e

9

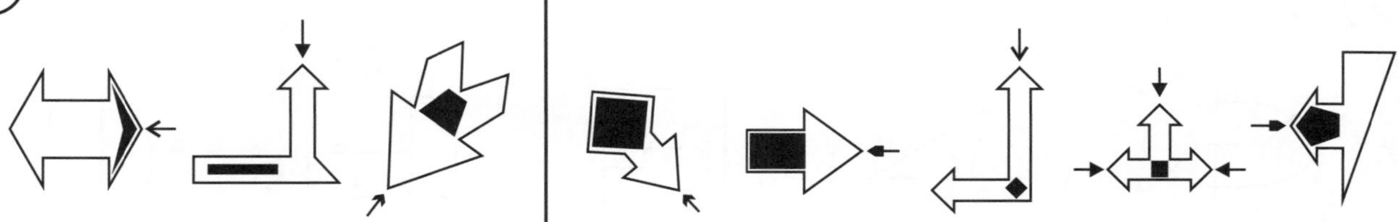

a b c d e

10

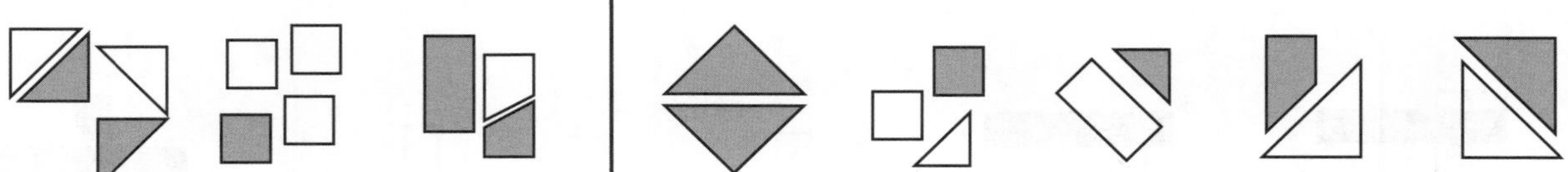

a b c d e

/ 10

Carry on to the next question → →

Section 4 — Odd One Out

Each of the questions below has five figures.
Find which figure in each row is most unlike the others.

Example:

a b c d e

Answer: b

(1)

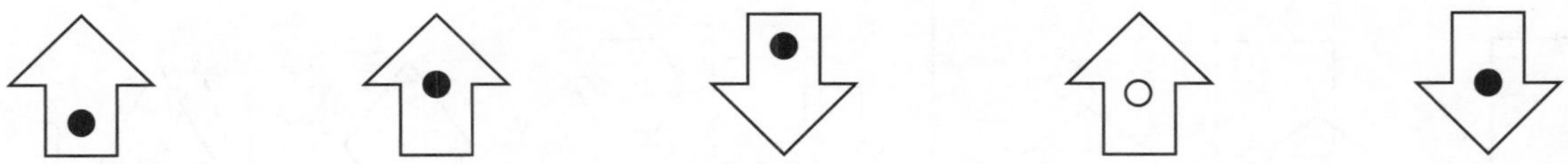

a b c d e

(2)

a b c d e

(3)

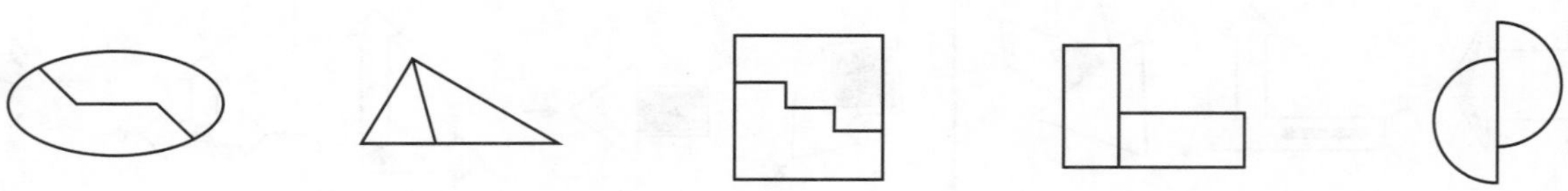

a b c d e

(4)

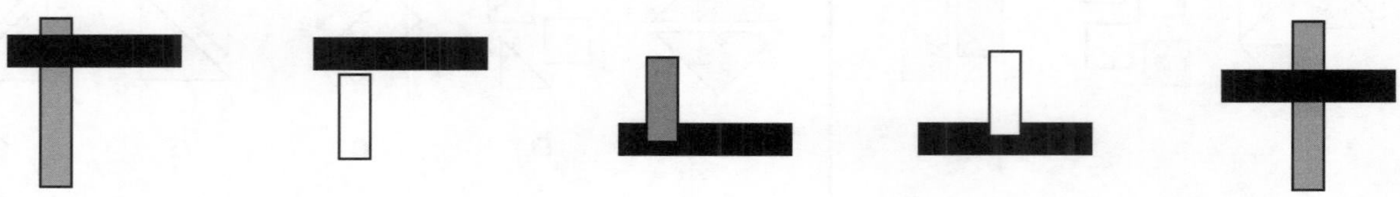

a b c d e

5

a b c d e

6

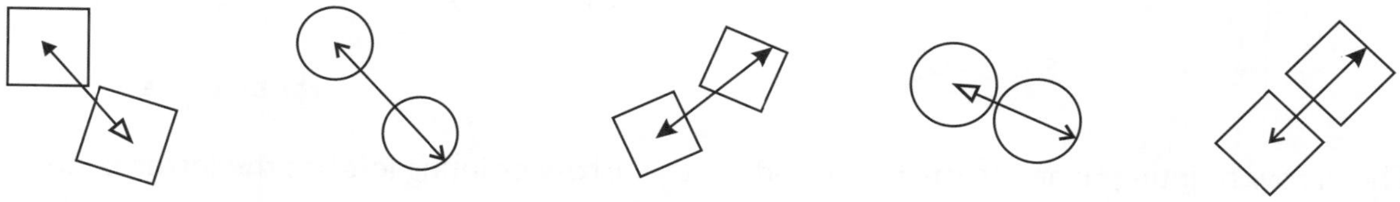

a b c d e

7

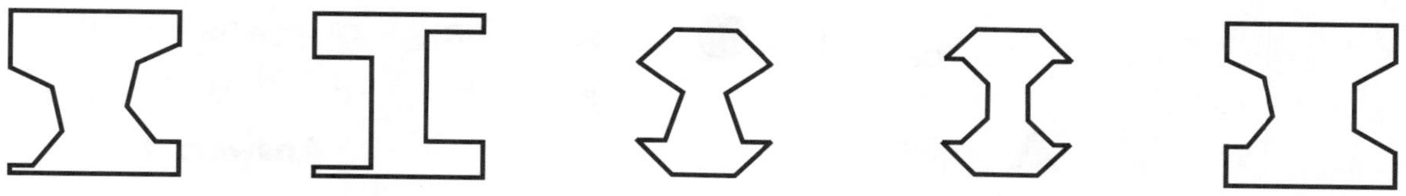

a b c d e

8

a b c d e

9

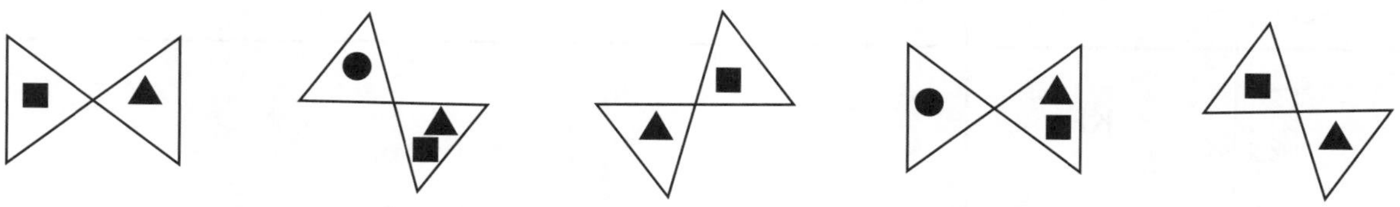

a b c d e

10

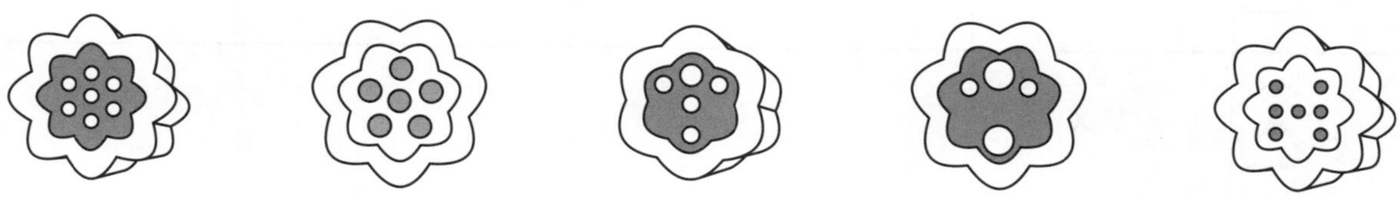

a b c d e

/ 10

Carry on to the next question → →

Section 5 — Vertical Code

Each question has some shapes on the left with code letters that describe them. You need to work out what the code letters mean. There is then a shape on its own next to a choice of five codes. Work out which code describes this shape.

Example:

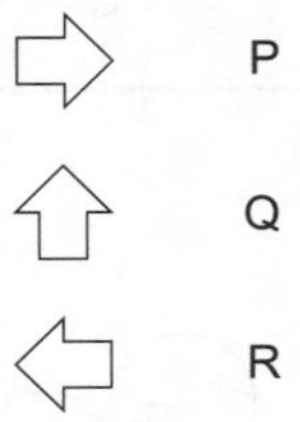

P	Q	T	S	R
a	**b**	**c**	**d**	**e**

Answer: a

The arrow pointing right has the letter code P, the arrow pointing left has the letter code R, and the arrow pointing up has the letter code Q. The new shape is an arrow pointing right, so the code must be P and the answer is a.

Example:

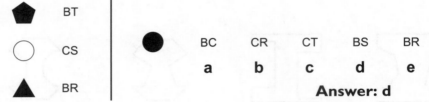

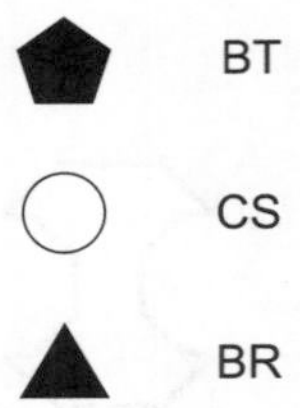

BC	CR	CT	BS	BR
a	**b**	**c**	**d**	**e**

Answer: d

Both black shapes have the letter code B, and the white shape has a C, so the first letter is for shading. The second letter code must be the code for shape. T stands for a pentagon, the letter S for a circle and the letter R for a triangle. The new shape must have a B because it is black, and an S because it is a circle. The code must be BS and the answer is d.

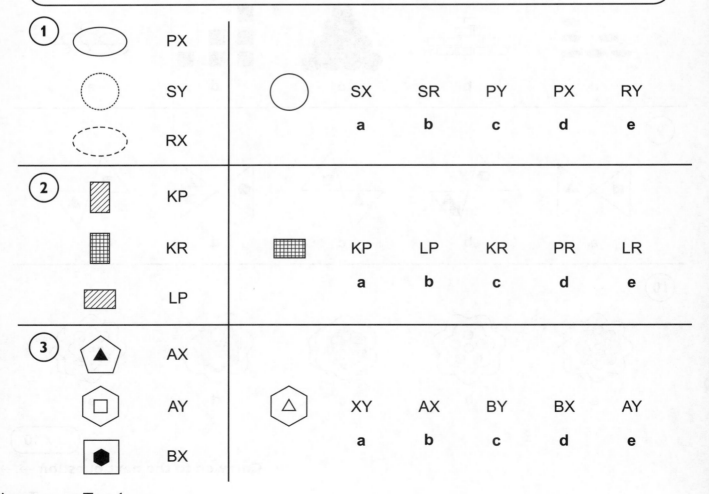

1

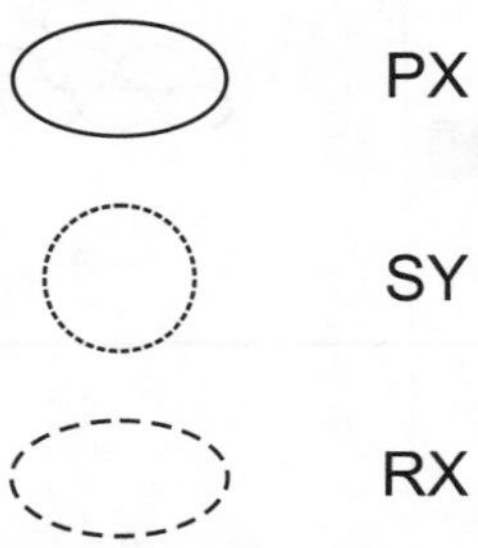

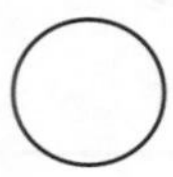

SX	SR	PY	PX	RY
a	**b**	**c**	**d**	**e**

2

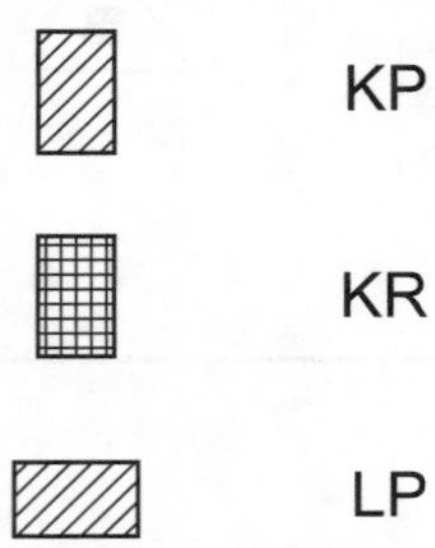

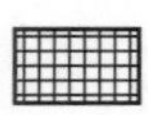

KP	LP	KR	PR	LR
a	**b**	**c**	**d**	**e**

3

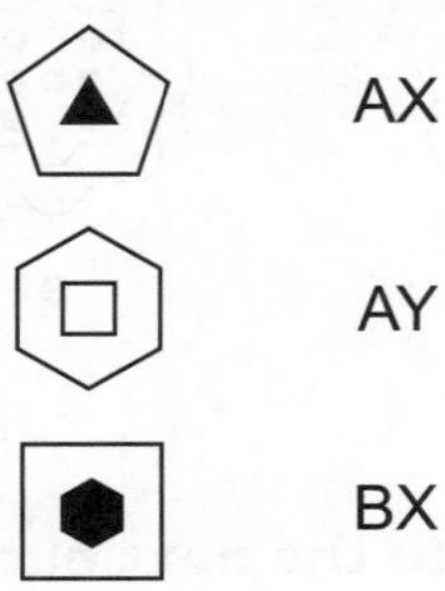

XY	AX	BY	BX	AY
a	**b**	**c**	**d**	**e**

4

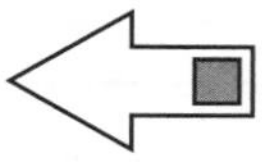 SZ

 RX

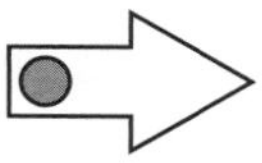 RY

 PY

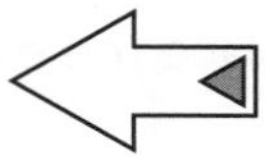

SX	PX	RZ	PZ	SY
a	**b**	**c**	**d**	**e**

5

 FNX

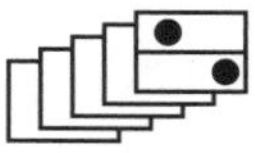 GNY

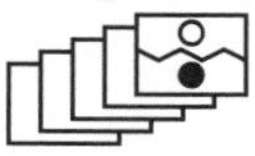 FMY

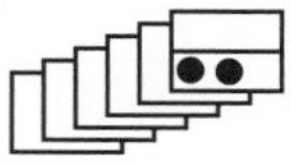

FNY	GNY	FNX	FMY	GNX
a	**b**	**c**	**d**	**e**

6

 GL

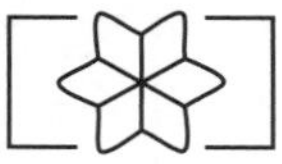 JP

 KX

 HL

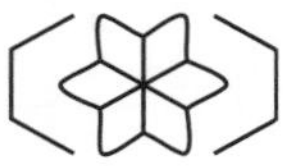

KL	JX	KP	JL	HP
a	**b**	**c**	**d**	**e**

7

 DU

 BU

 AW

 CV

AU	BU	BV	CU	DV
a	**b**	**c**	**d**	**e**

8

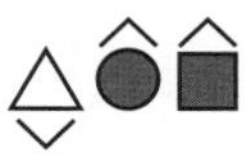 AS

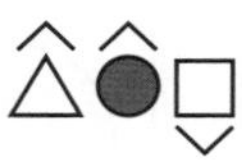 BP

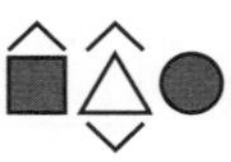 AR

 AS

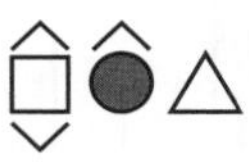

BR	BS	AR	BP	AP
a	**b**	**c**	**d**	**e**

/ 8

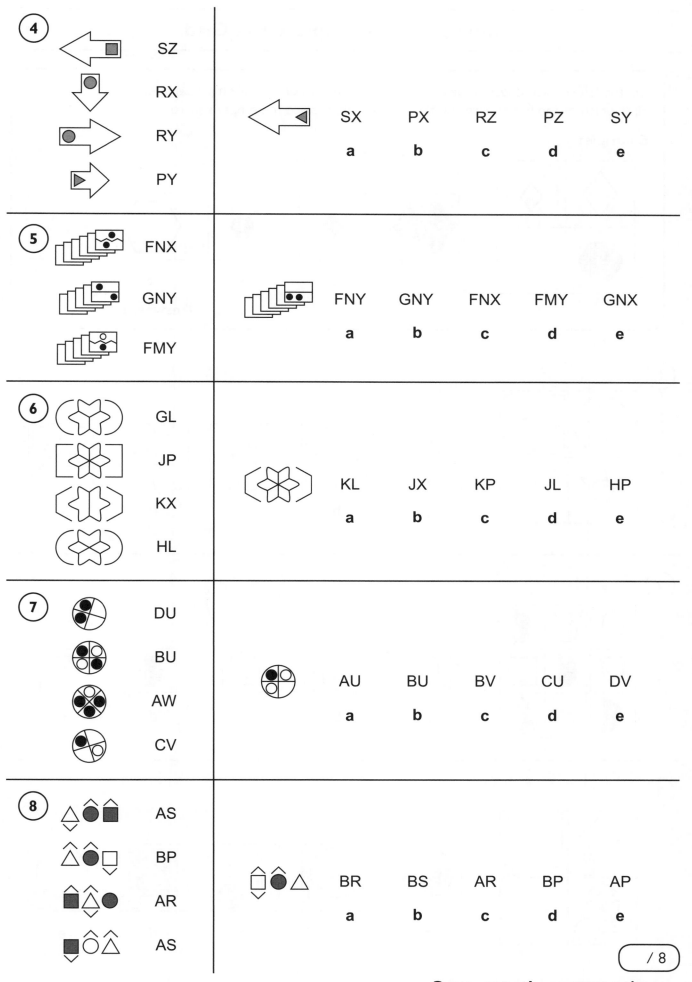

Carry on to the next question → →

Section 6 — Complete the Grid

On the left of each question below is a big square with one small empty square.
Find which of the five squares on the right should replace the empty square.

Example:

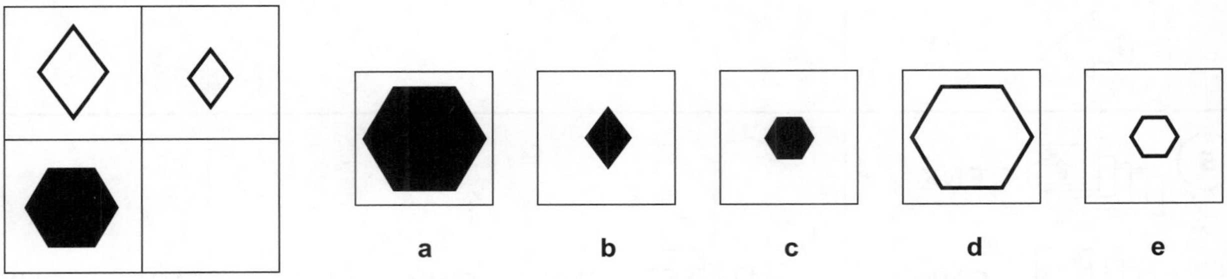

Answer: c

1

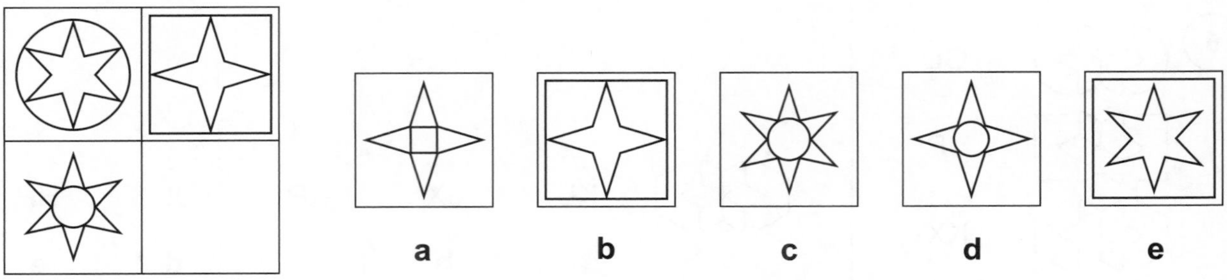

2

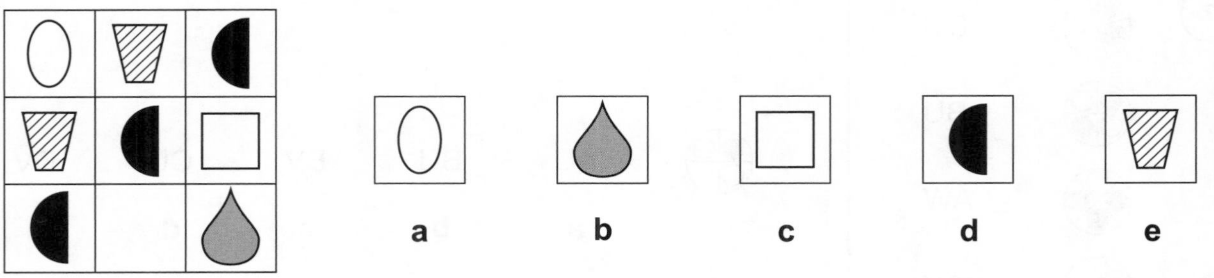

3

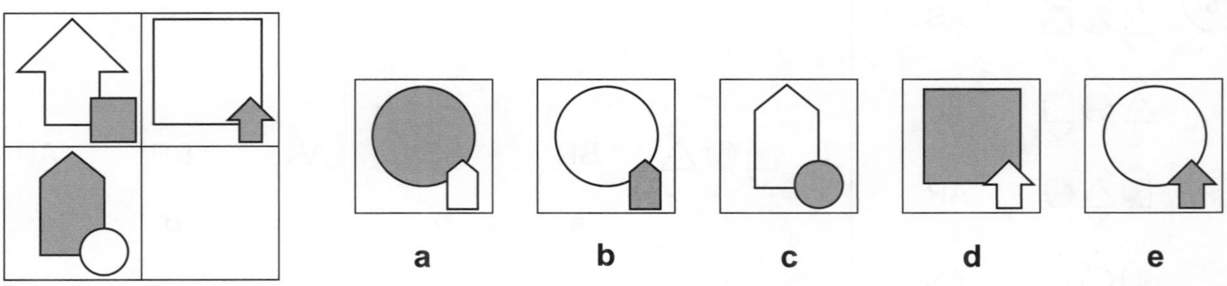

4

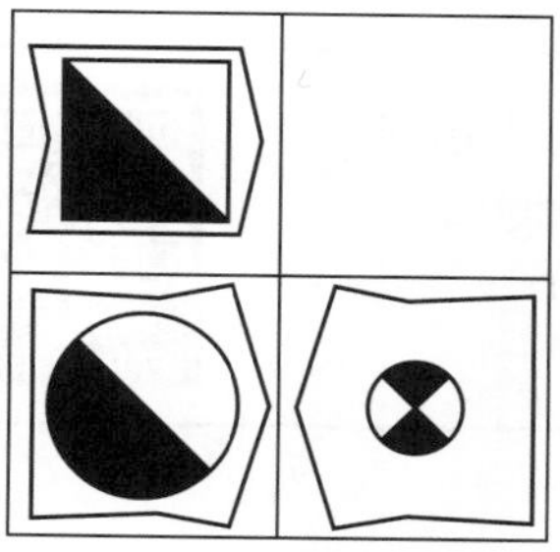

a b c d e

5

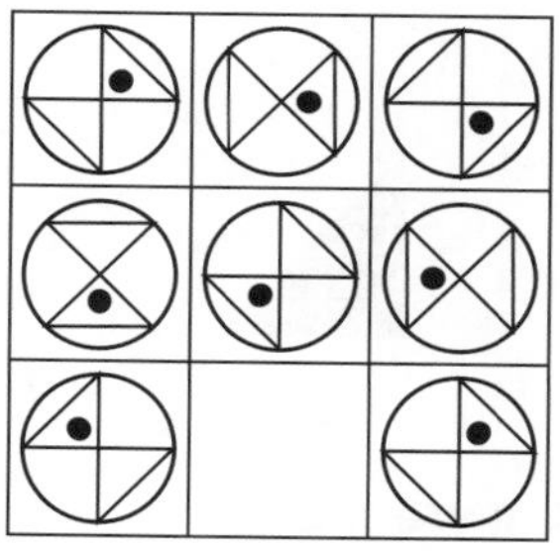

a b c d e

6

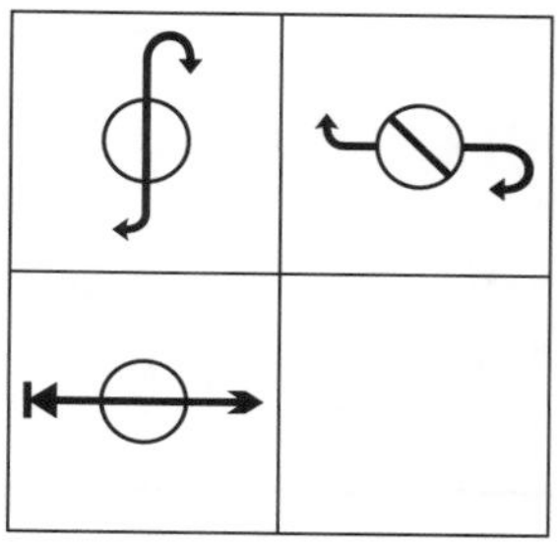

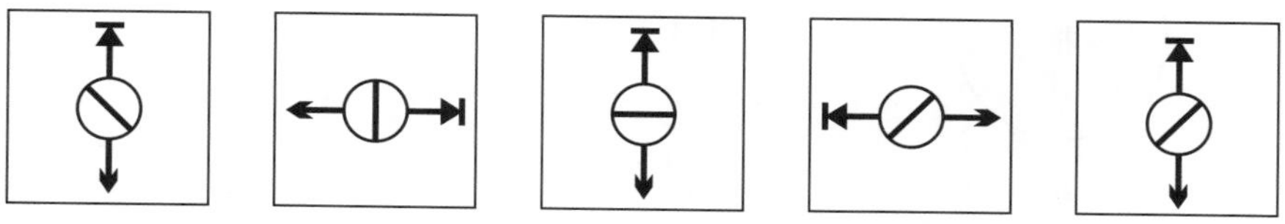

a b c d e

7

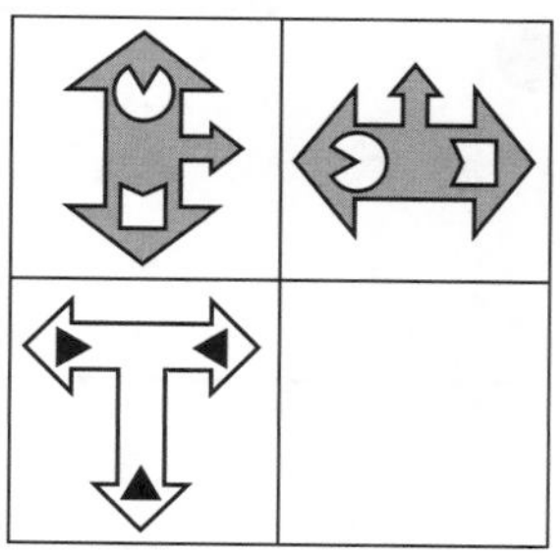

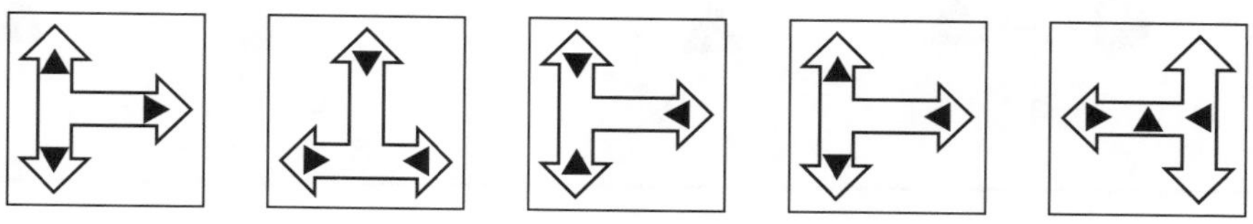

a b c d e

8

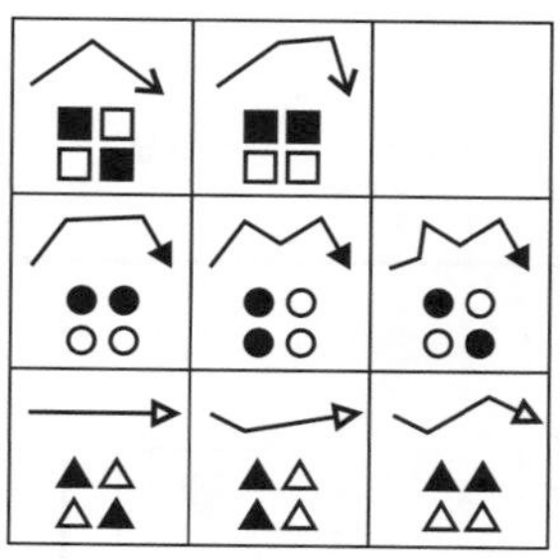

a b c d e

/ 8

Total / 56

End of Test

Assessment Test 2

You can print **multiple-choice answer sheets** for these questions from our website — go to cgpbooks.co.uk/11plus/answer-sheets or scan the QR code on the right. If you'd prefer to answer them in standard write-in format, just circle the letter underneath your answer. The test should take around 30 minutes.

Answer Sheets

Section 1 — Odd One Out

Each of the questions below has five figures.
Find which figure in each row is most unlike the others.

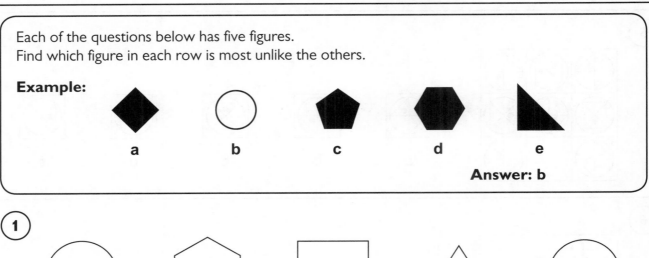

Example:

a b c d e

Answer: b

1

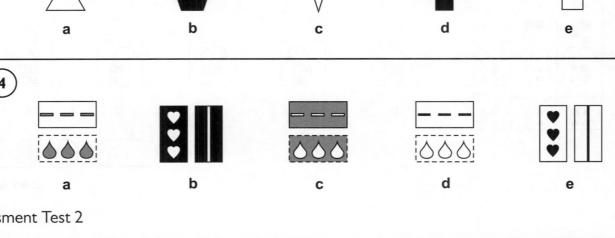

a b c d e

2

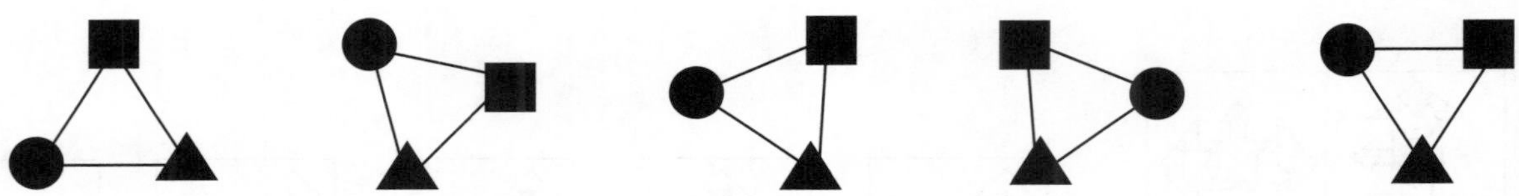

a b c d e

3

a b c d e

4

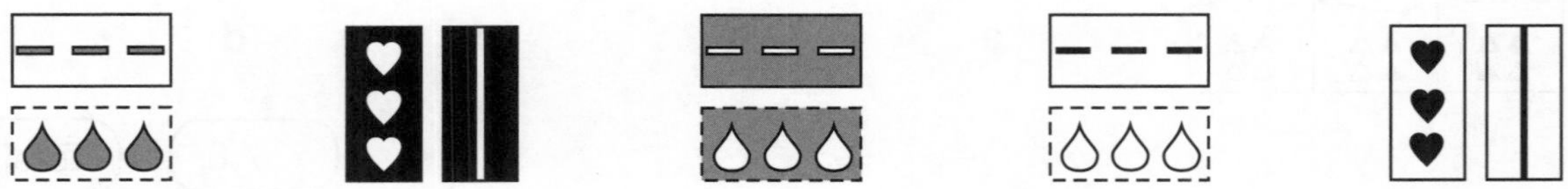

a b c d e

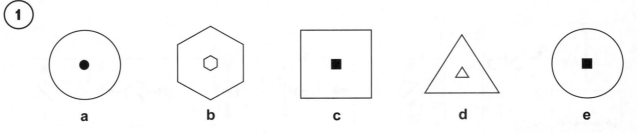

5

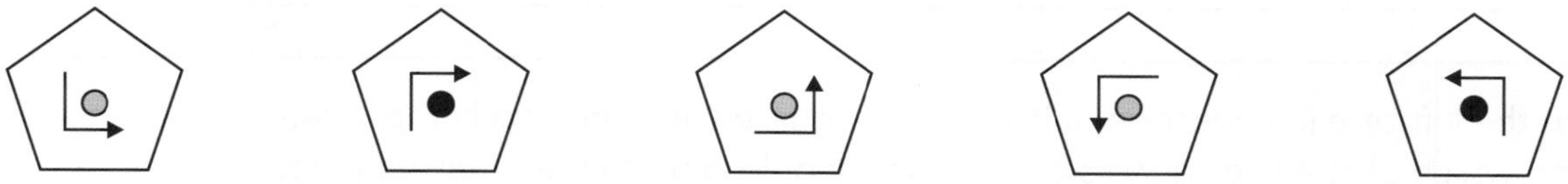

a b c d e

6

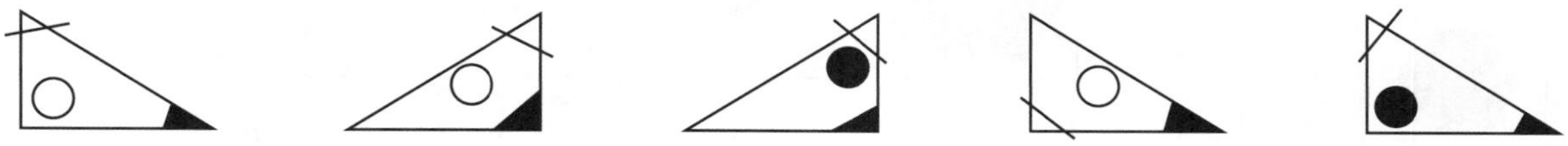

a b c d e

7

a b c d e

8

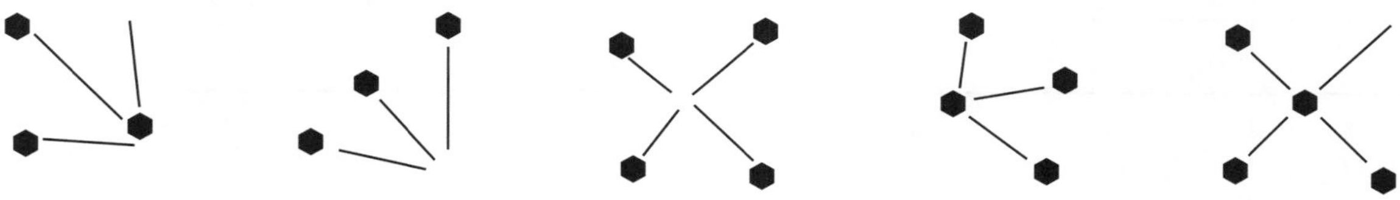

a b c d e

9

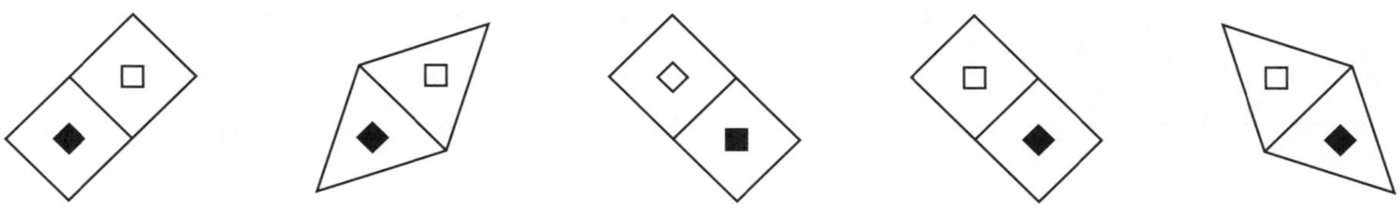

a b c d e

10

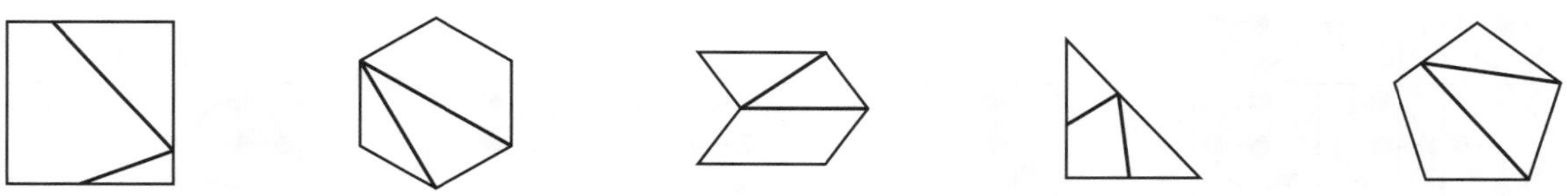

a b c d e

/ 10

Carry on to the next question →→

Section 2 — Complete the Grid

On the left of each question below is a big square with one small empty square.
Find which of the five squares on the right should replace the empty square.

Example:

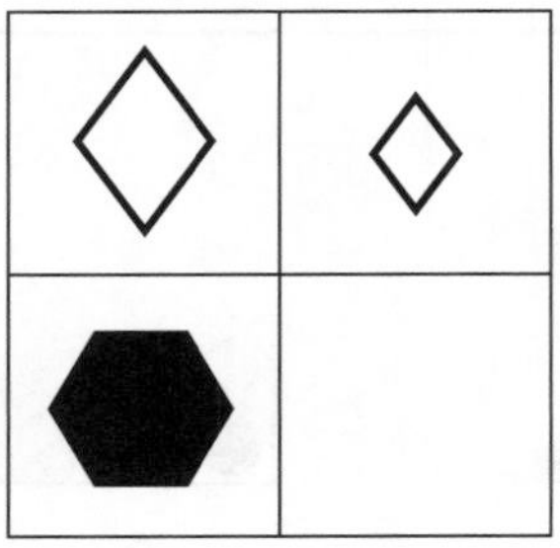

a b c d e

Answer: c

(1)

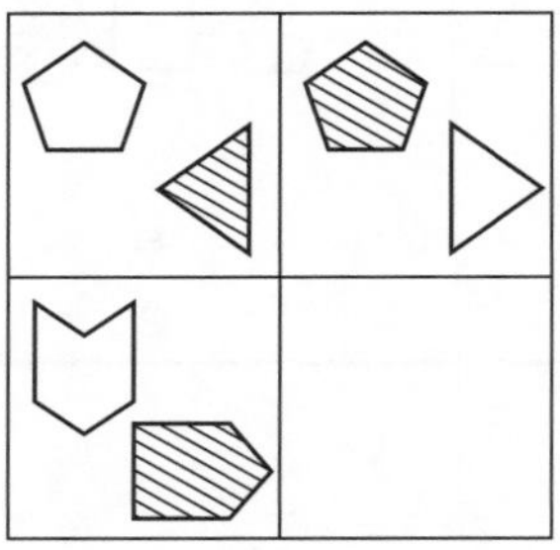

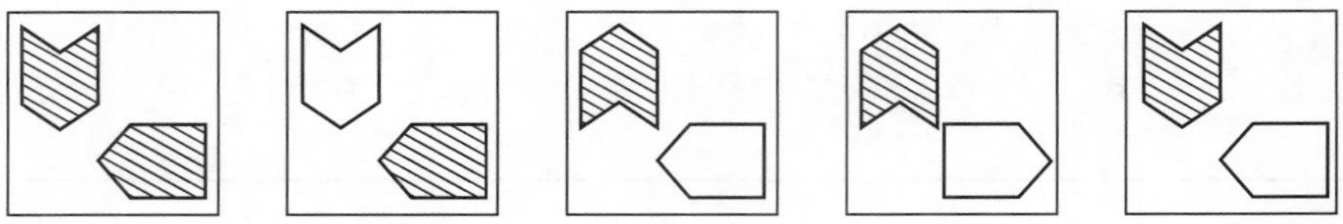

a b c d e

(2)

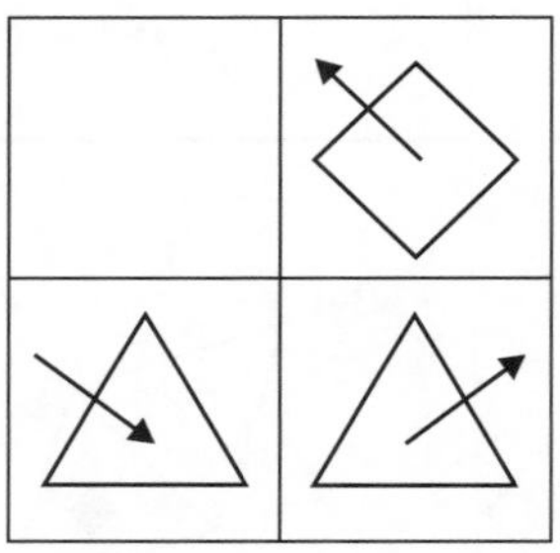

a b c d e

(3)

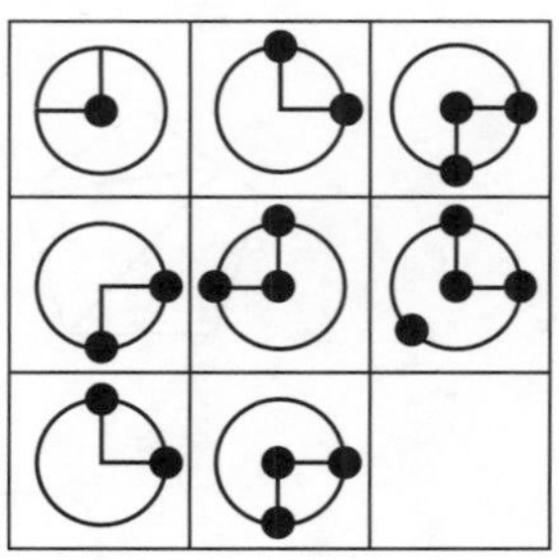

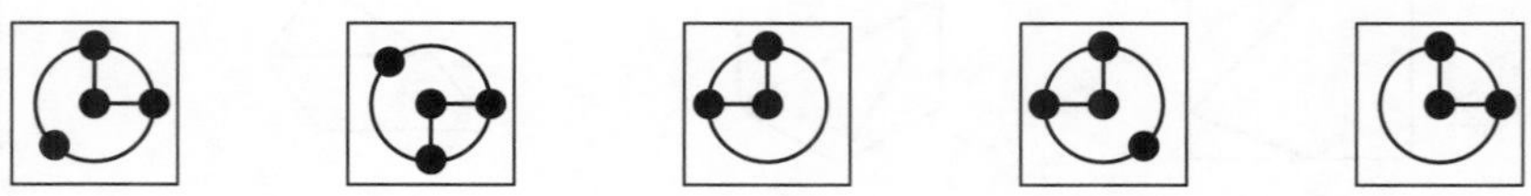

a b c d e

4

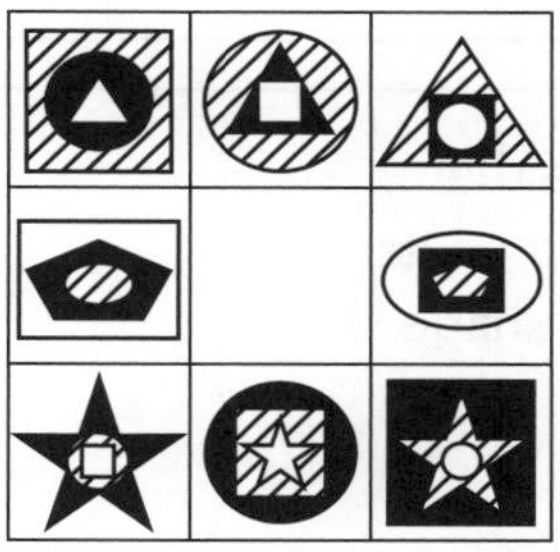

a b c d e

5

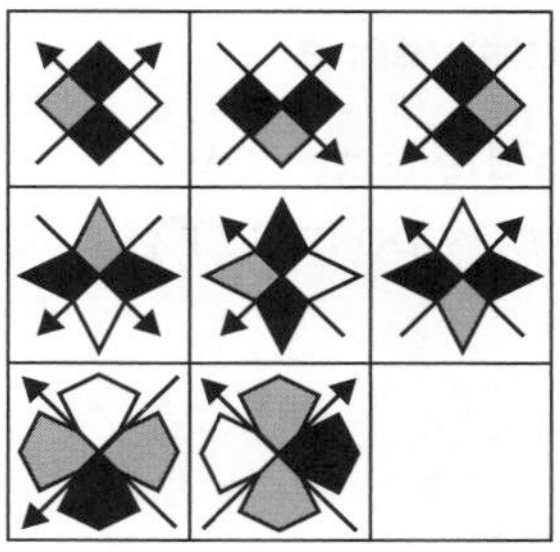

a b c d e

6

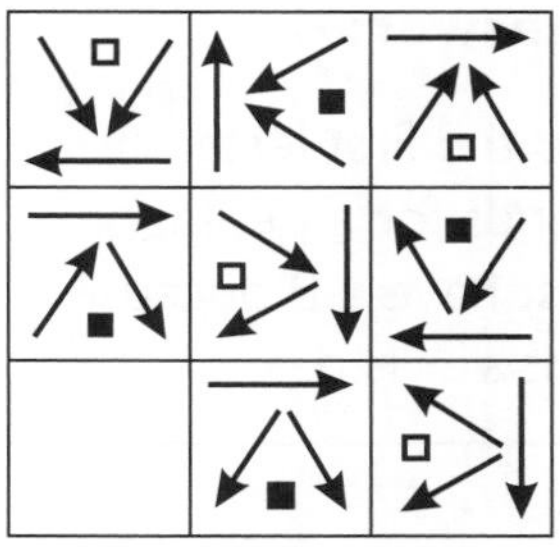

a b c d e

7

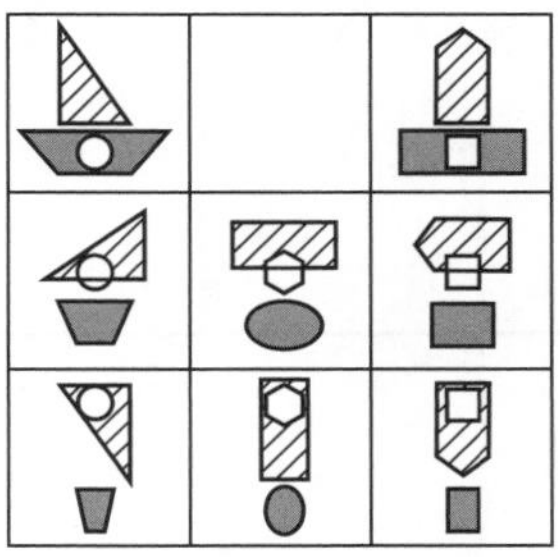

a b c d e

8

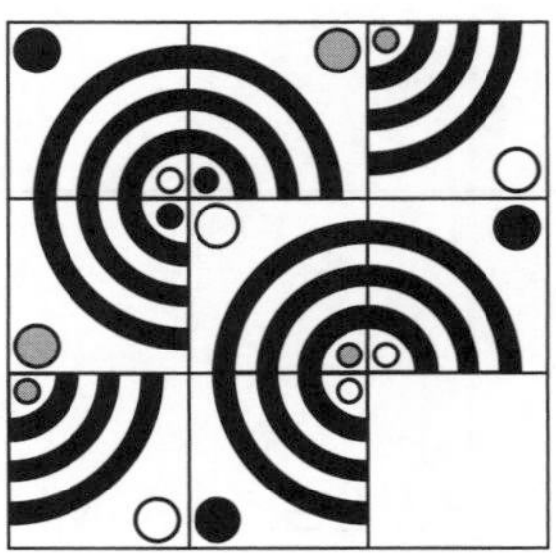

a b c d e

/ 8

Carry on to the next question → →

Section 3 — Vertical Code

Each question has some shapes on the left with code letters that describe them. You need to work out what the code letters mean. There is then a shape on its own next to a choice of five codes. Work out which code describes this shape.

Example:

P

Q

R

P	Q	T	S	R
a	**b**	**c**	**d**	**e**

Answer: a

The arrow pointing right has the letter code P, the arrow pointing left has the letter code R, and the arrow pointing up has the letter code Q. The new shape is an arrow pointing right, so the code must be P and the answer is a.

Example:

BT

CS

BR

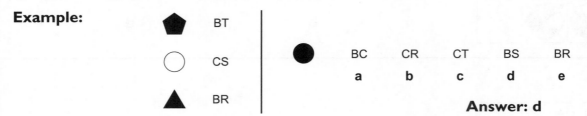

BC	CR	CT	BS	BR
a	**b**	**c**	**d**	**e**

Answer: d

Both black shapes have the letter code B, and the white shape has a C, so the first letter is for shading. The second letter code must be the code for shape. T stands for a pentagon, the letter S for a circle and the letter R for a triangle. The new shape must have a B because it is black, and an S because it is a circle. The code must be BS and the answer is d.

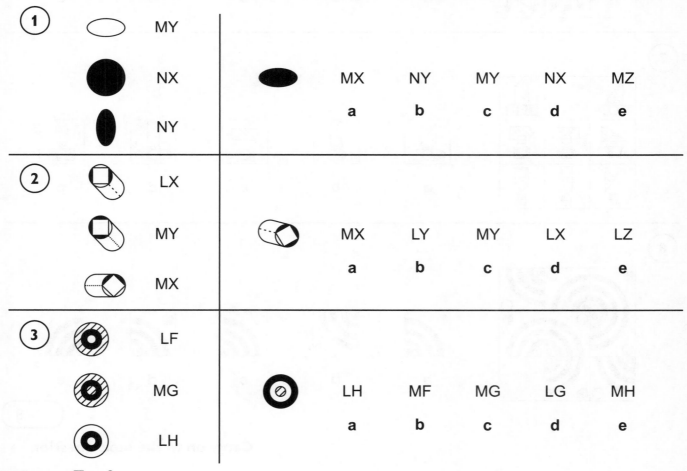

1

MY

NX

NY

MX	NY	MY	NX	MZ
a	**b**	**c**	**d**	**e**

2

LX

MY

MX

MX	LY	MY	LX	LZ
a	**b**	**c**	**d**	**e**

3

LF

MG

LH

LH	MF	MG	LG	MH
a	**b**	**c**	**d**	**e**

4

RVC

SWD

TVD

SVC

a	b	c	d	e
TVC	RWD	RWC	RVD	TWC

5

WL

WK

VM

a	b	c	d	e
VK	WL	VL	WK	VM

6

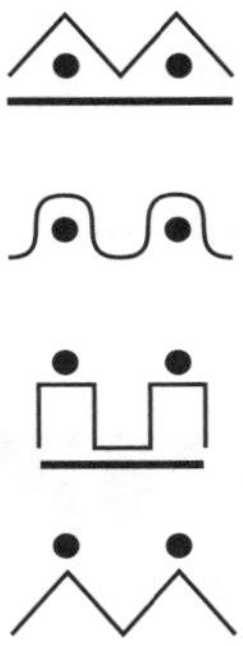

RVY

SVZ

TWY

RWZ

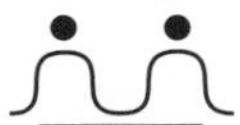

a	b	c	d	e
RWY	SVY	SWY	SVZ	RVZ

7

BCG

ACG

BDG

BDF

a	b	c	d	e
ADF	ADG	BDG	ADH	BCF

8

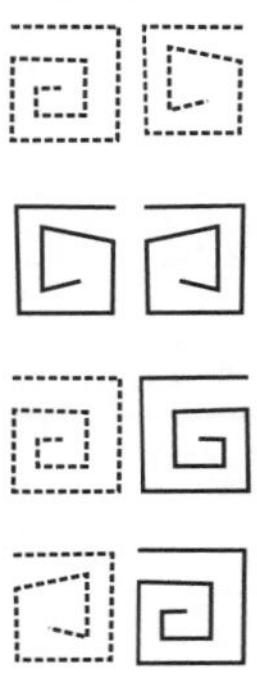

TWX

SWY

RWY

RVX

a	b	c	d	e
SWX	SVY	TVX	RWY	SWY

/ 8

Carry on to the next question → →

Section 4 — Complete the Series

Each of these questions has five squares on the left that are arranged in order.
One of the squares is missing. One of the squares on the right should go in its place.
Find which one of the five squares on the right should go in place of the empty square.

Example:

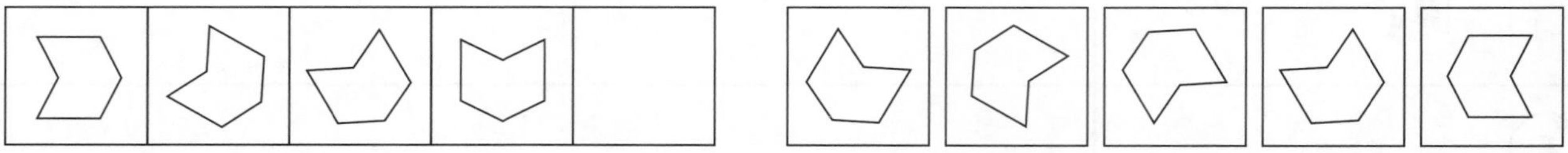

a b c d e

Answer: a

(1)

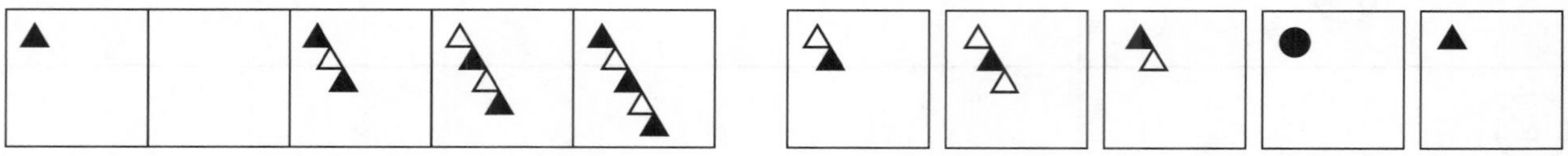

a b c d e

(2)

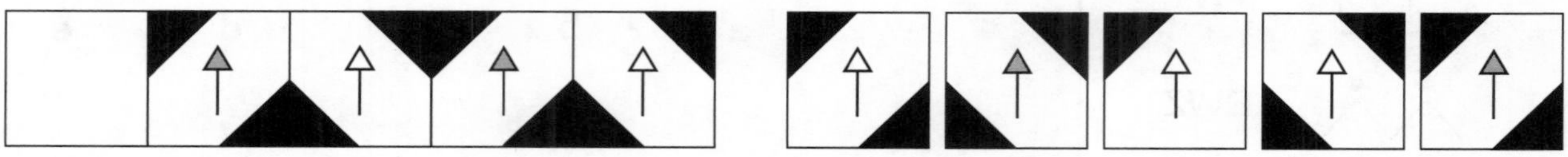

a b c d e

(3)

a b c d e

(4)

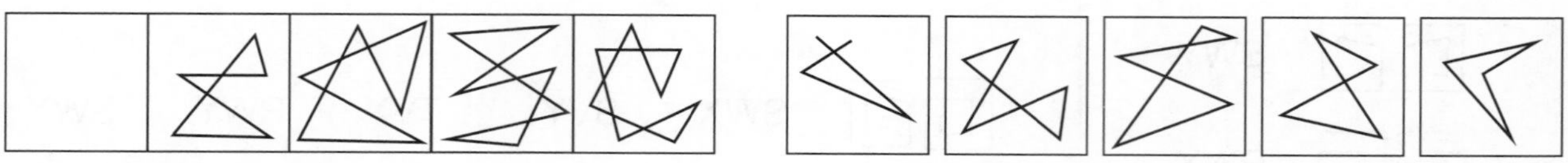

a b c d e

5

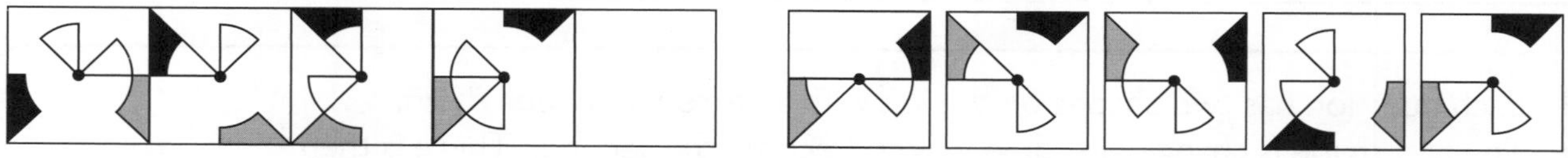

a b c d e

6

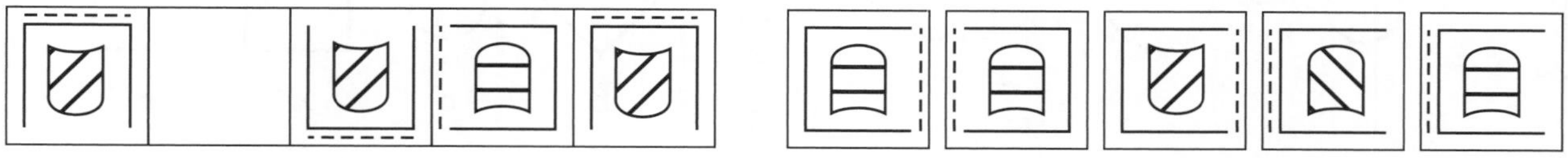

a b c d e

7

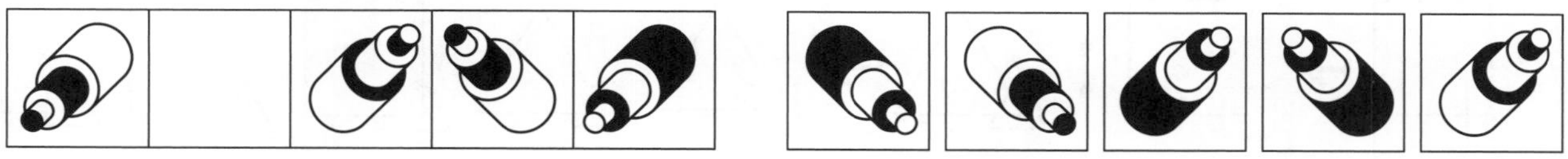

a b c d e

8

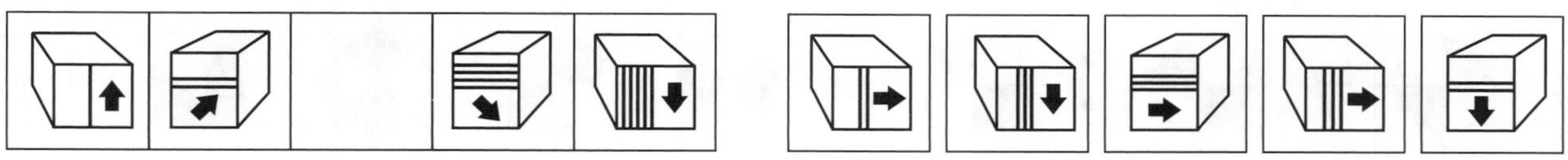

a b c d e

9

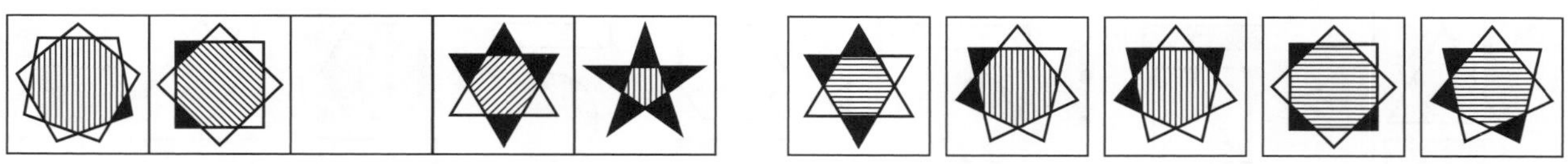

a b c d e

10

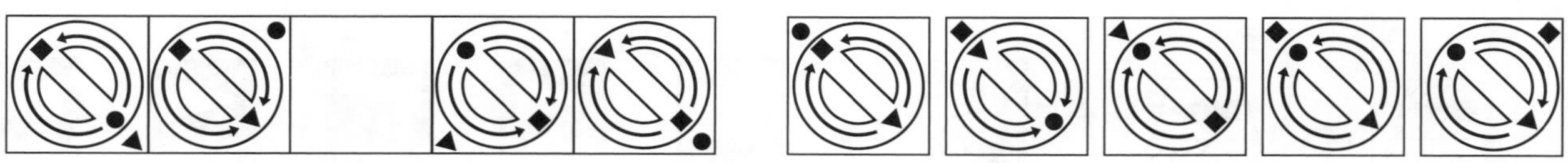

a b c d e

/ 10

Carry on to the next question → →

Section 5 — Complete the Pair

Each question has two shapes on the left with an arrow between them. The first shape is changed in some way to become the second. There is then a third shape followed by an arrow and a choice of five shapes. Choose the shape on the right that relates to the third shape like the second does to the first.

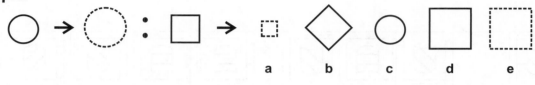

Example:

a b c d e

Answer: e

1

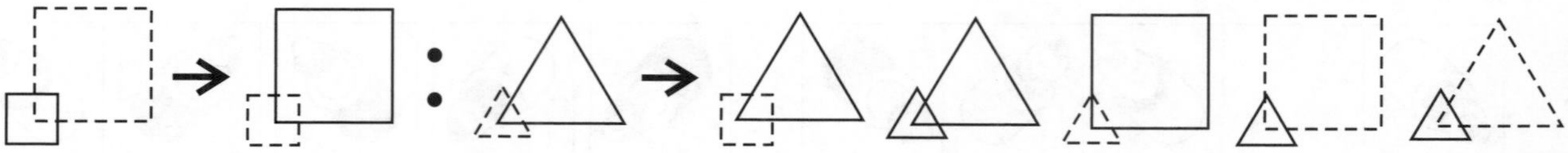

a b c d e

2

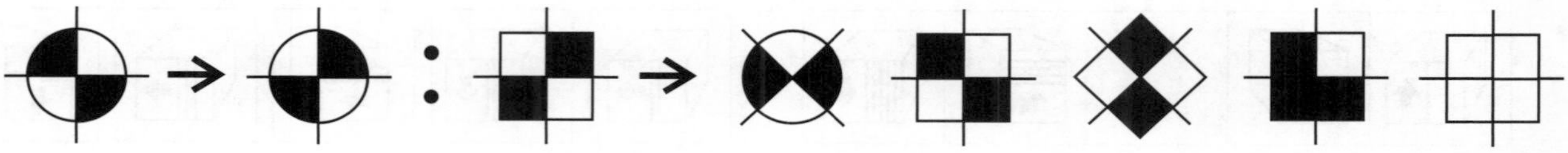

a b c d e

3

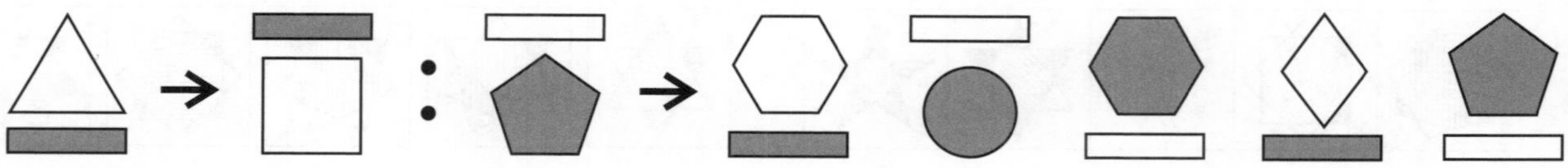

a b c d e

4

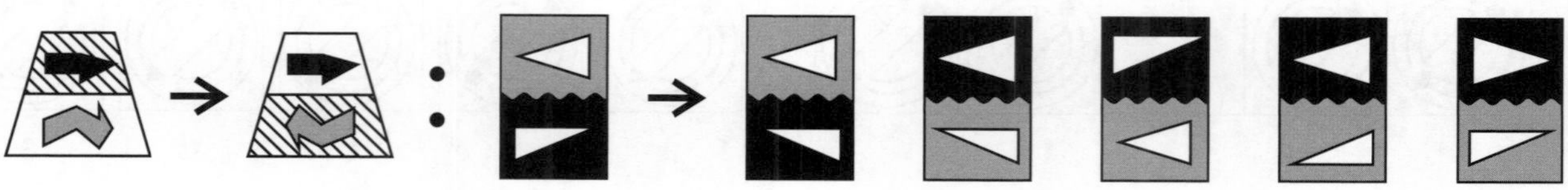

a b c d e

(5)

a b c d e

(6)

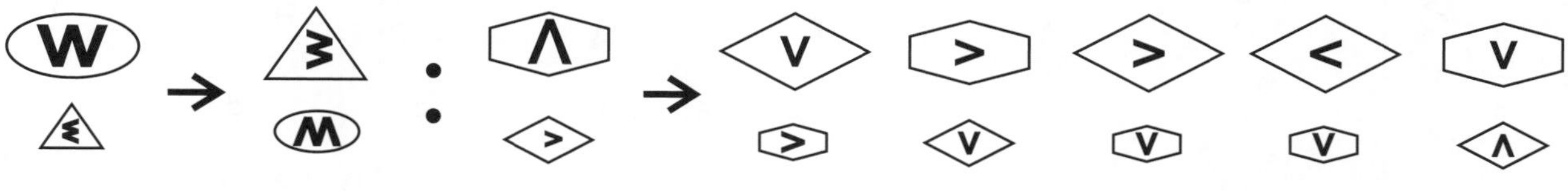

a b c d e

(7)

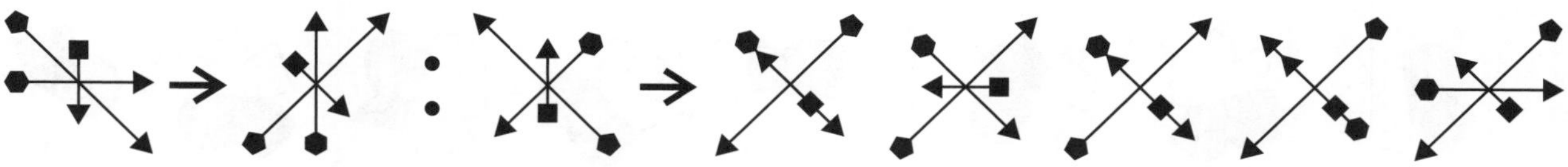

a b c d e

(8)

a b c d e

(9)

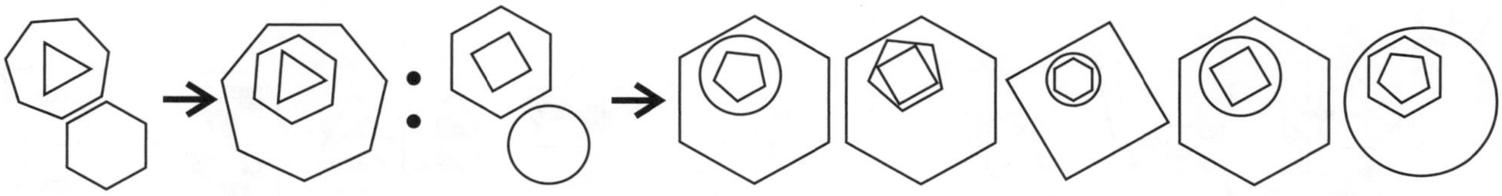

a b c d e

(10)

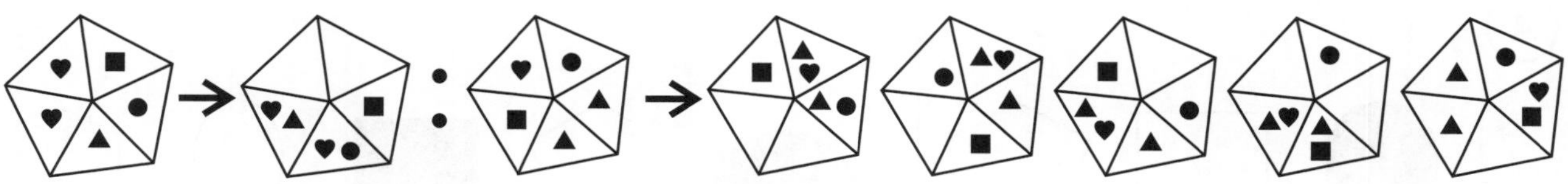

a b c d e

/ 10

Carry on to the next question → →

Section 6 — Find the Figure Like the First Three

For each of the questions below there are three figures that are like each other in some way. Find which of the five figures on the right is most like the three figures on the left.

Example:

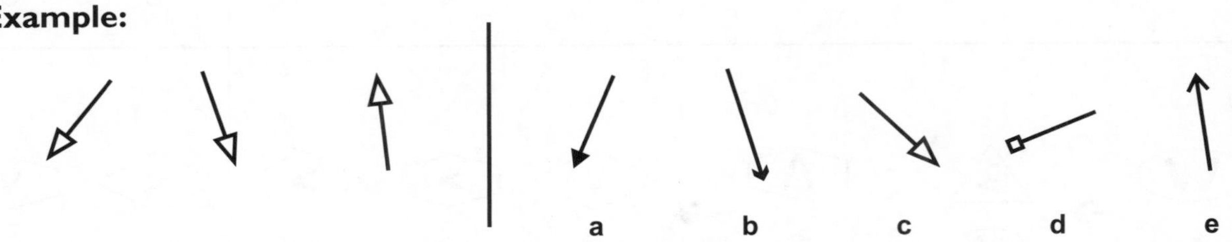

Answer: c

1

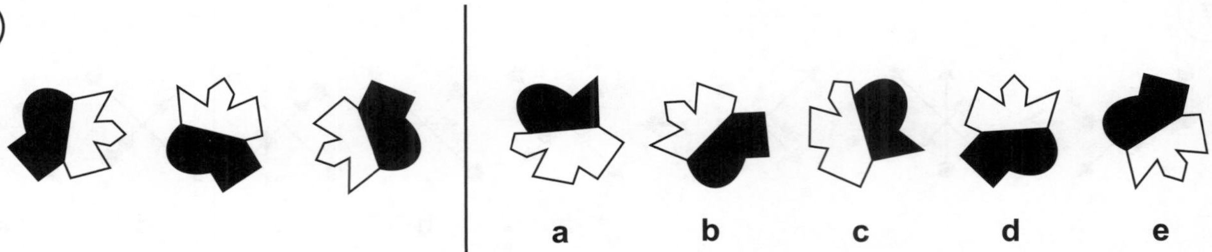

2

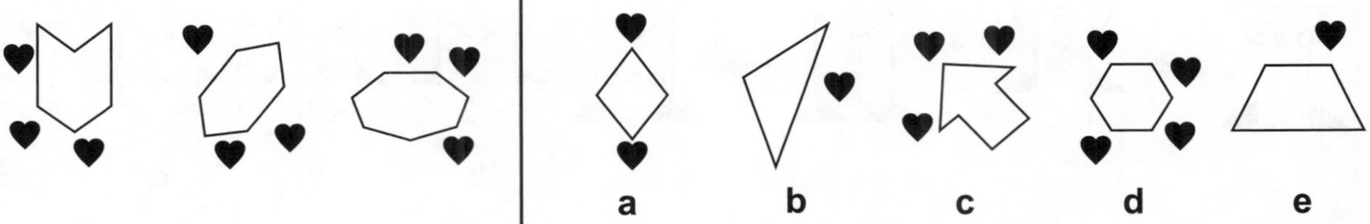

3

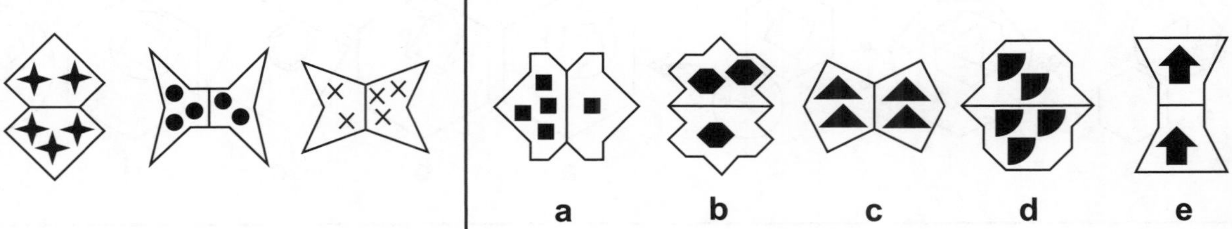

4

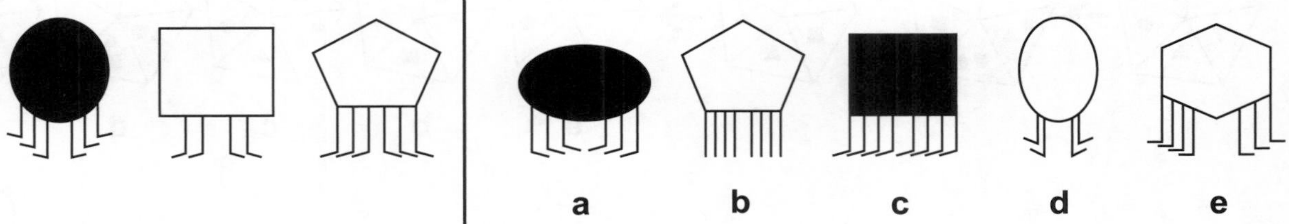

5

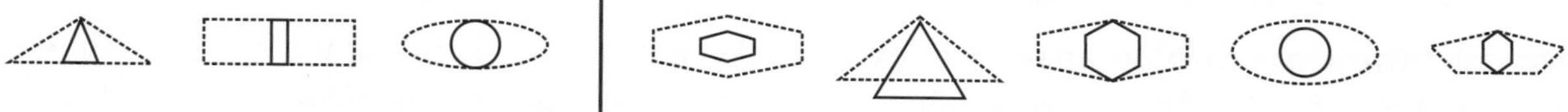

a b c d e

6

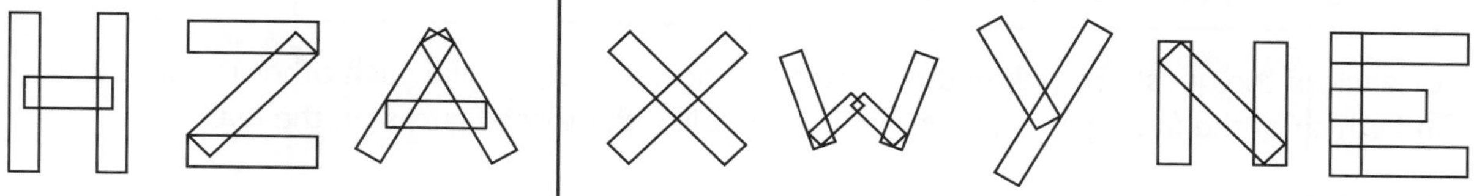

a b c d e

7

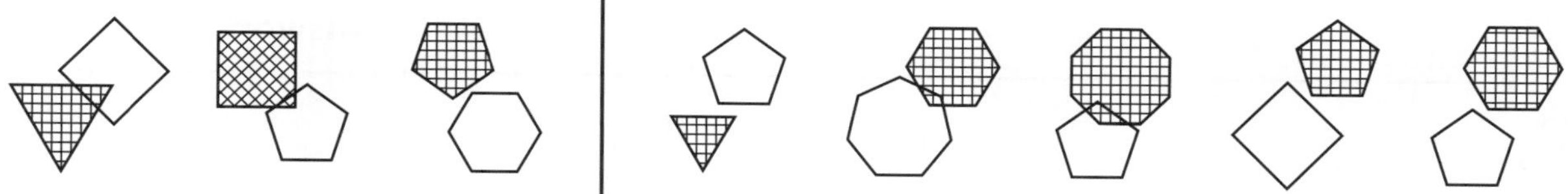

a b c d e

8

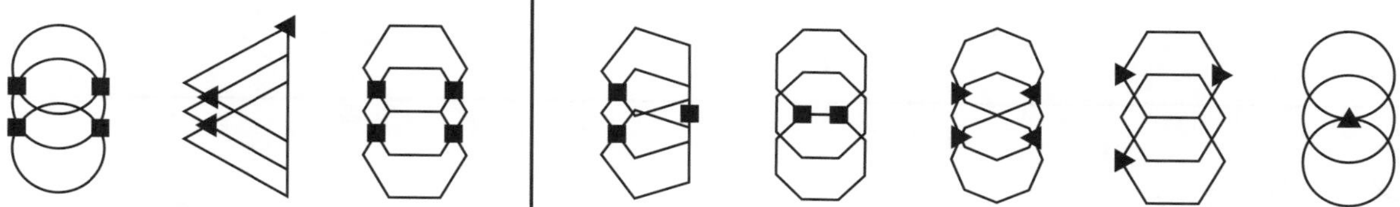

a b c d e

9

a b c d e

10

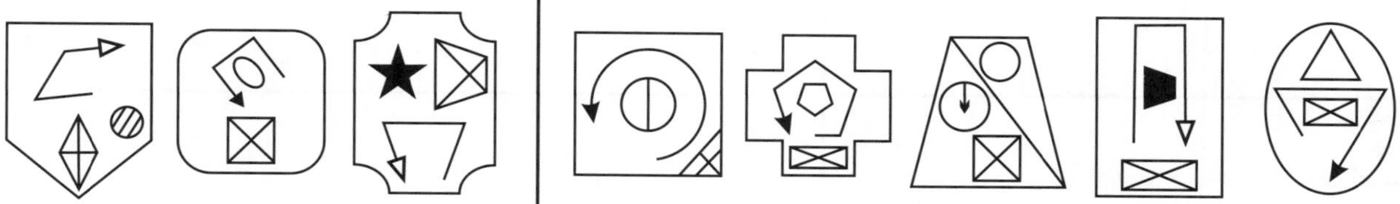

a b c d e

/ 10

Total / 56

End of Test

Assessment Test 3

You can print **multiple-choice answer sheets** for these questions from our website — go to cgpbooks.co.uk/11plus/answer-sheets or scan the QR code on the right. If you'd prefer to answer them in standard write-in format, just circle the letter underneath your answer. The test should take around 30 minutes.

Answer Sheets

Section 1 — Find the Figure Like the First Three

For each of the questions below there are three figures that are like each other in some way. Find which of the five figures on the right is most like the three figures on the left.

Example:

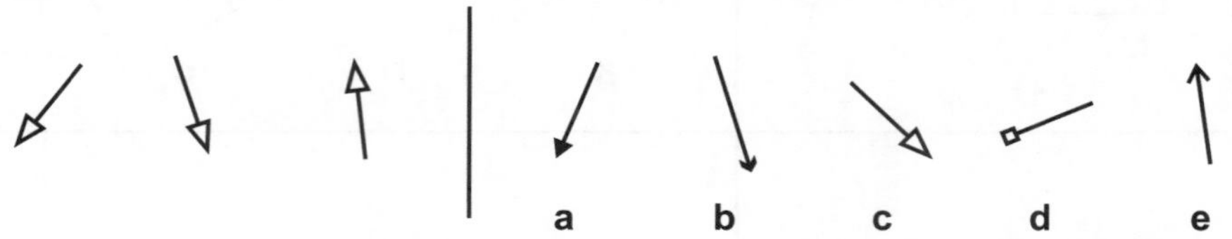

Answer: c

1

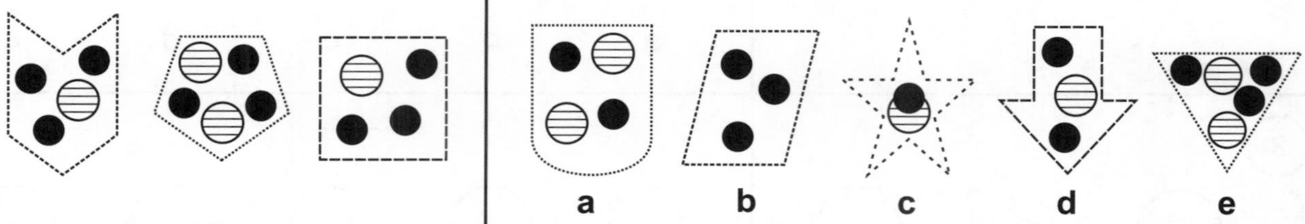

2

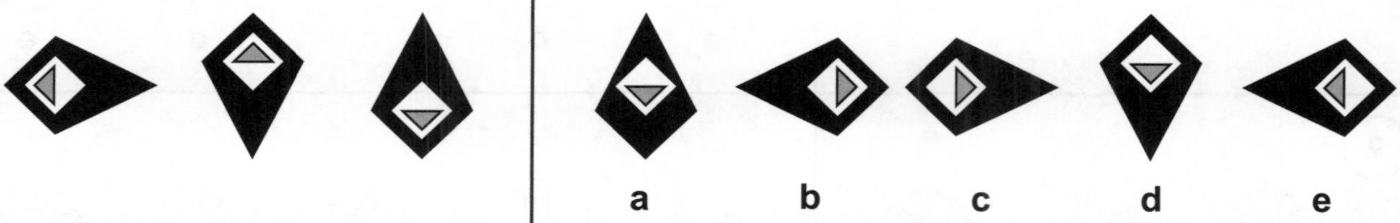

3

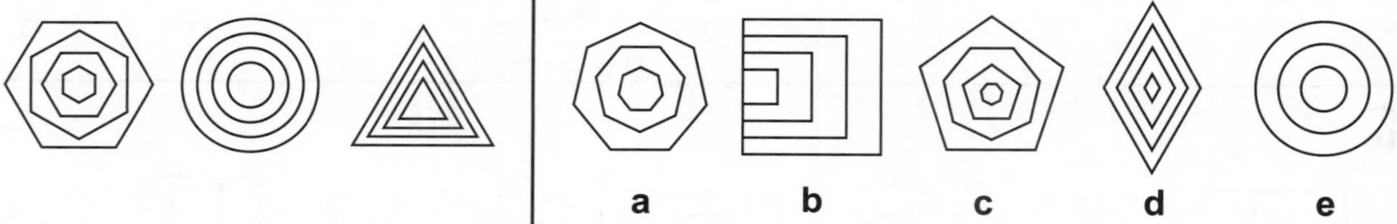

4

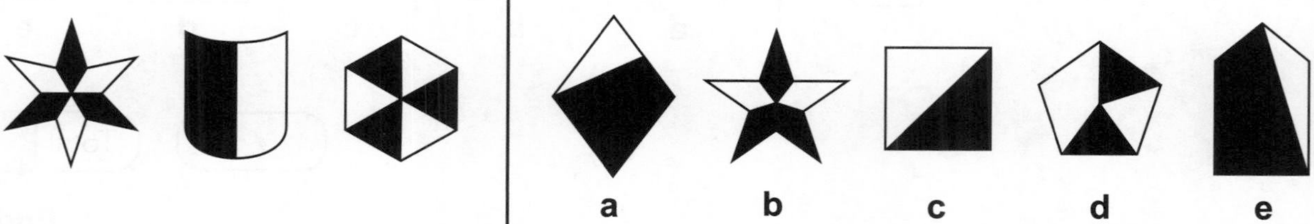

5

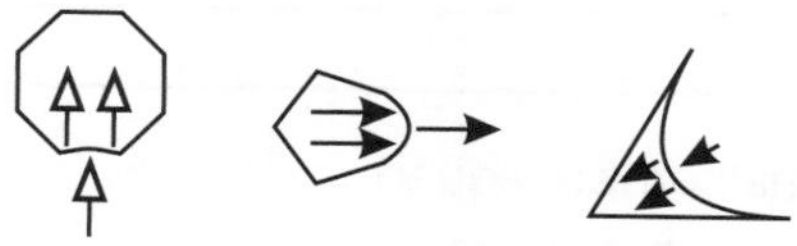

a b c d e

6

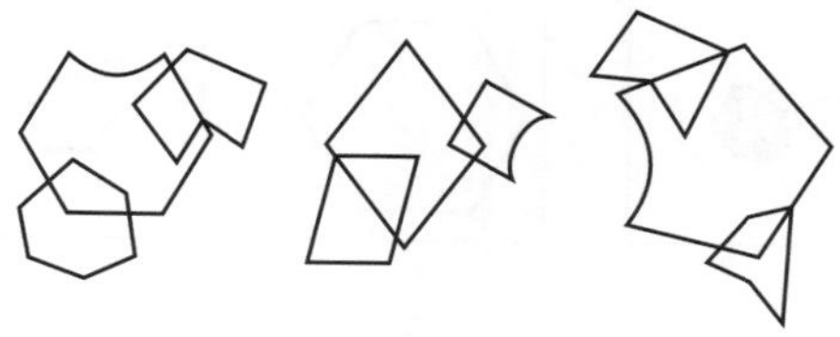

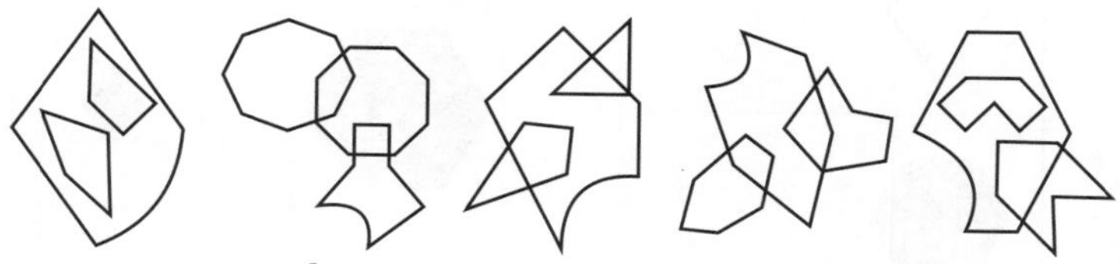

a b c d e

7

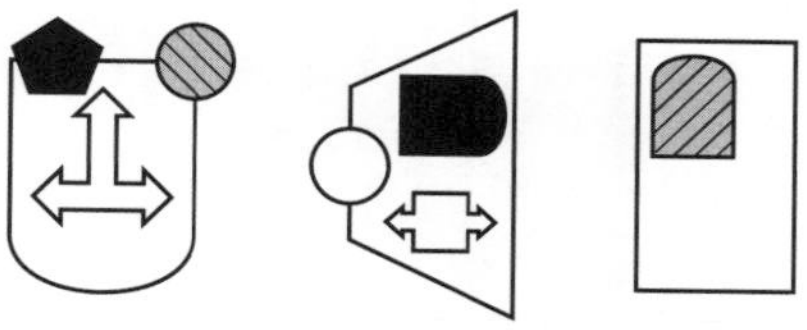

a b c d e

8

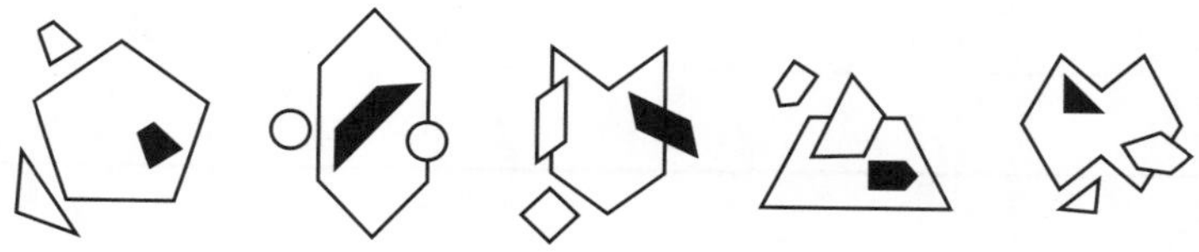

a b c d e

9

a b c d e

10

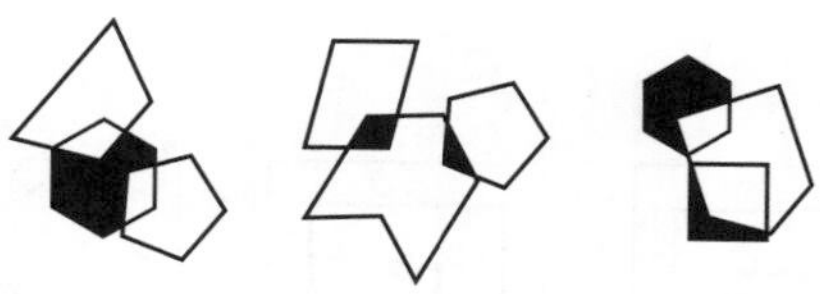

a b c d e

/ 10

Carry on to the next question → →

Section 2 — Complete the Grid

On the left of each question below is a big square with one small empty square.
Find which of the five squares on the right should replace the empty square.

Example:

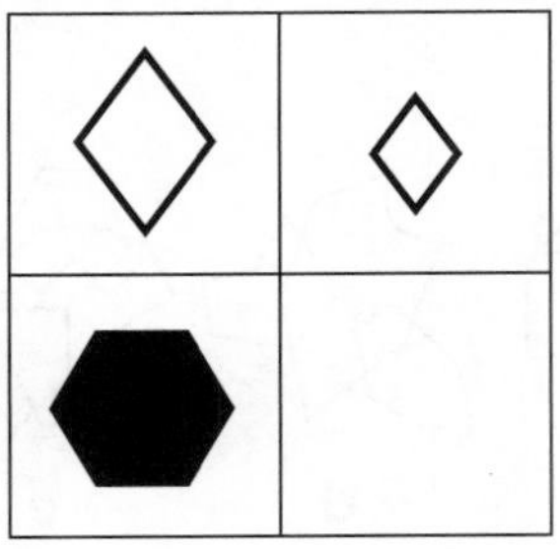

a b c d e

Answer: c

1

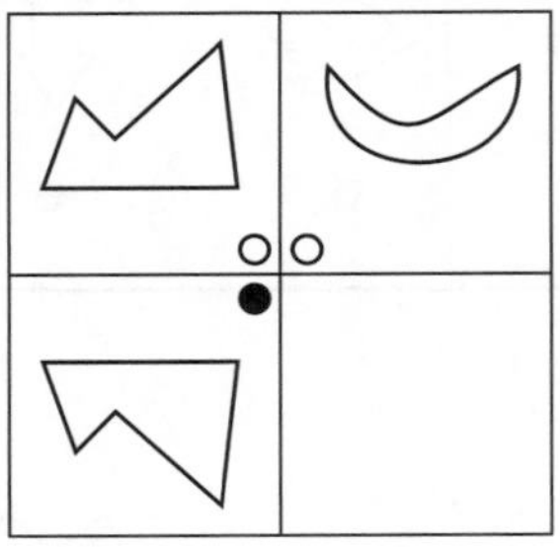

a b c d e

2

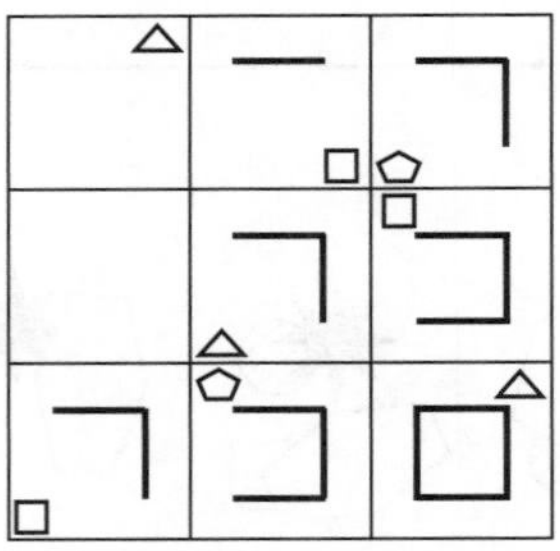

a b c d e

3

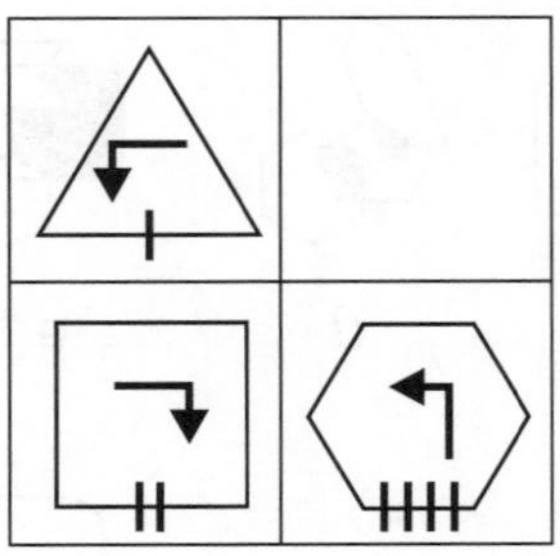

a b c d e

4

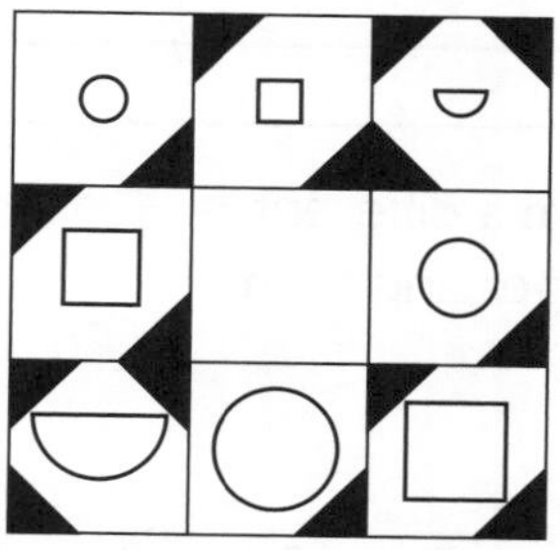

a b c d e

5

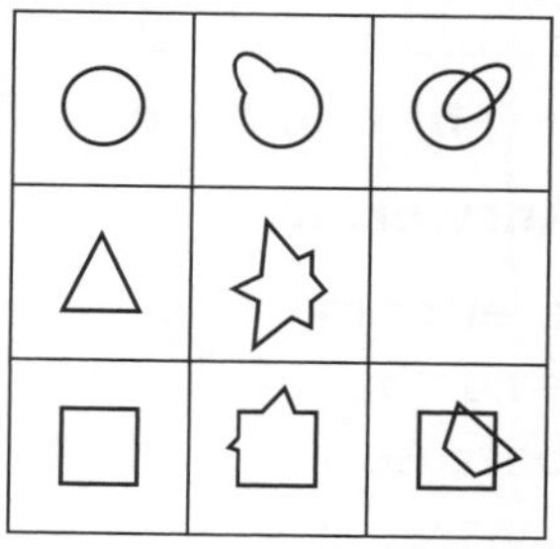

a b c d e

6

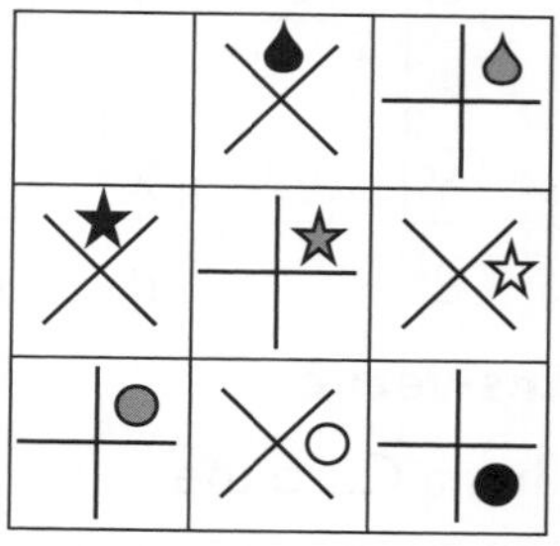

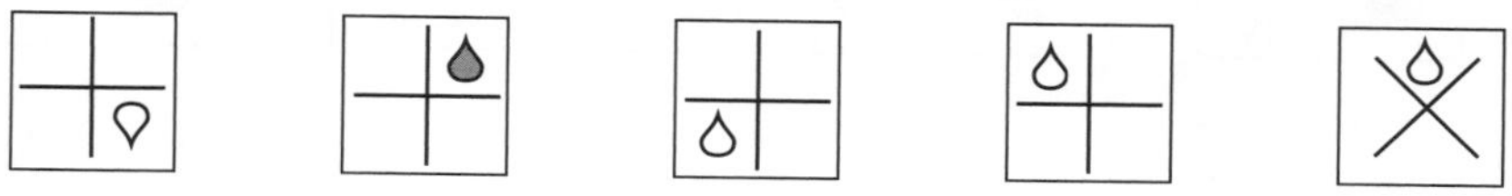

a b c d e

7

a b c d e

8

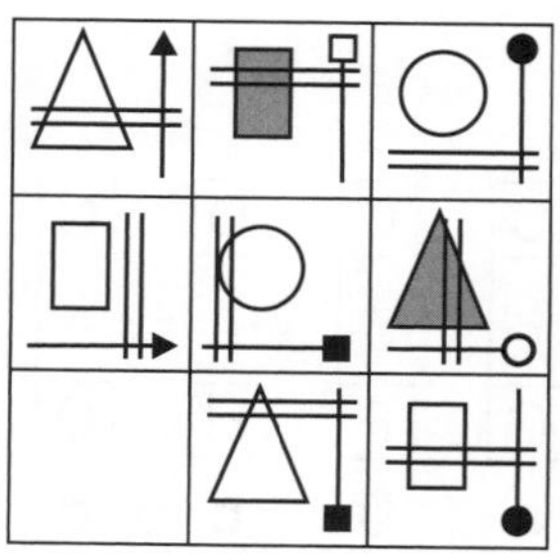

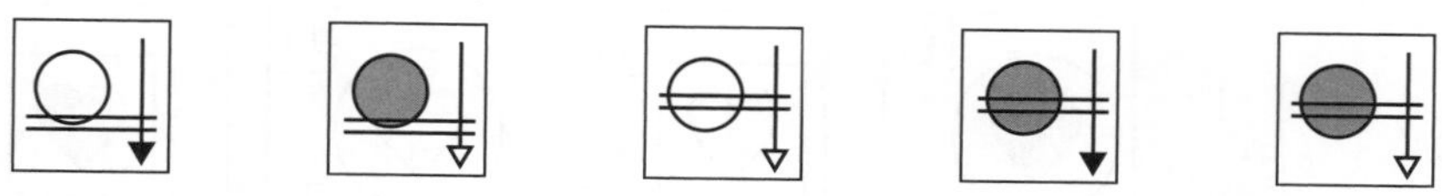

a b c d e

/ 8

Carry on to the next question → →

Section 3 — Horizontal Code

In the boxes on the left are shapes with code letters. The top letters have a different meaning to the bottom ones. Work out how the letters go with the shapes and then find the code for the new shape from the five codes on the right.

Example:

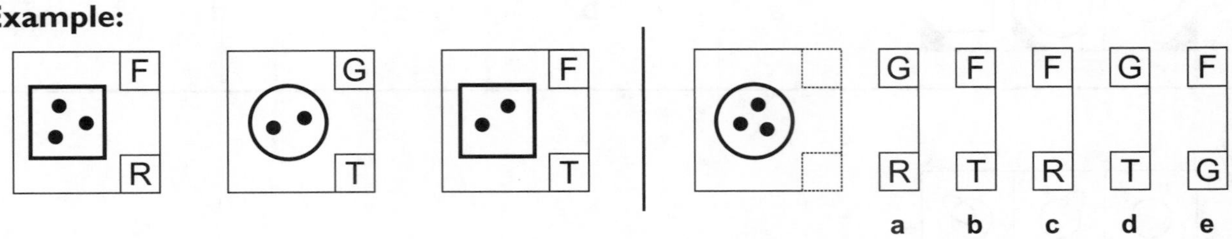

Answer: a

Both squares have an F at the top, but the circle has a G, so the top code letter must stand for shape. This means that the bottom code letter must be for the number of dots. R is for 3 dots and T is for 2 dots. The new shape must have a G because it is a circle and an R because it has 3 dots. The code must be GR and the answer is a.

Example:

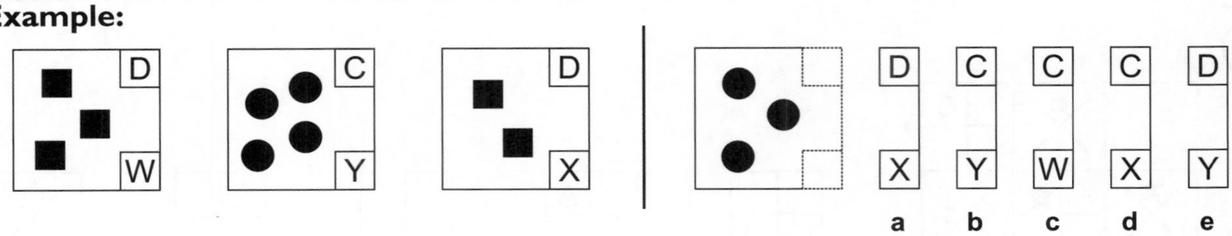

Answer: c

Both figures with squares have a D at the top, and the figure with circles has a C, so the top code letter must be for shape. The bottom code letter must be for the number of shapes. W is for 3 shapes, Y is for 4 and X is for 2. The new figure must have a C because it is made of circles and a W because there are 3 of them. The code must be CW and the answer is c.

1

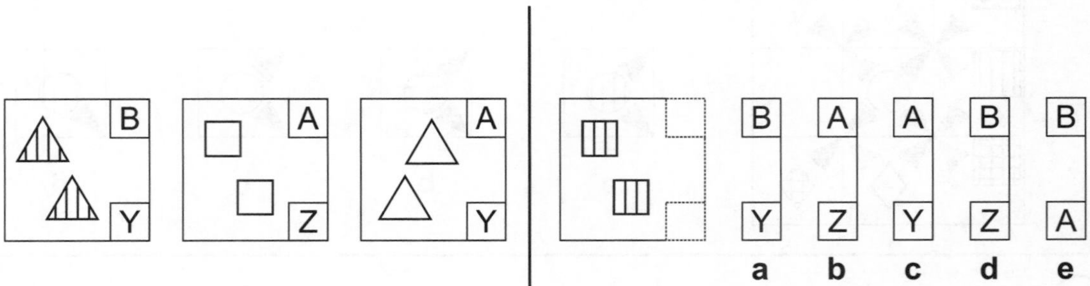

2

3

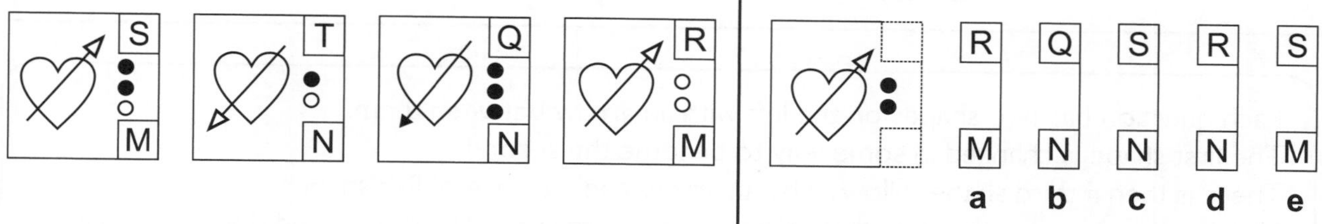

4

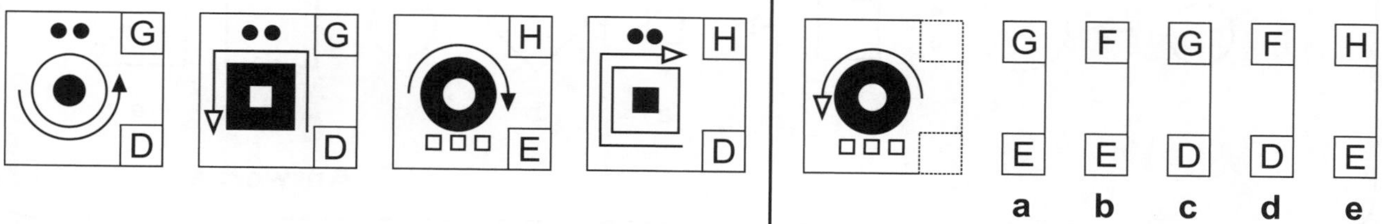

5

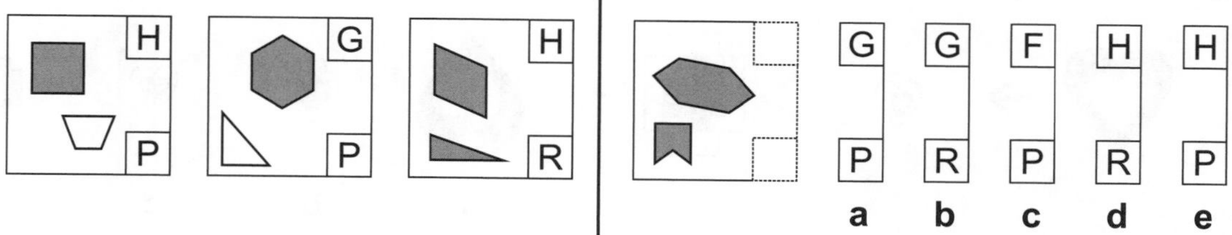

6

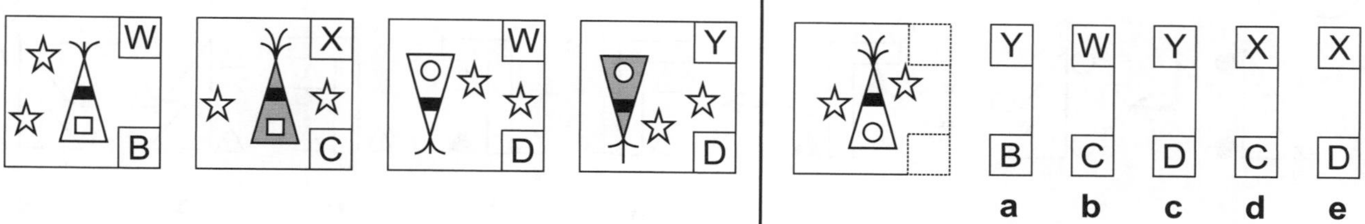

7

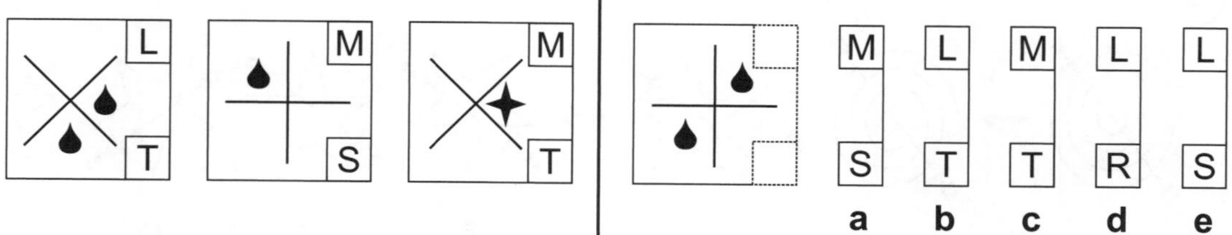

8

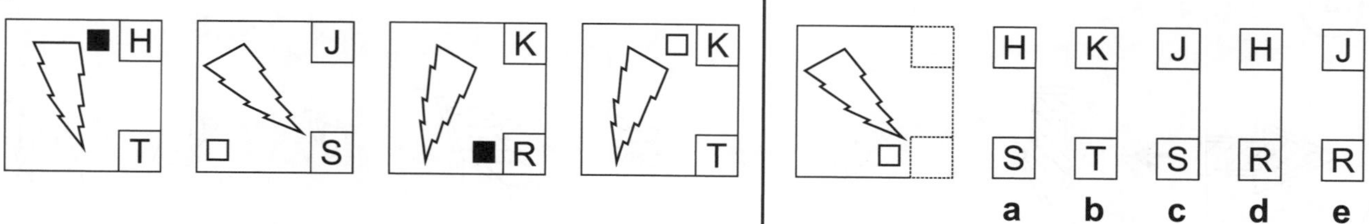

/ 8

Carry on to the next question →→

Section 4 — Complete the Pair

Each question has two shapes on the left with an arrow between them.
The first shape is changed in some way to become the second.
There is then a third shape followed by an arrow and a choice of five shapes.
Choose the shape on the right that relates to the third shape like the second does to the first.

Example:

a b c d e

Answer: e

1

a b c d e

2

a b c d e

3

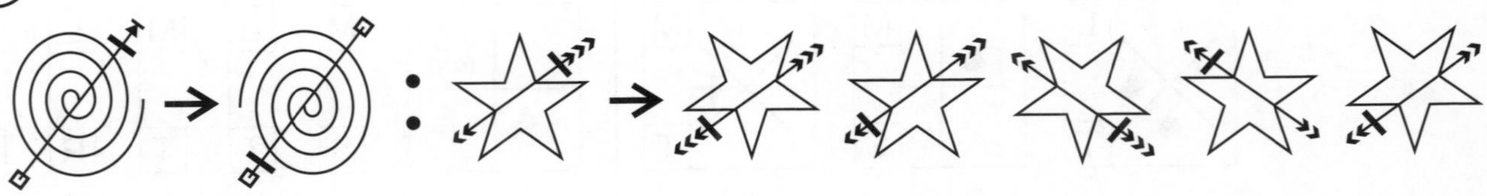

a b c d e

4

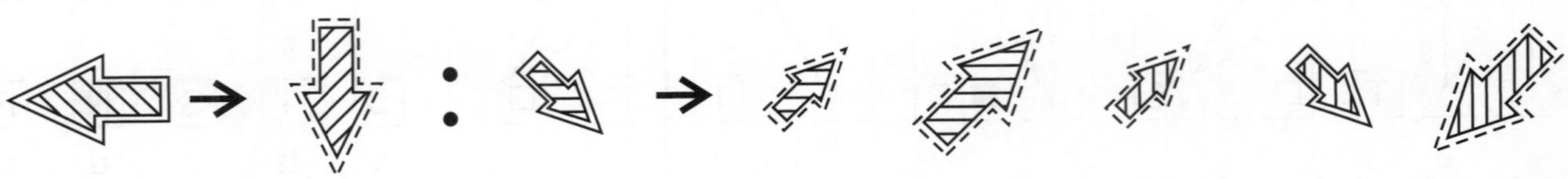

a b c d e

5

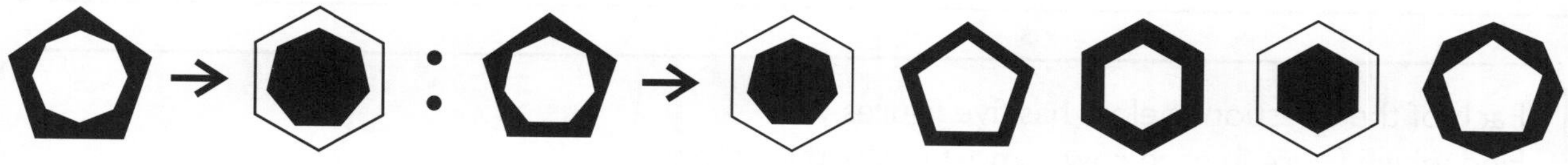

a b c d e

6

a b c d e

7

a b c d e

8

a b c d e

9

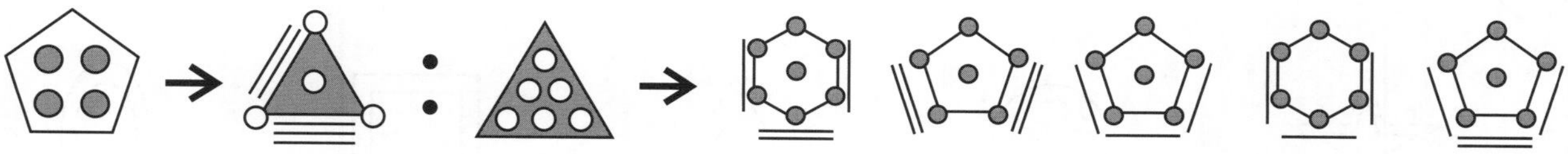

a b c d e

10

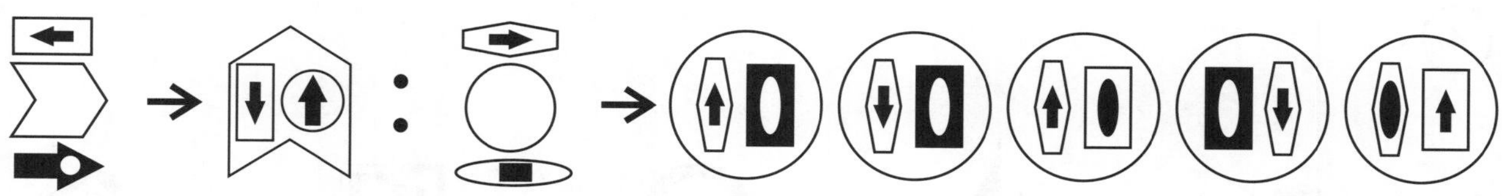

a b c d e

/ 10

Carry on to the next question → →

Section 5 — Odd One Out

Each of the questions below has five figures.
Find which figure in each row is most unlike the others.

Example:

a b c d e

Answer: b

1

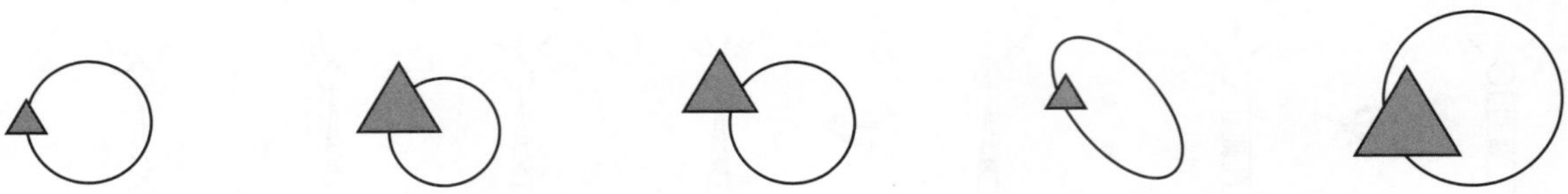

a b c d e

2

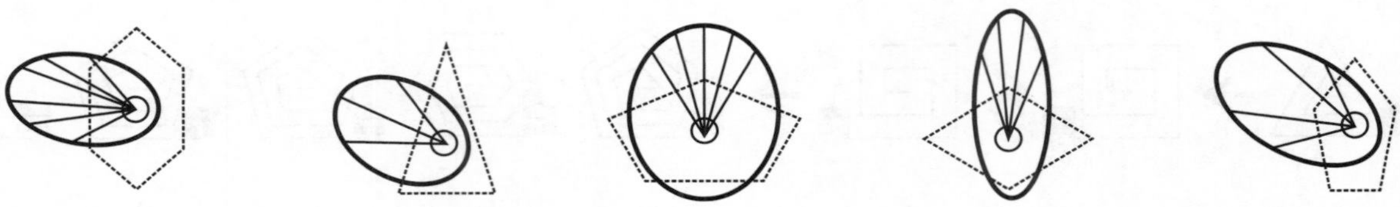

a b c d e

3

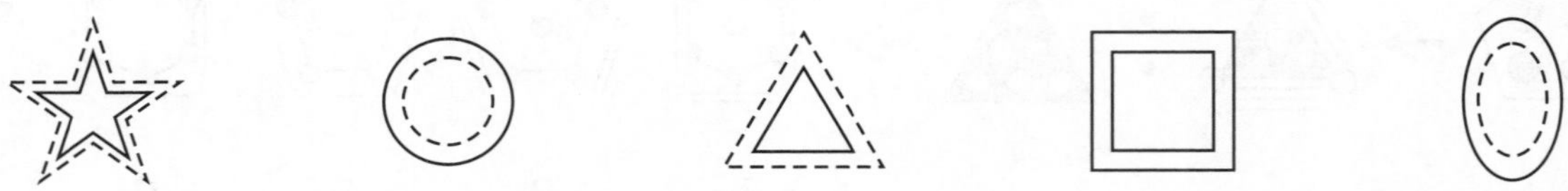

a b c d e

4

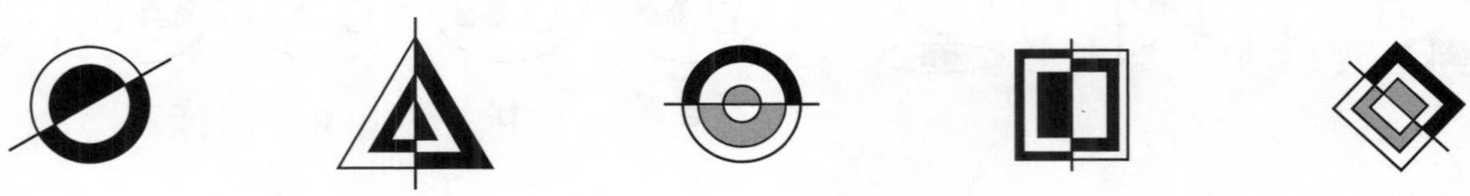

a b c d e

5

a b c d e

6

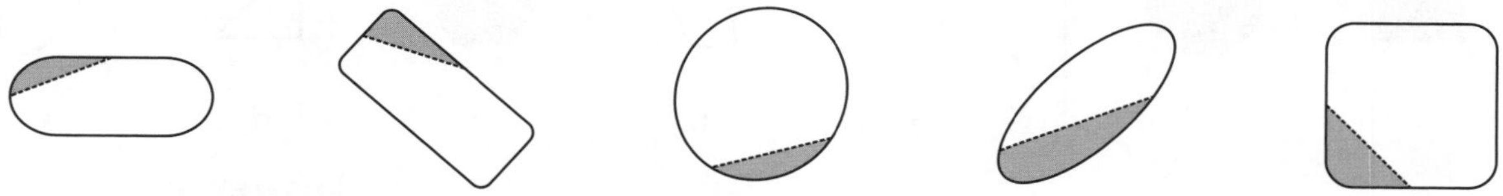

a b c d e

7

a b c d e

8

a b c d e

9

a b c d e

10

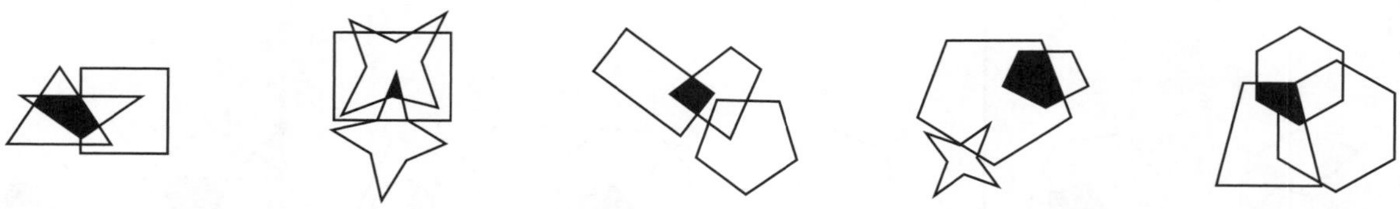

a b c d e

/ 10

Carry on to the next question → →

Section 6 — Find the Figure Like the First Two

For each question below there are two figures that are like each other in some way.
Find which of the five figures on the right is most like the two figures on the left.

Example:

a b c d e

Answer: c

(1)

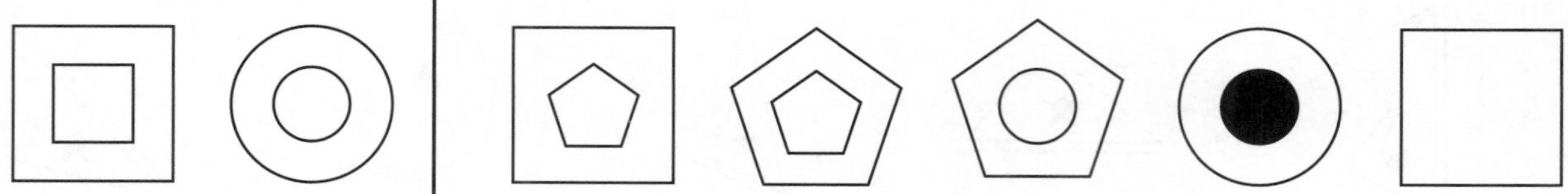

a b c d e

(2)

a b c d e

(3)

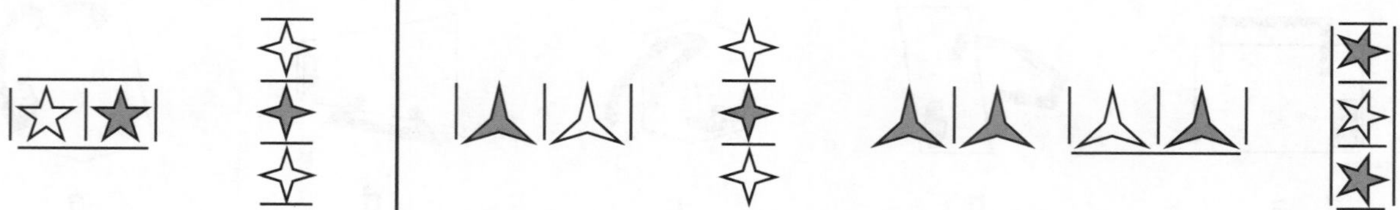

a b c d e

(4)

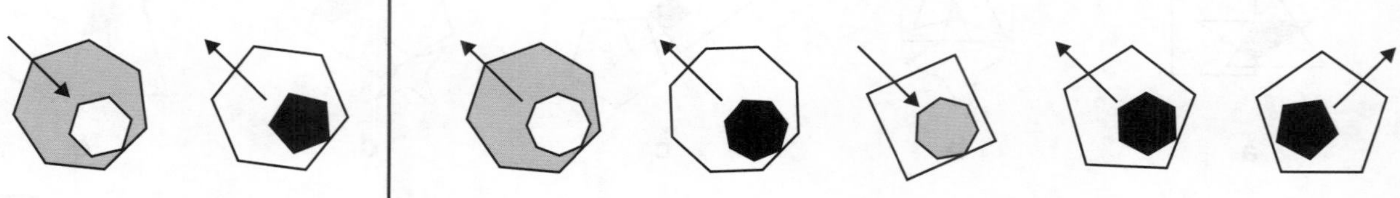

a b c d e

5

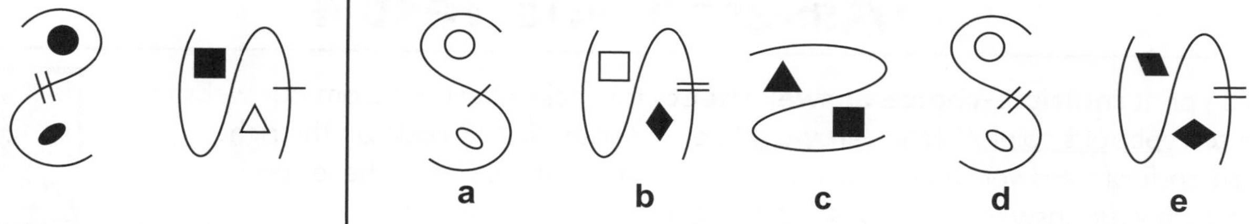

6

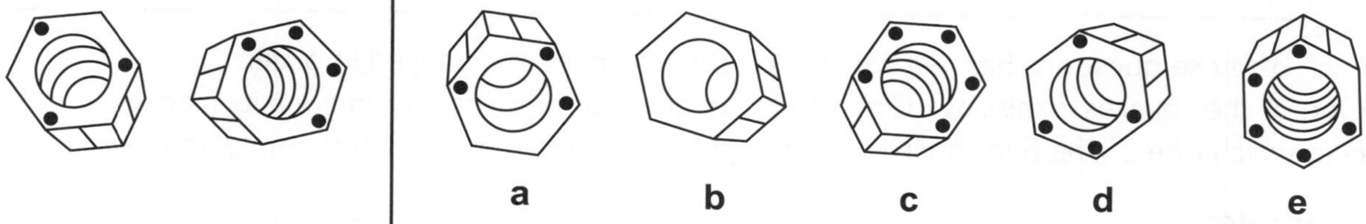

7

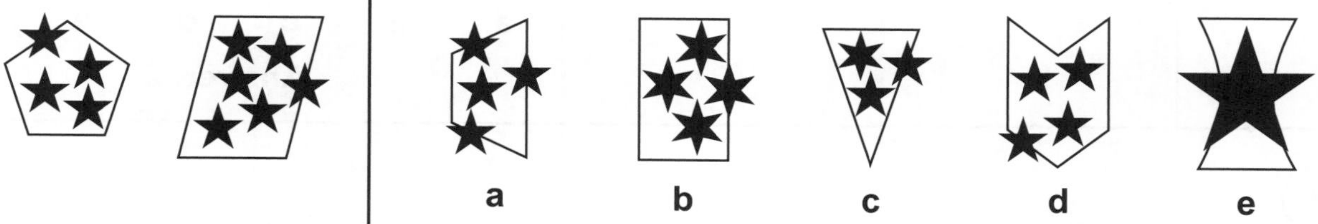

8

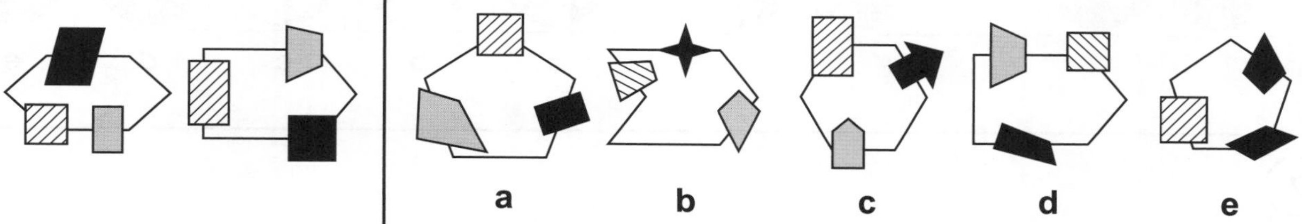

9

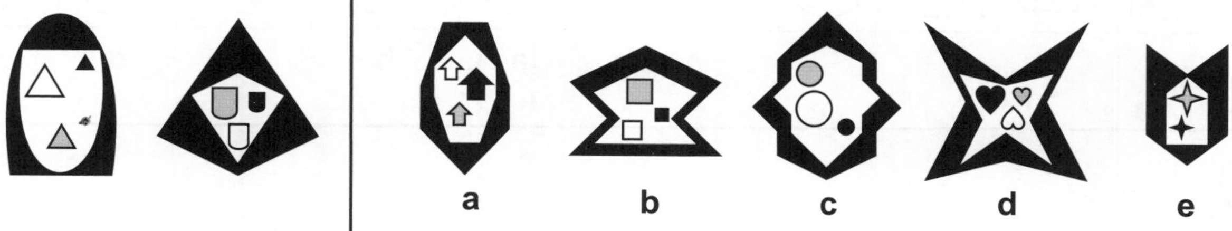

10

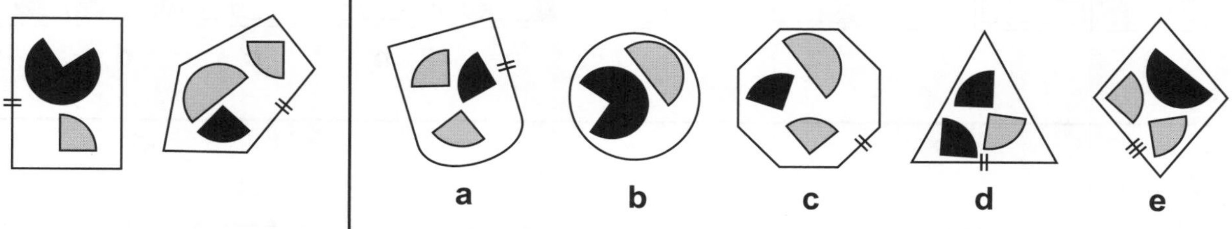

/ 10 | Total / 56

End of Test

Assessment Test 4

You can print **multiple-choice answer sheets** for these questions from our website — go to cgpbooks.co.uk/11plus/answer-sheets or scan the QR code on the right.
If you'd prefer to answer them in standard write-in format, just circle the letter underneath your answer. The test should take around 30 minutes.

Answer Sheets

Section 1 — Complete the Series

Each of these questions has five squares on the left that are arranged in order.
One of the squares is missing. One of the squares on the right should go in its place.
Find which one of the five squares on the right should go in place of the empty square.

Example:

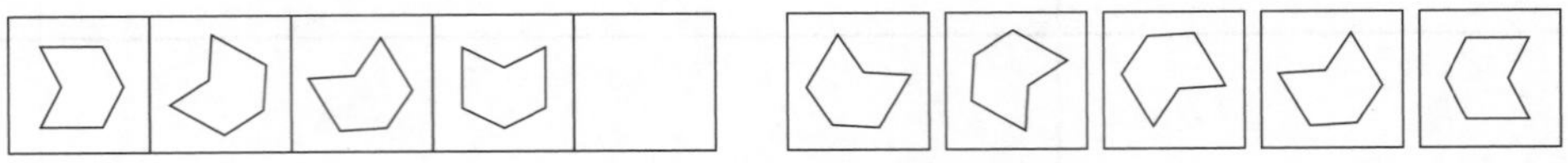

a b c d e

Answer: a

1

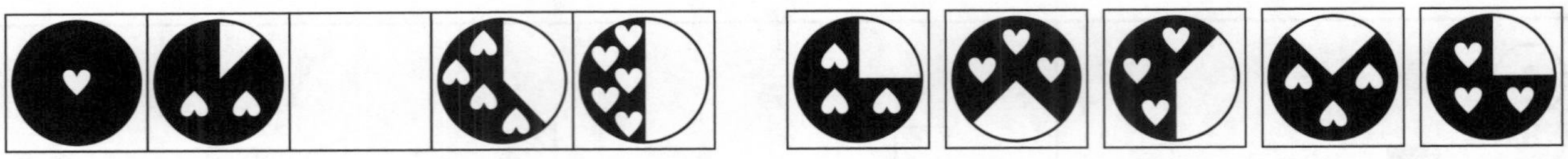

a b c d e

2

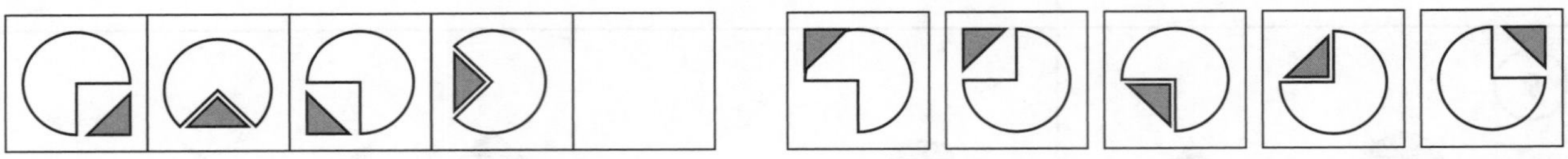

a b c d e

3

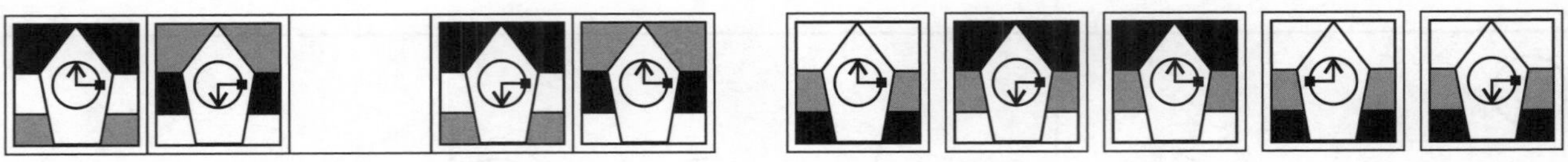

a b c d e

4

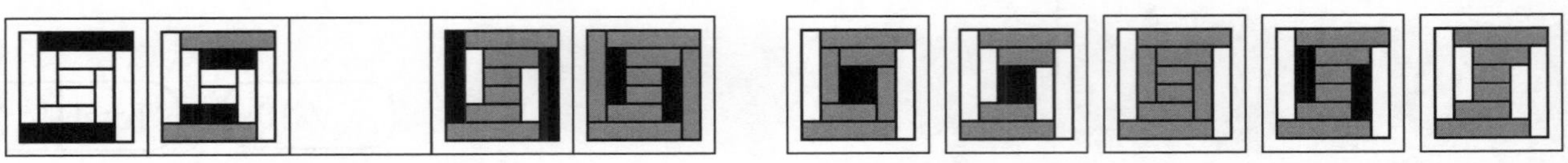

a b c d e

5

a b c d e

6

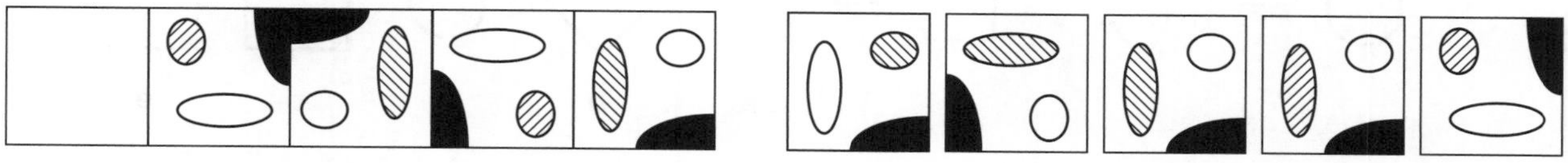

a b c d e

7

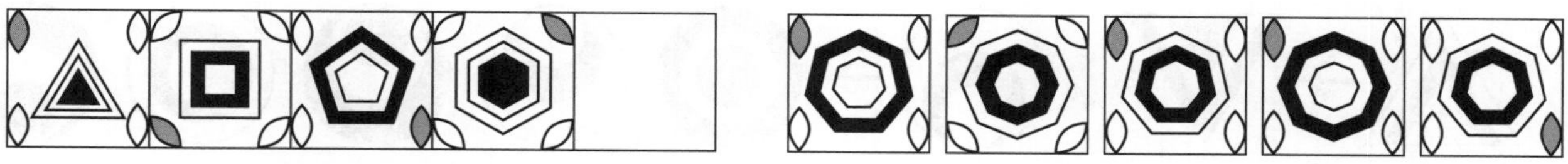

a b c d e

8

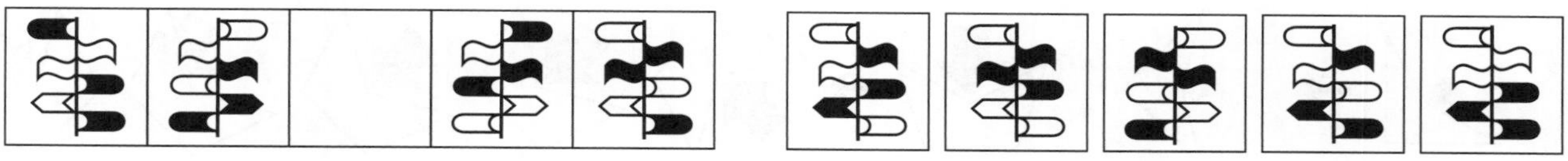

a b c d e

9

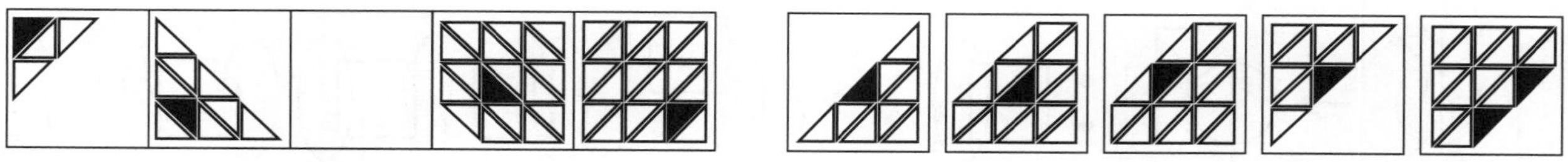

a b c d e

10

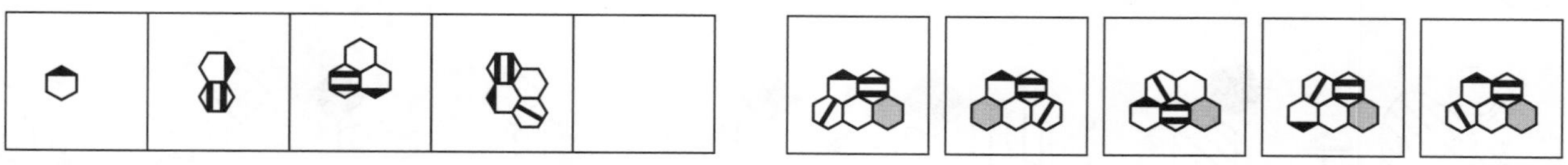

a b c d e

/ 10

Carry on to the next question → →

Section 2 — Complete the Pair

Each question has two shapes on the left with an arrow between them.
The first shape is changed in some way to become the second.
There is then a third shape followed by an arrow and a choice of five shapes.
Choose the shape on the right that relates to the third shape like the second does to the first.

Example:

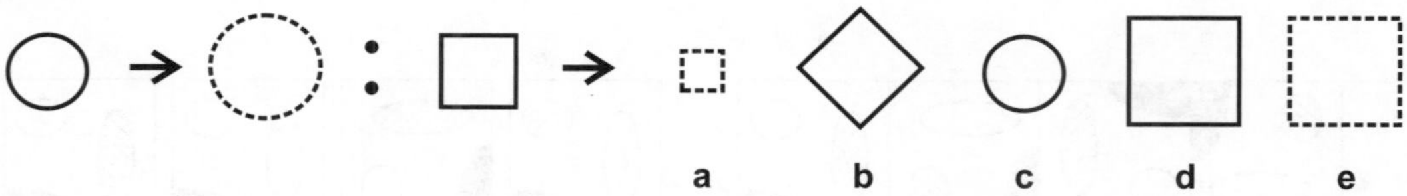

Answer: e

1

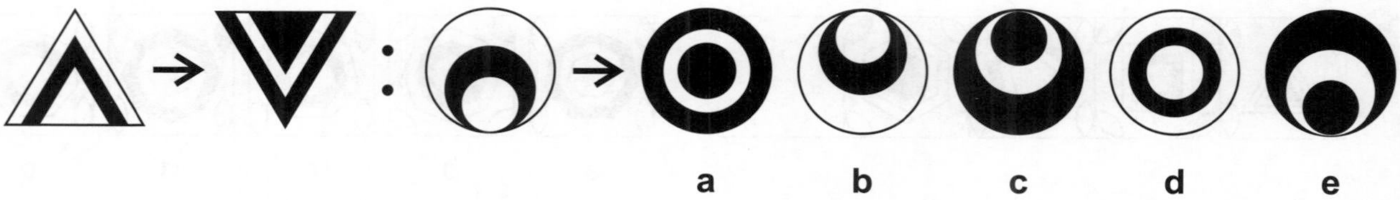

2

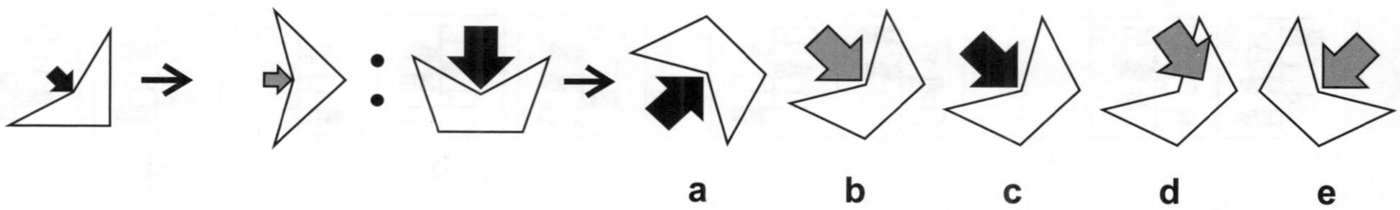

3

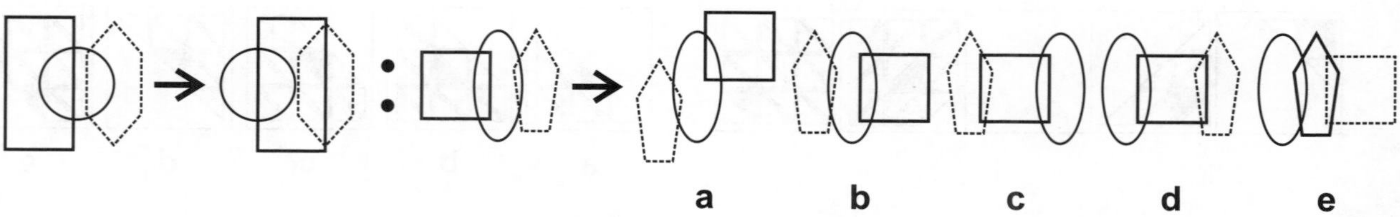

4

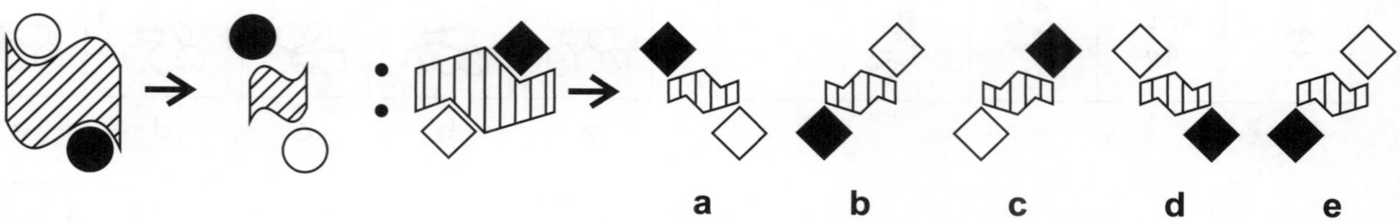

5

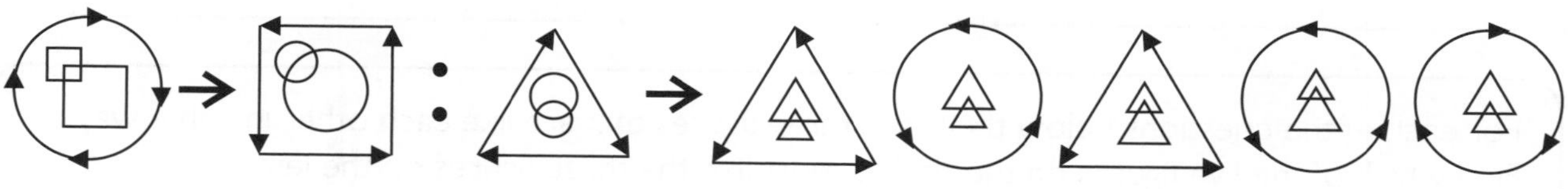

a b c d e

6

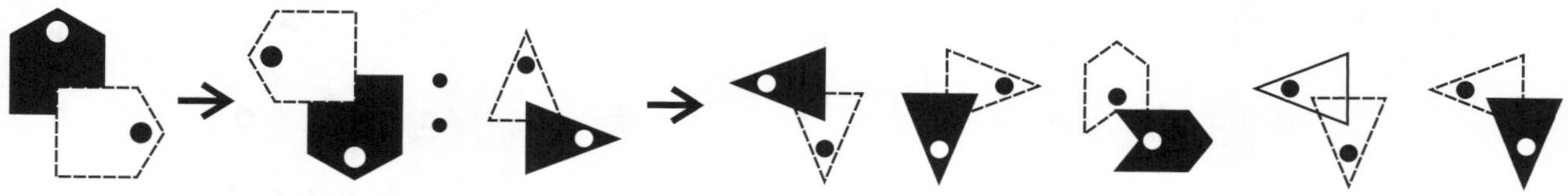

a b c d e

7

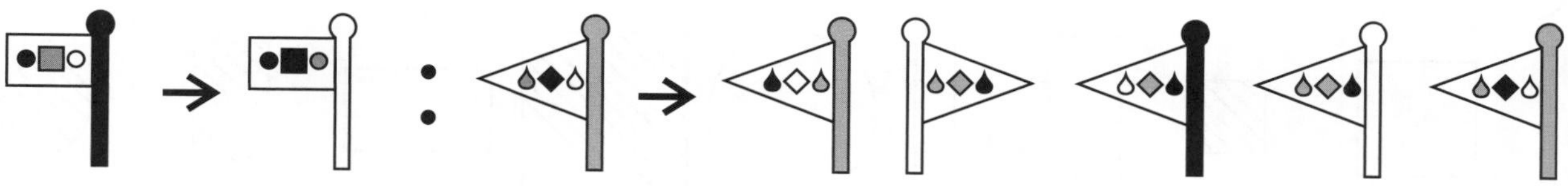

a b c d e

8

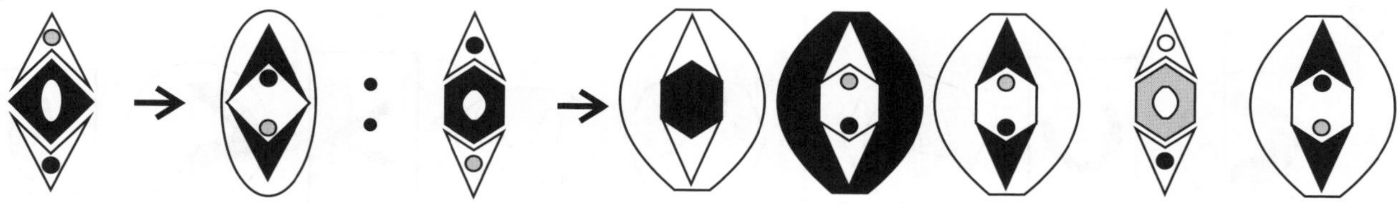

a b c d e

9

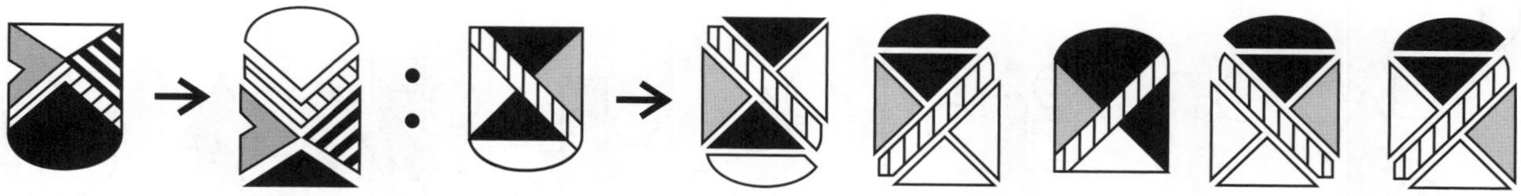

a b c d e

10

a b c d e

/ 10

Carry on to the next question → →

Section 3 — Find the Figure Like the First Three

For each of the questions below there are three figures that are like each other in some way.
Find which of the five figures on the right is most like the three figures on the left.

Example:

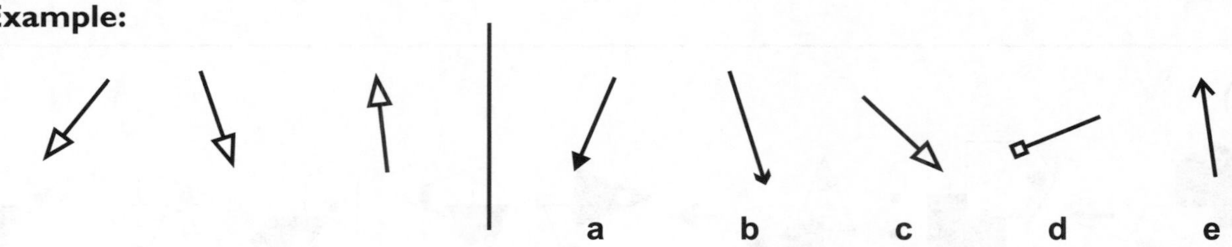

Answer: c

1

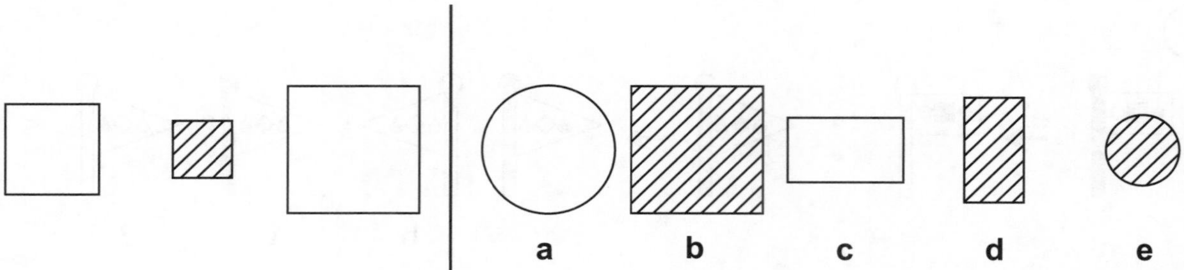

2

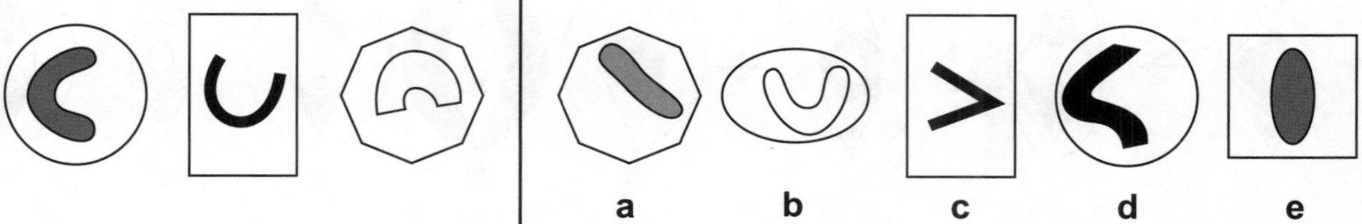

3

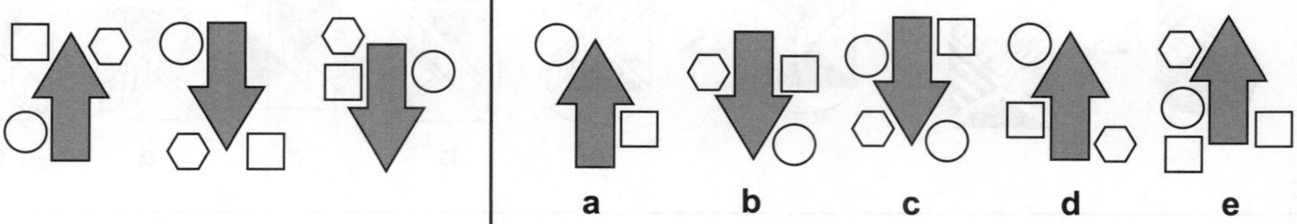

4

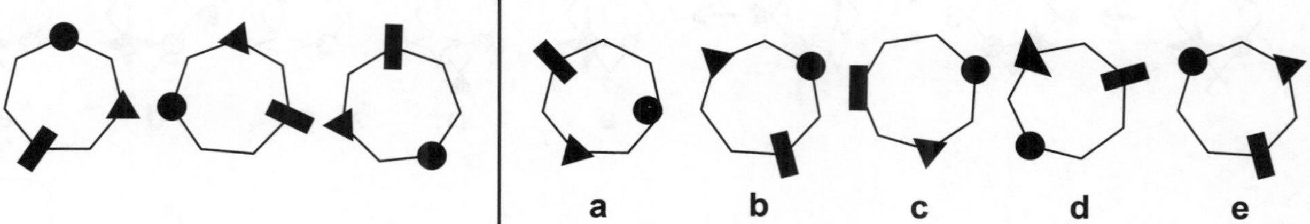

5

a b c d e

6

a b c d e

7

a b c d e

8

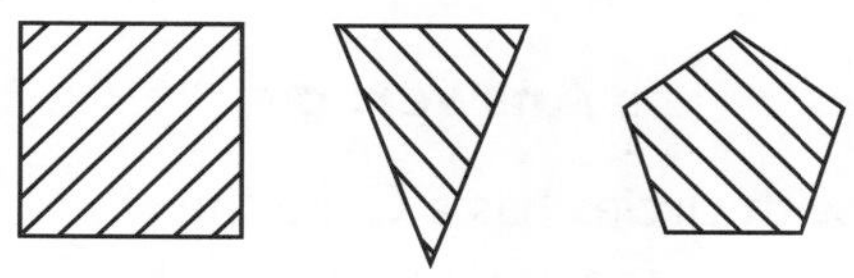

a b c d e

9

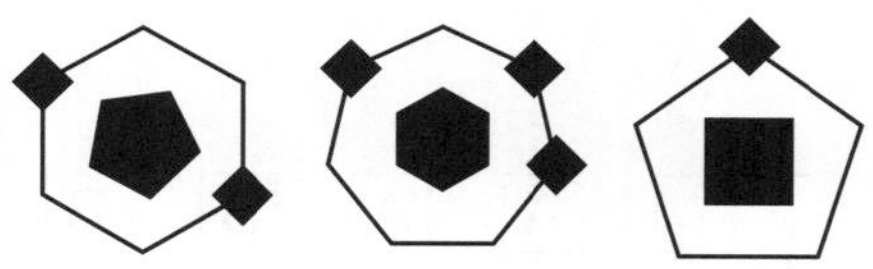

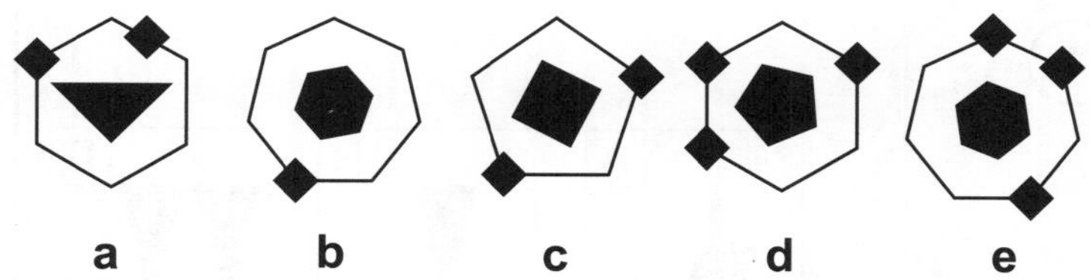

a b c d e

10

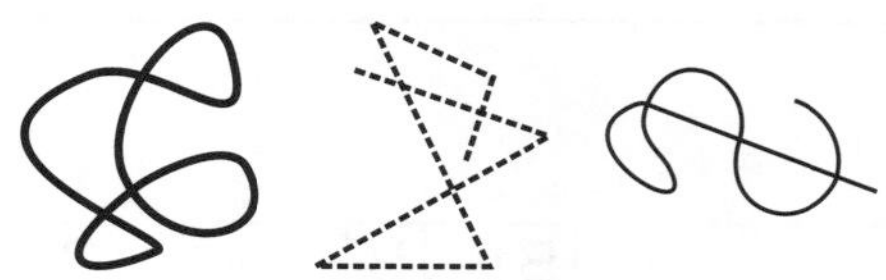

a b c d e

/ 10

Carry on to the next question → →

Section 4 — Horizontal Code

In the boxes on the left are shapes with code letters. The top letters have a different meaning to the bottom ones. Work out how the letters go with the shapes and then find the code for the new shape from the five codes on the right.

Example:

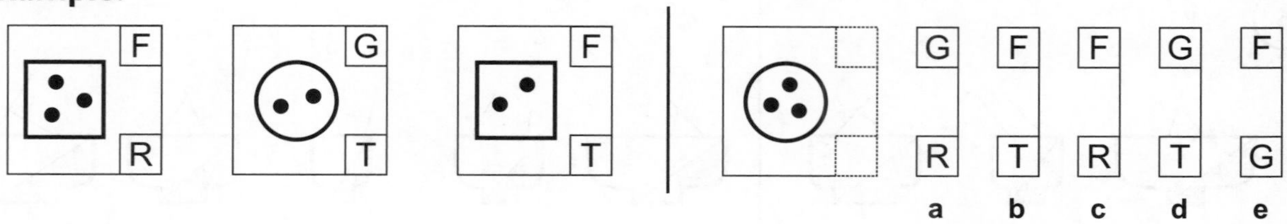

Answer: a

Both squares have an F at the top, but the circle has a G, so the top code letter must stand for shape. This means that the bottom code letter must be for the number of dots. R is for 3 dots and T is for 2 dots. The new shape must have a G because it is a circle and an R because it has 3 dots. The code must be GR and the answer is a.

Example:

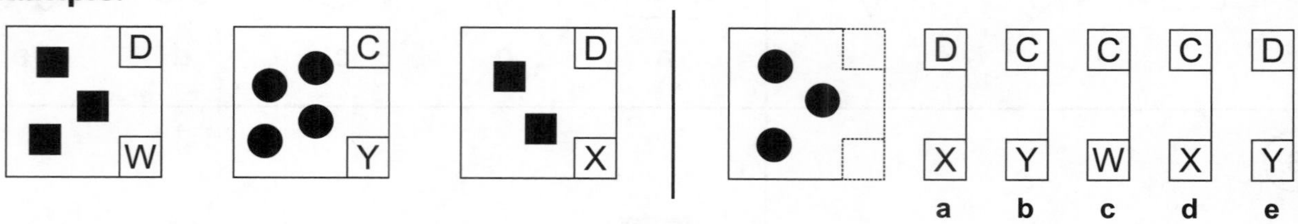

Answer: c

Both figures with squares have a D at the top, and the figure with circles has a C, so the top code letter must be for shape. The bottom code letter must be for the number of shapes. W is for 3 shapes, Y is for 4 and X is for 2. The new figure must have a C because it is made of circles and a W because there are 3 of them. The code must be CW and the answer is c.

1

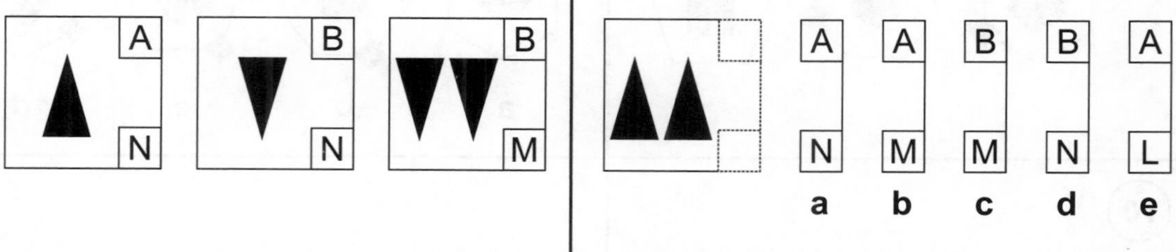

2

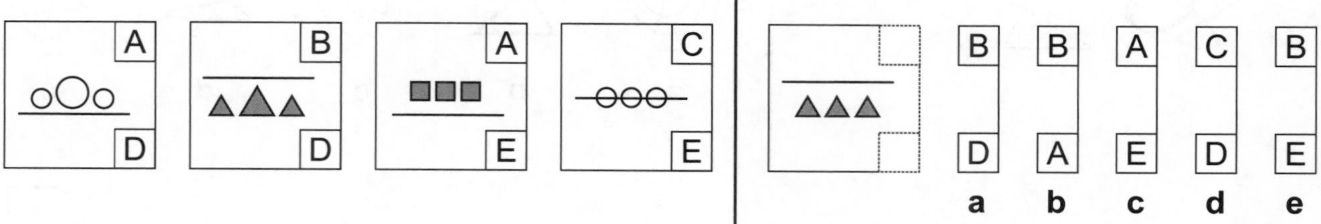

3

a b c d e

4

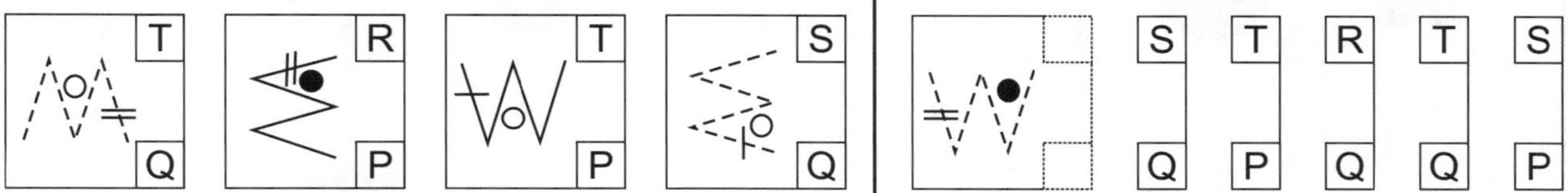

a b c d e

5

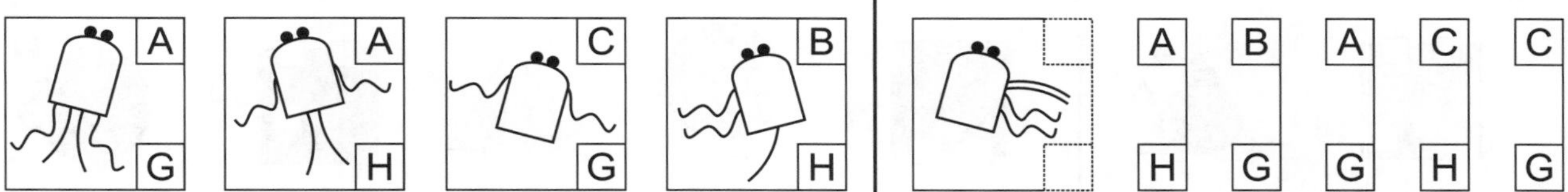

a b c d e

6

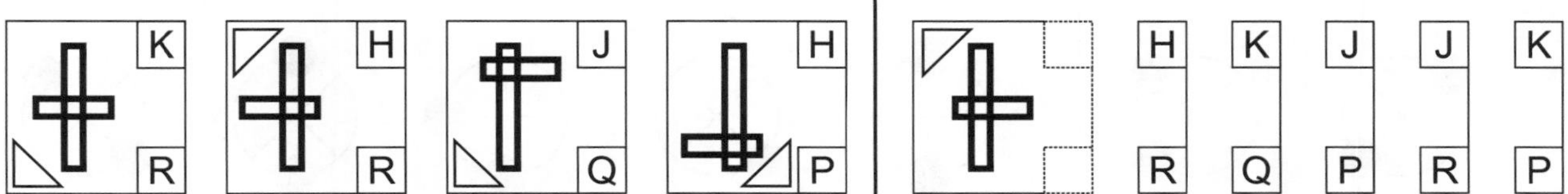

a b c d e

7

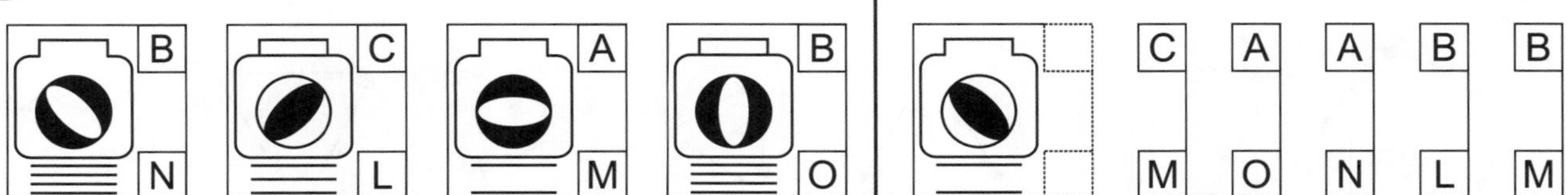

a b c d e

8

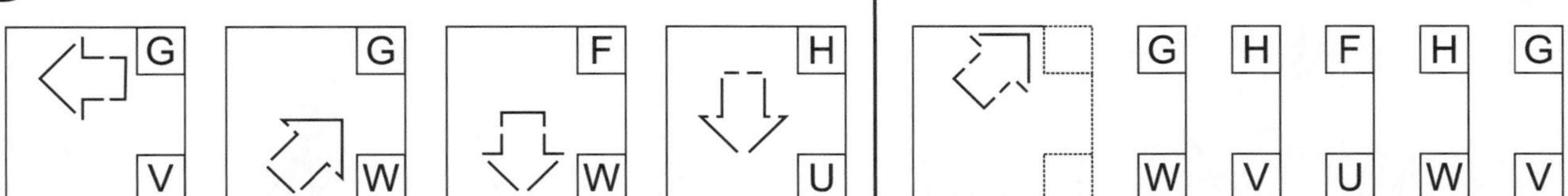

a b c d e

/ 8

Carry on to the next question → →

Section 5 — Find the Figure Like the First Two

For each question below there are two figures that are like each other in some way.
Find which of the five figures on the right is most like the two figures on the left.

Example:

a b c d e

Answer: c

(1)

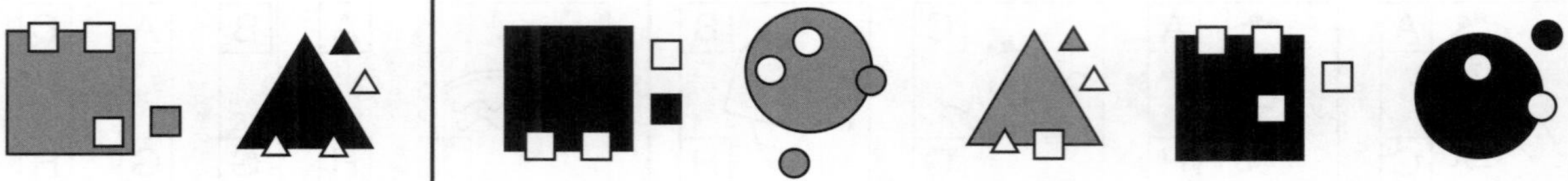

a b c d e

(2)

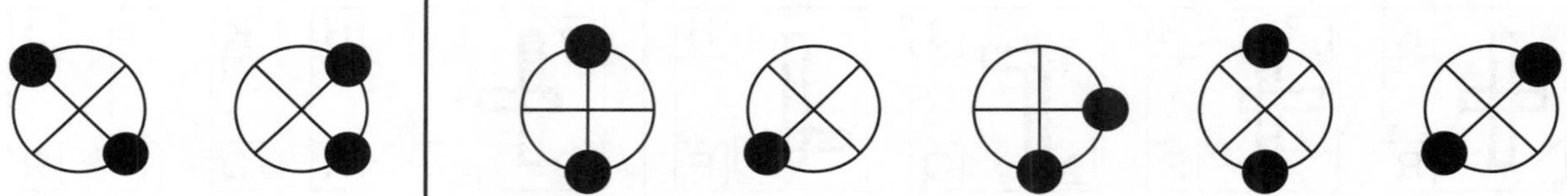

a b c d e

(3)

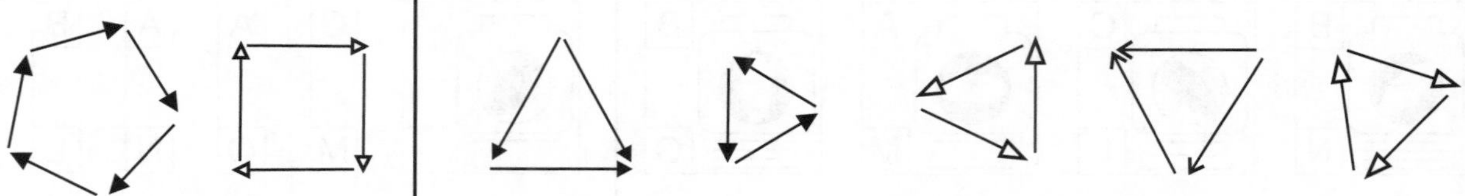

a b c d e

(4)

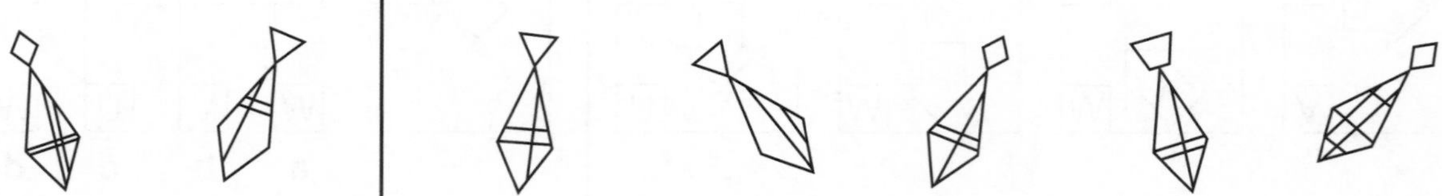

a b c d e

5

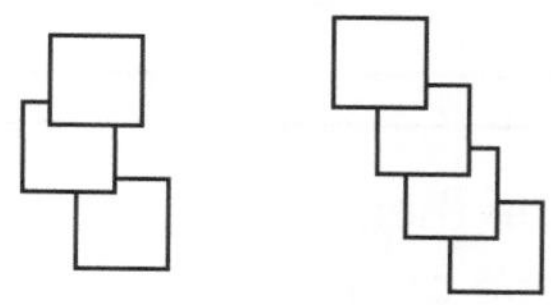

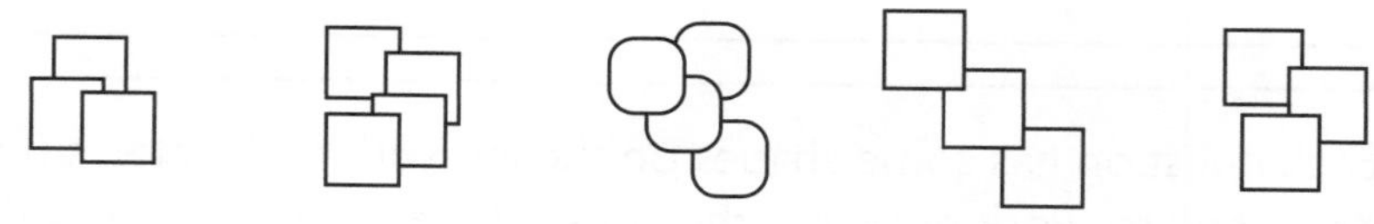

a b c d e

6

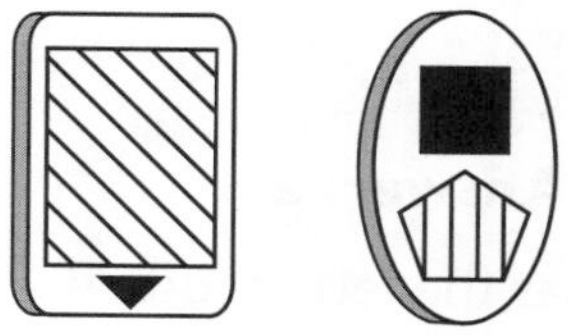

a b c d e

7

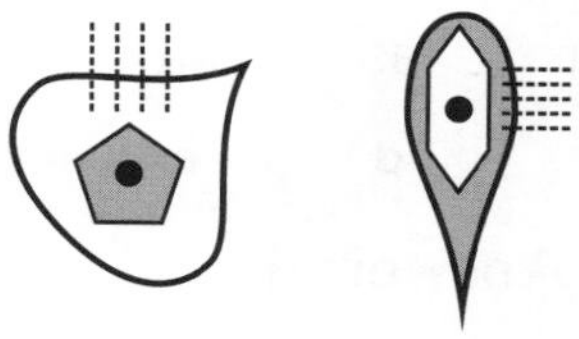

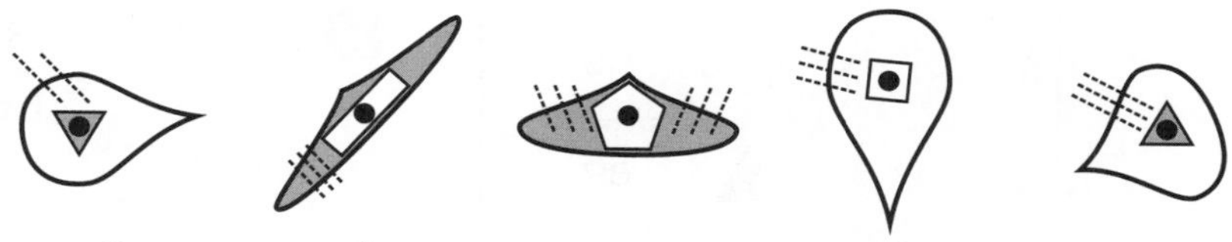

a b c d e

8

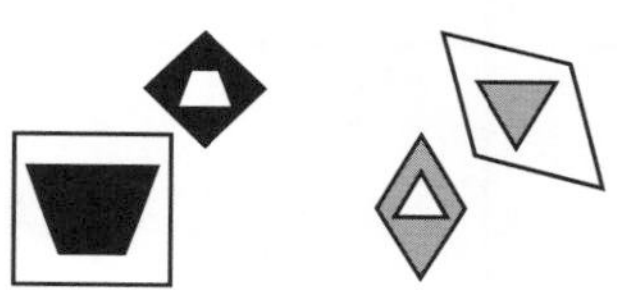

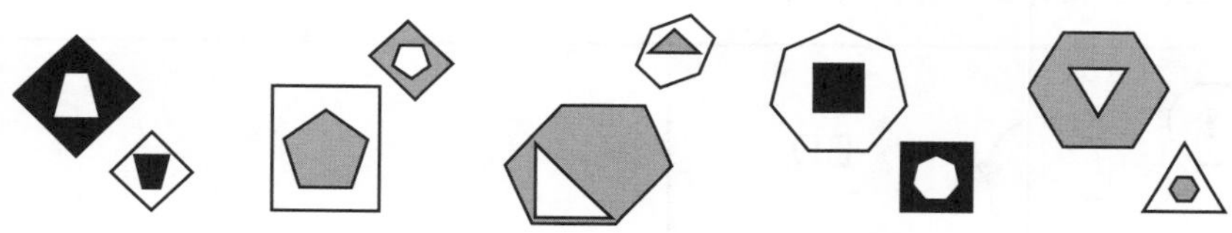

a b c d e

9

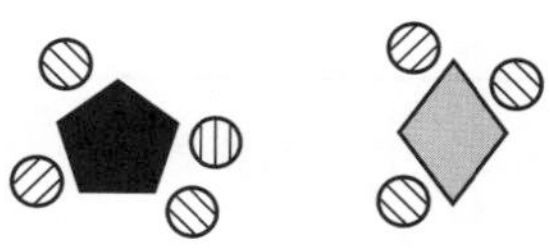

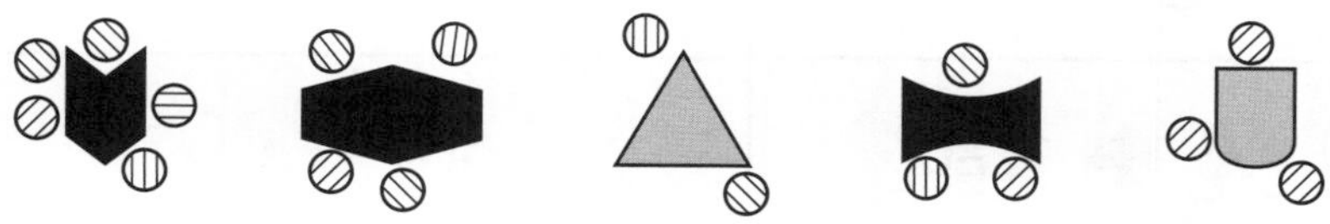

a b c d e

10

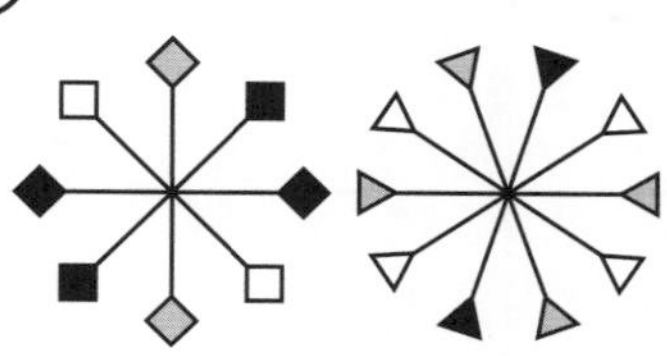

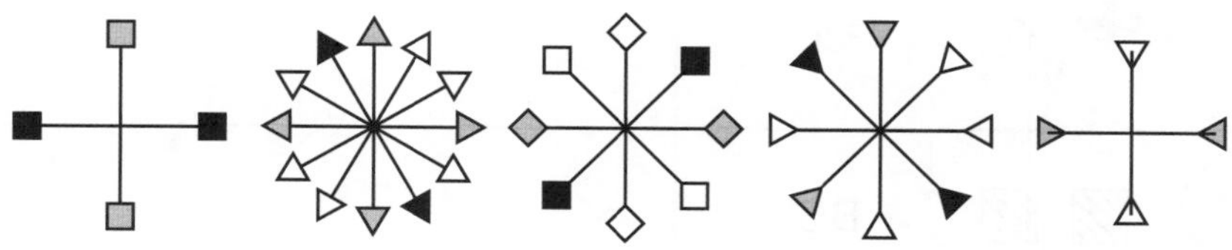

a b c d e

/ 10

Carry on to the next question →→

Section 6 — Vertical Code

Each question has some shapes on the left with code letters that describe them. You need to work out what the code letters mean. There is then a shape on its own next to a choice of five codes. Work out which code describes this shape.

Example:

P
Q
R

P	Q	T	S	R
a	**b**	**c**	**d**	**e**

Answer: a

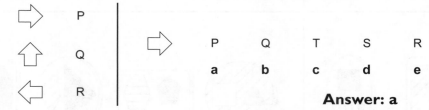

The arrow pointing right has the letter code P, the arrow pointing left has the letter code R, and the arrow pointing up has the letter code Q. The new shape is an arrow pointing right, so the code must be P and the answer is a.

Example:

BT
CS
BR

BC	CR	CT	BS	BR
a	**b**	**c**	**d**	**e**

Answer: d

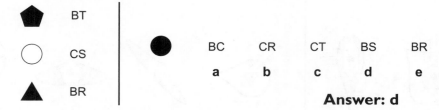

Both black shapes have the letter code B, and the white shape has a C, so the first letter is for shading. The second letter code must be the code for shape. T stands for a pentagon, the letter S for a circle and the letter R for a triangle. The new shape must have a B because it is black, and an S because it is a circle. The code must be BS and the answer is d.

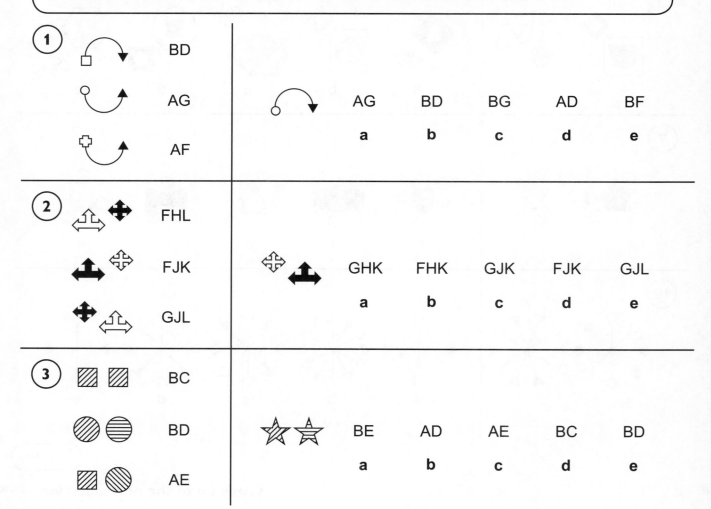

1

BD
AG
AF

AG	BD	BG	AD	BF
a	**b**	**c**	**d**	**e**

2

FHL
FJK
GJL

GHK	FHK	GJK	FJK	GJL
a	**b**	**c**	**d**	**e**

3

BC
BD
AE

BE	AD	AE	BC	BD
a	**b**	**c**	**d**	**e**

4

 HY						
 GZ		JX	GY	GZ	HZ	JY
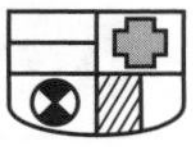 GX		**a**	**b**	**c**	**d**	**e**
 JZ						

5

 XQ						
 ZP		XP	YQ	YP	ZQ	XQ
 XP		**a**	**b**	**c**	**d**	**e**
 YQ						

6

 ELV						
 DNU		EKV	DKW	DNW	DMU	EKW
 DMW		**a**	**b**	**c**	**d**	**e**
 EKU						

7

 CPH						
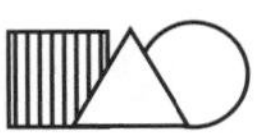 CPG	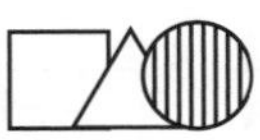	BPH	APG	CQG	APH	AQH
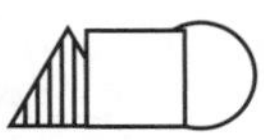 AQJ		**a**	**b**	**c**	**d**	**e**
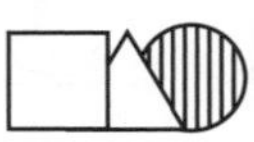 BPJ						

8

 CP						
 DQ		CQ	DQ	CP	DR	DP
 CQ		**a**	**b**	**c**	**d**	**e**

/ 8 Total / 56

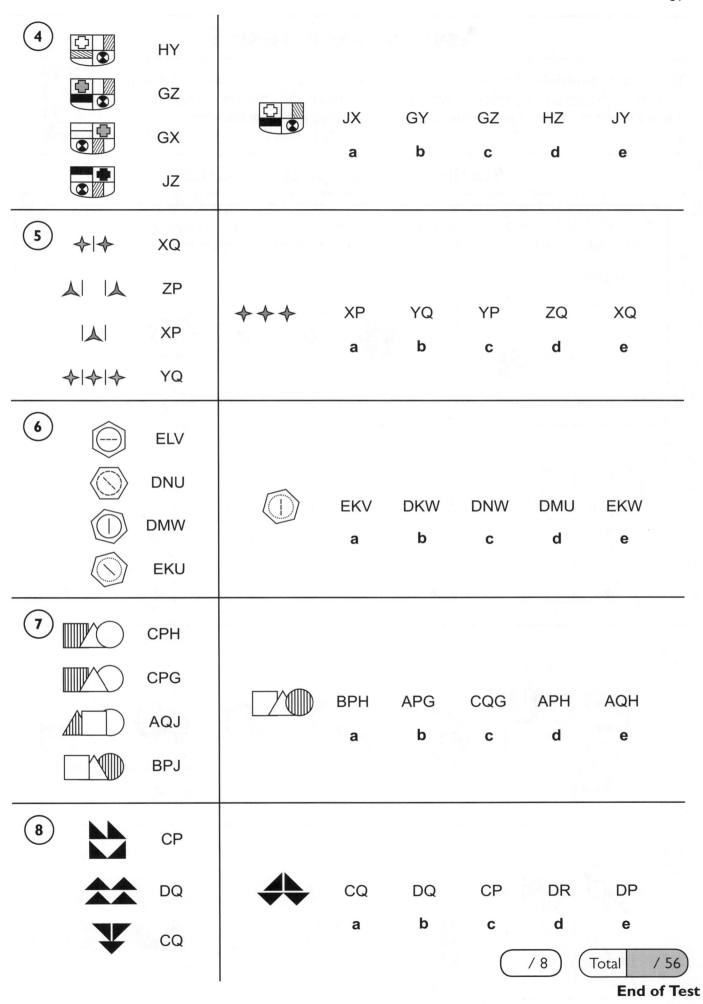

End of Test

Assessment Test 5

You can print **multiple-choice answer sheets** for these questions from our website — go to cgpbooks.co.uk/11plus/answer-sheets or scan the QR code on the right. If you'd prefer to answer them in standard write-in format, just circle the letter underneath your answer. The test should take around 30 minutes.

Answer Sheets

Section 1 — Complete the Grid

On the left of each question below is a big square with one small empty square. Find which of the five squares on the right should replace the empty square.

Example:

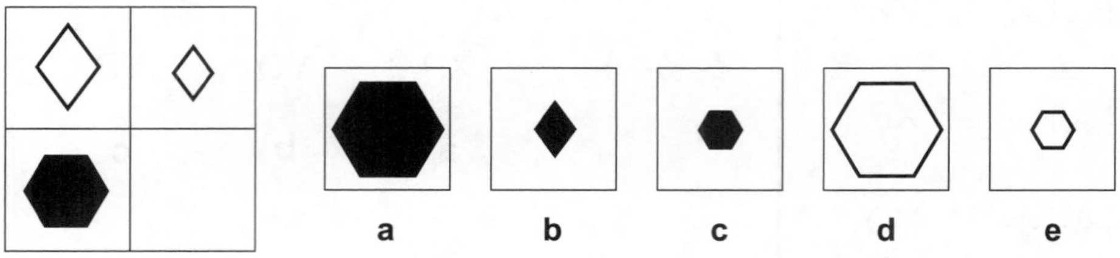

a b c d e

Answer: c

(1)

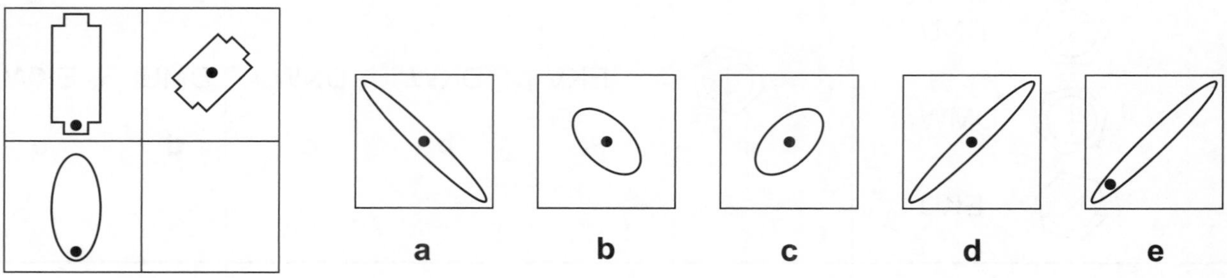

a b c d e

(2)

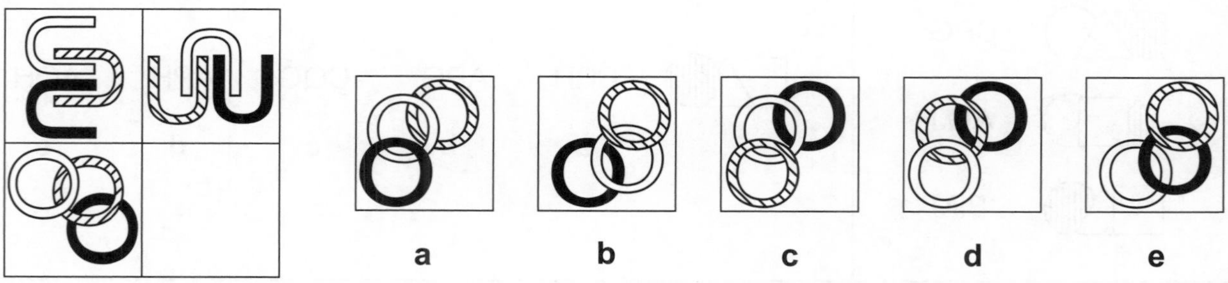

a b c d e

(3)

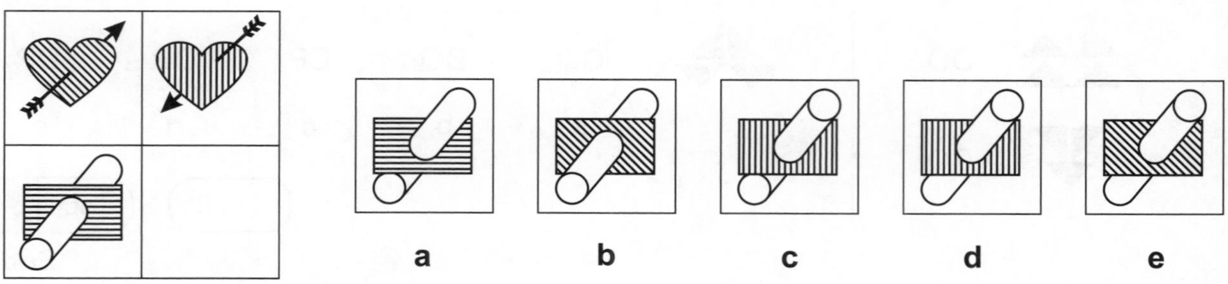

a b c d e

4

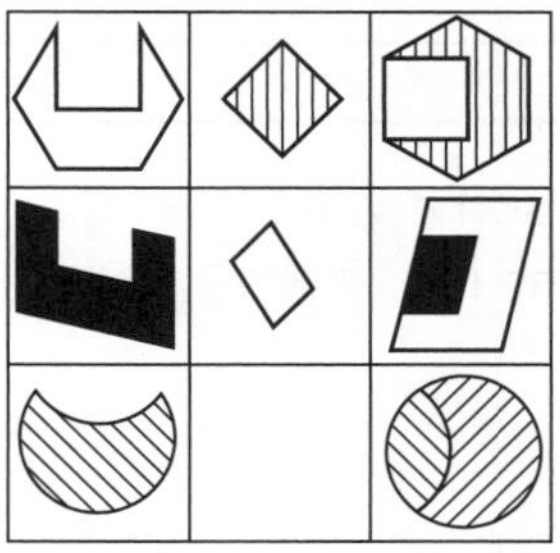

a b c d e

5

a b c d e

6

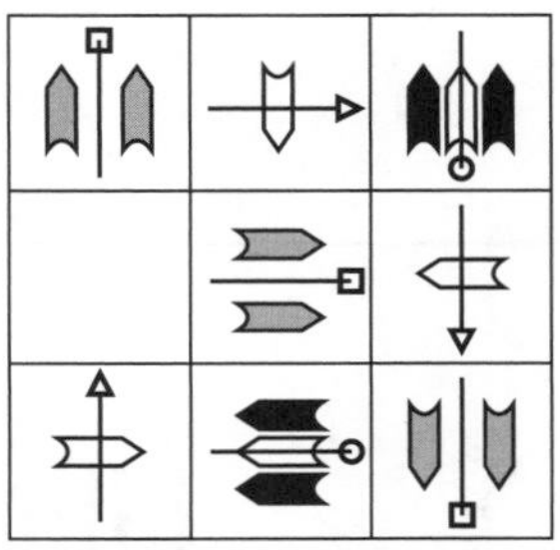

a b c d e

7

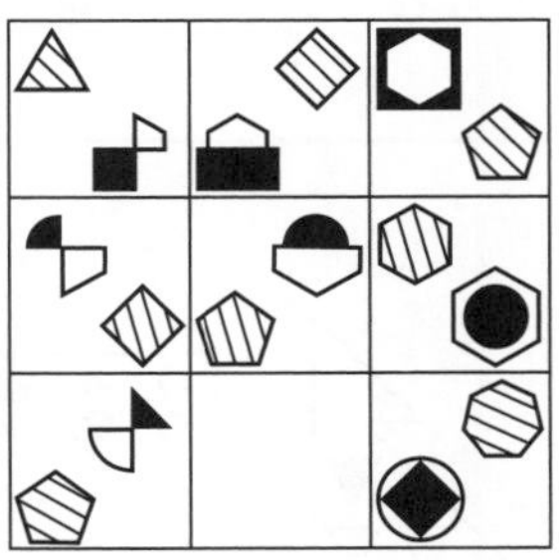

a b c d e

8

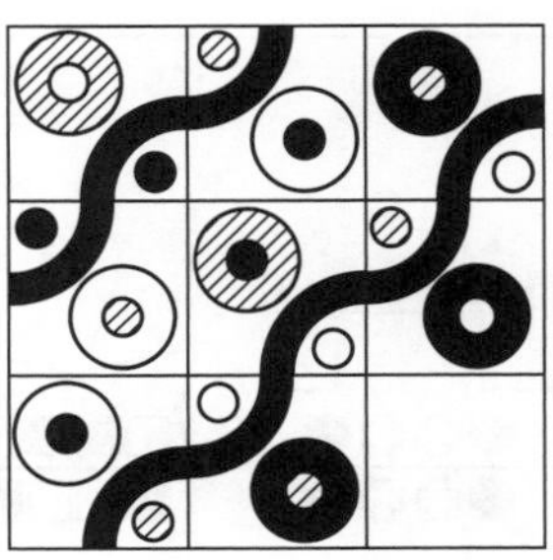

a b c d e

/ 8

Carry on to the next question → →

Section 2 — Find the Figure Like the First Two

For each question below there are two figures that are like each other in some way.
Find which of the five figures on the right is most like the two figures on the left.

Example:

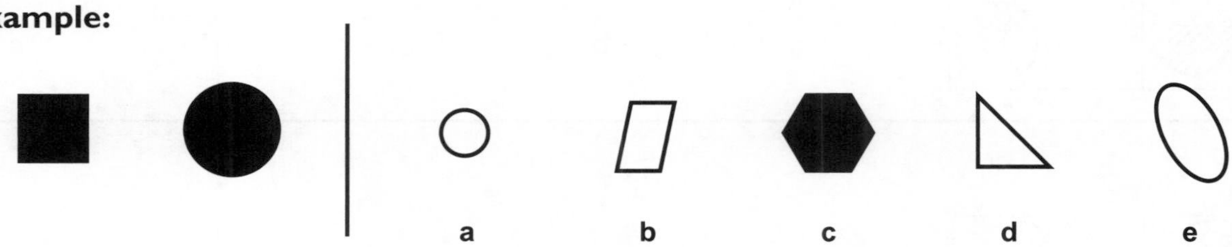

a b c d e

Answer: c

1

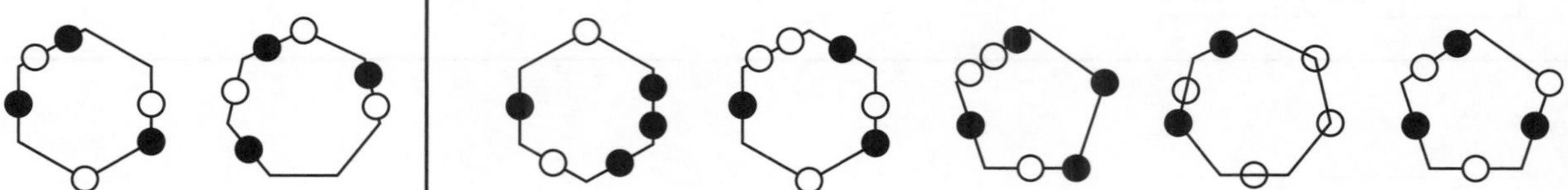

a b c d e

2

a b c d e

3

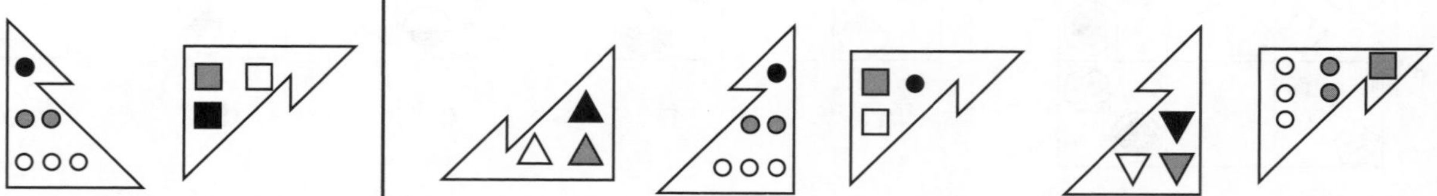

a b c d e

4

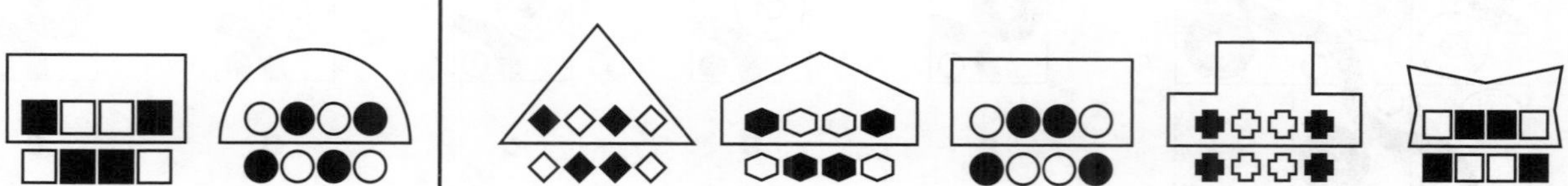

a b c d e

5

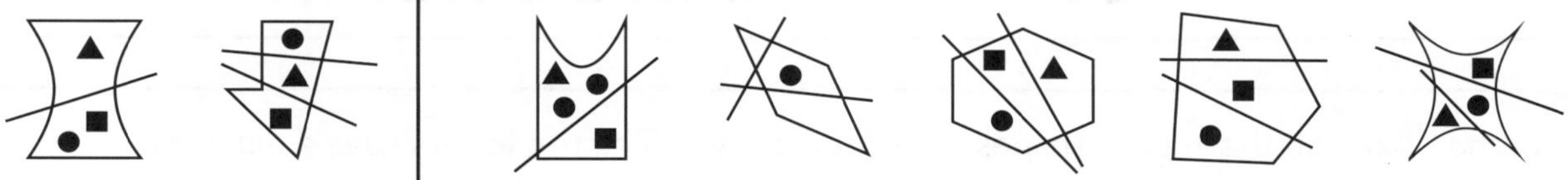

a b c d e

6

a b c d e

7

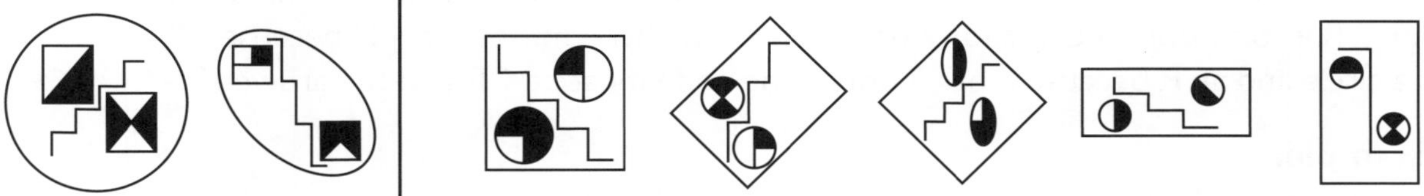

a b c d e

8

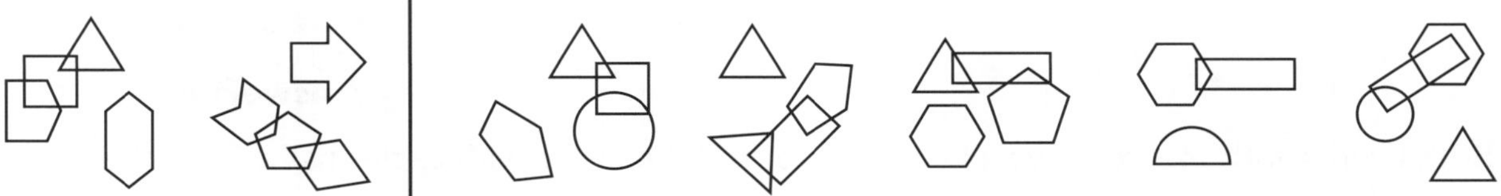

a b c d e

9

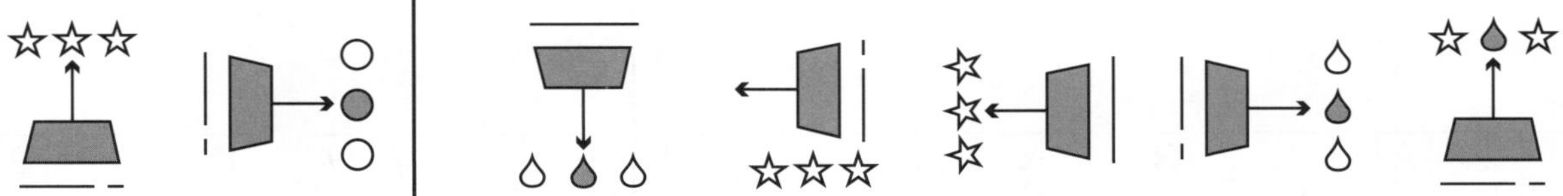

a b c d e

10

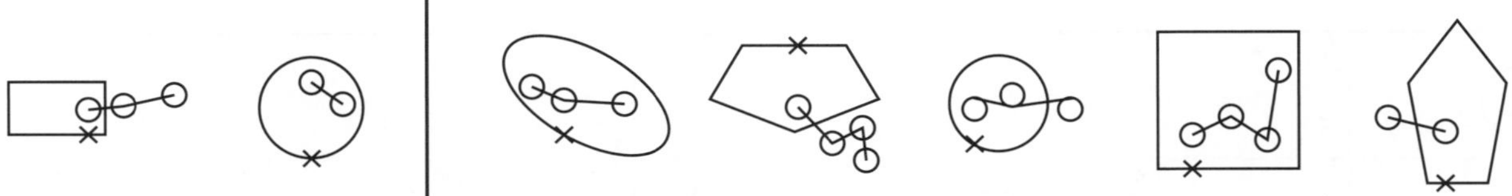

a b c d e

/ 10

Carry on to the next question → →

Section 3 — Horizontal Code

In the boxes on the left are shapes with code letters. The top letters have a different meaning to the bottom ones. Work out how the letters go with the shapes and then find the code for the new shape from the five codes on the right.

Example:

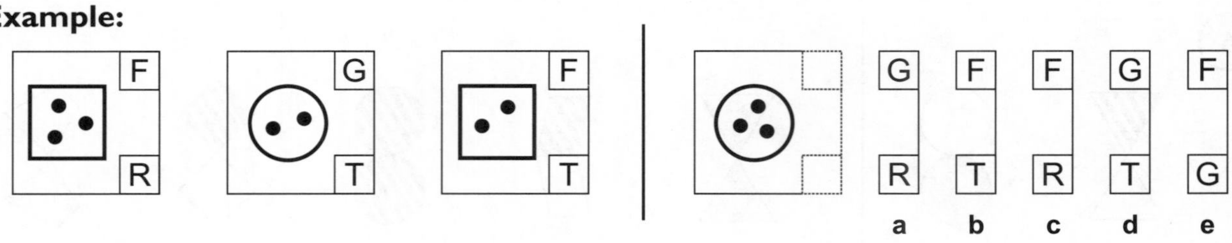

Answer: a

Both squares have an F at the top, but the circle has a G, so the top code letter must stand for shape. This means that the bottom code letter must be for the number of dots. R is for 3 dots and T is for 2 dots. The new shape must have a G because it is a circle and an R because it has 3 dots. The code must be GR and the answer is a.

Example:

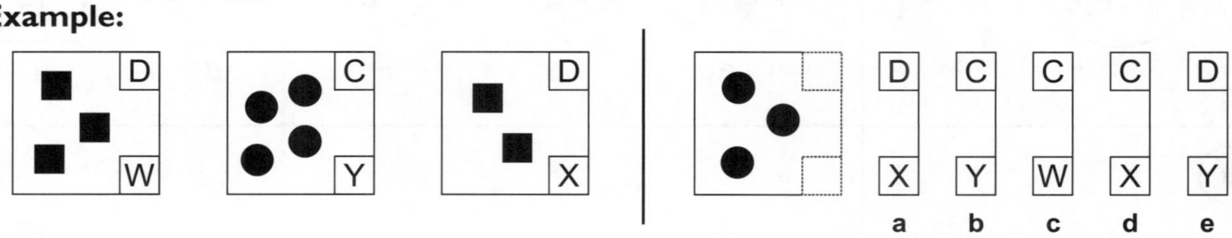

Answer: c

Both figures with squares have a D at the top, and the figure with circles has a C, so the top code letter must be for shape. The bottom code letter must be for the number of shapes. W is for 3 shapes, Y is for 4 and X is for 2. The new figure must have a C because it is made of circles and a W because there are 3 of them. The code must be CW and the answer is c.

1

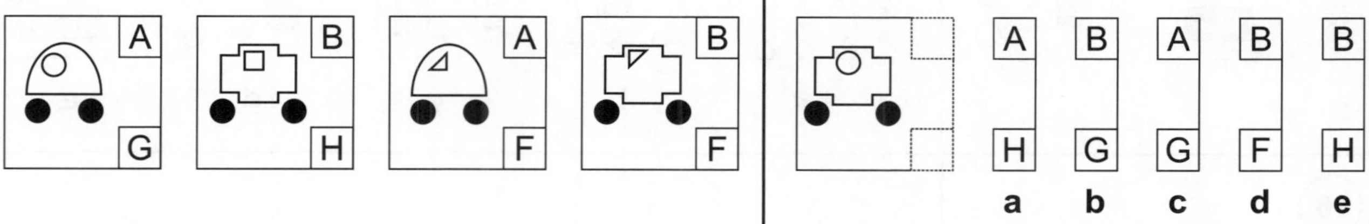

2

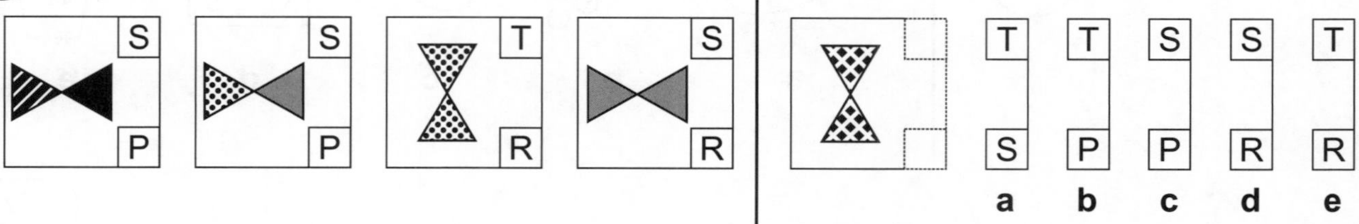

3

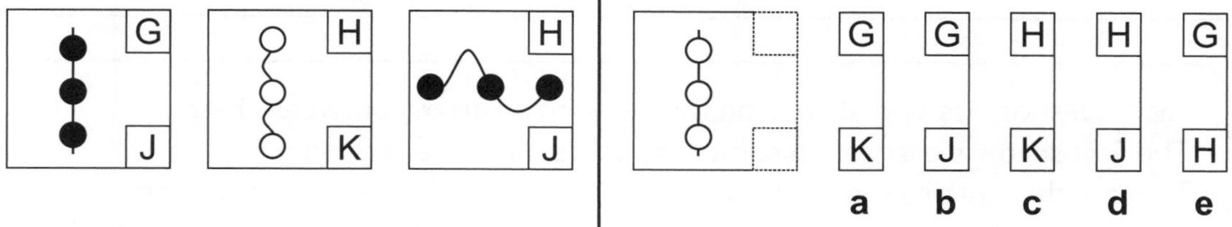

4

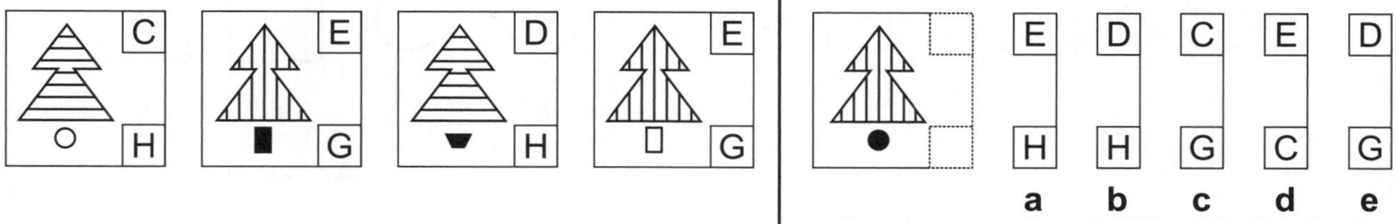

5

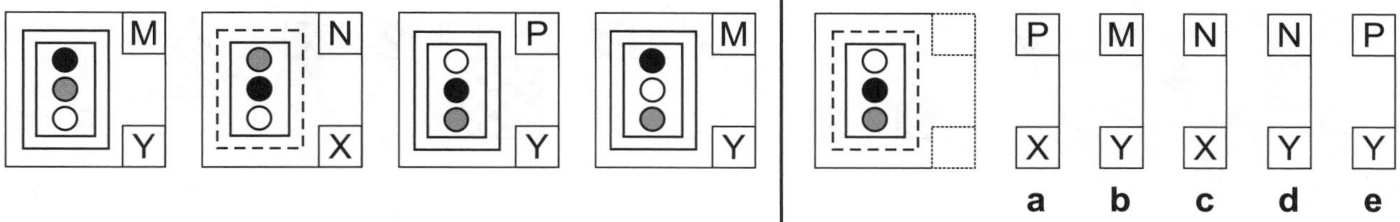

6

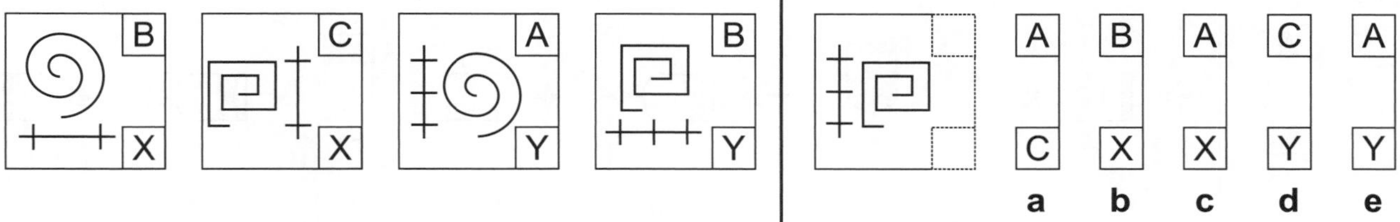

7

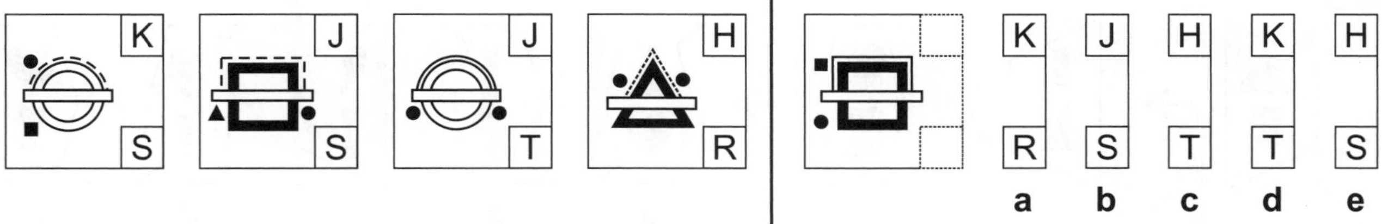

8

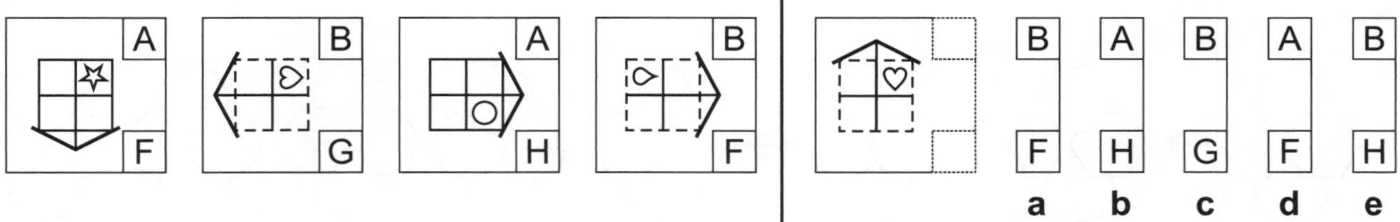

/ 8

Carry on to the next question →→

Section 4 — Complete the Pair

Each question has two shapes on the left with an arrow between them.
The first shape is changed in some way to become the second.
There is then a third shape followed by an arrow and a choice of five shapes.
Choose the shape on the right that relates to the third shape like the second does to the first.

Example:

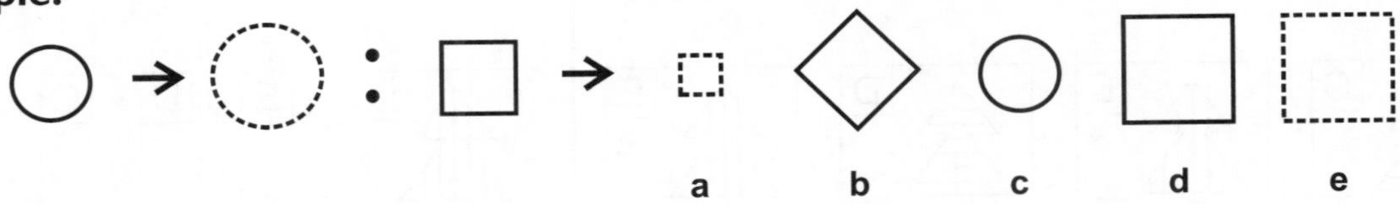

Answer: e

(1)

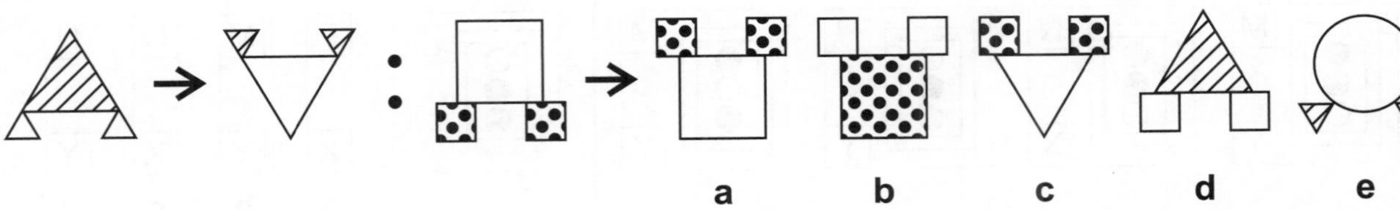

(2)

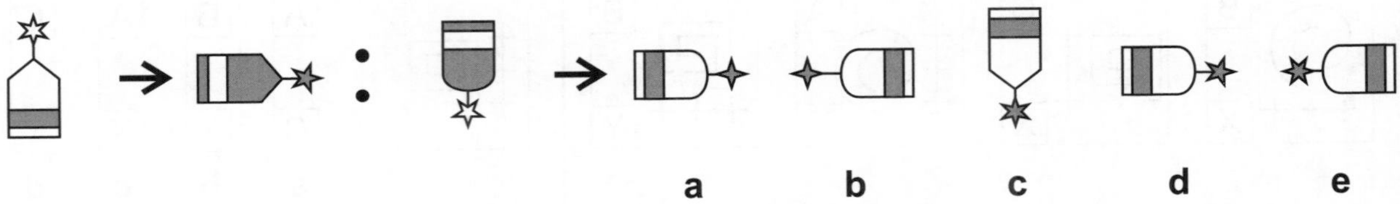

(3)

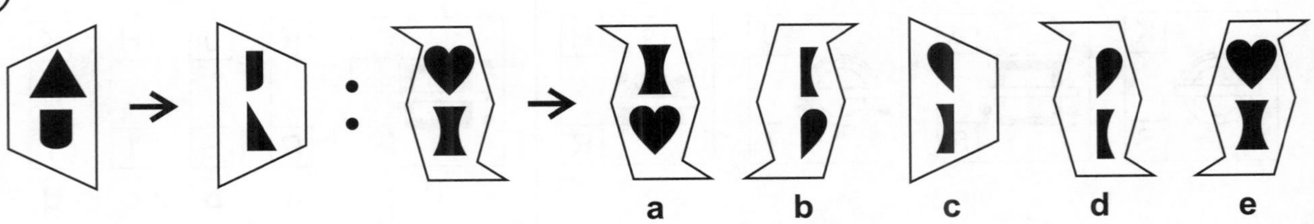

(4)

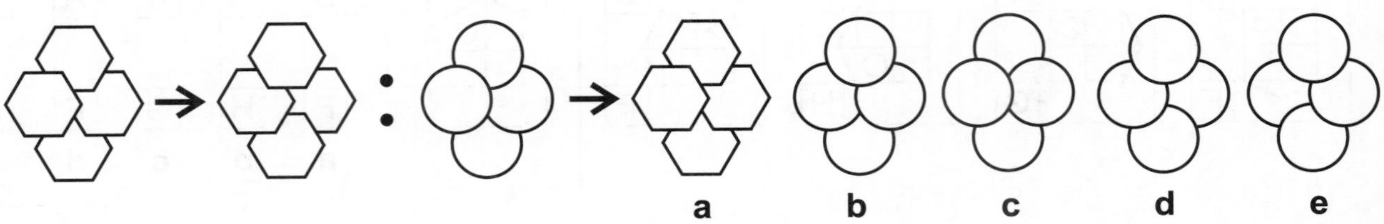

5

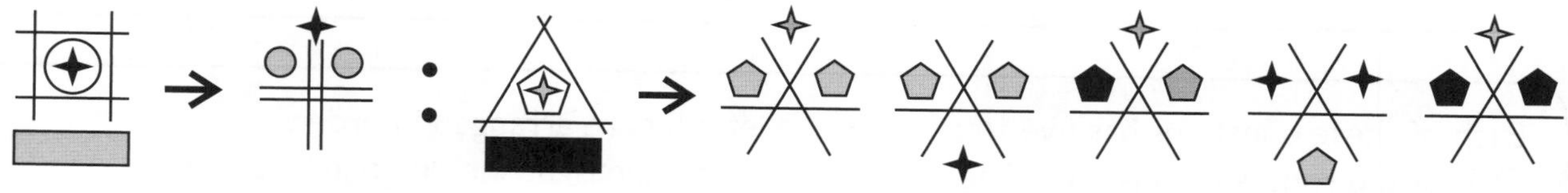

a b c d e

6

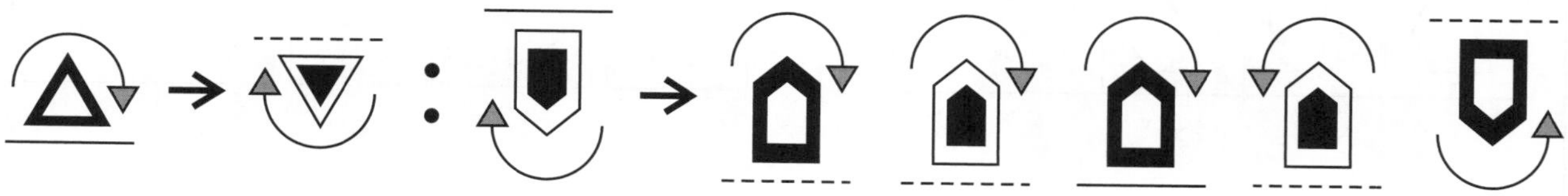

a b c d e

7

a b c d e

8

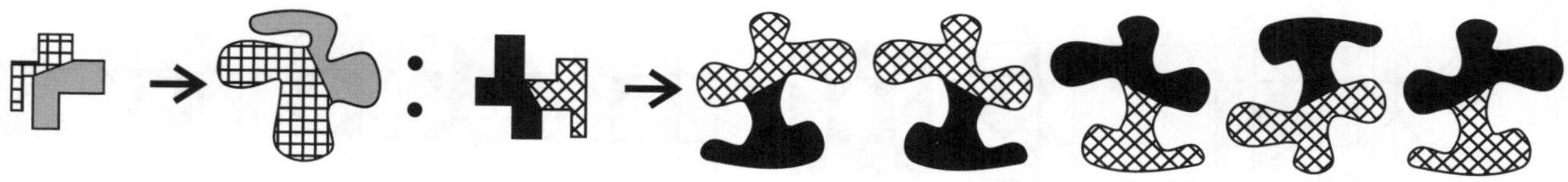

a b c d e

9

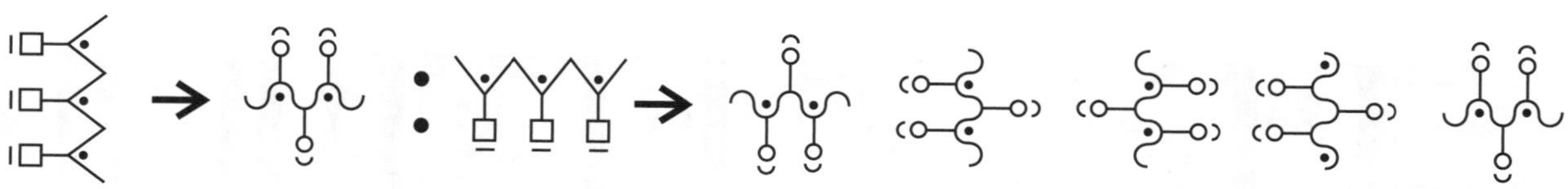

a b c d e

10

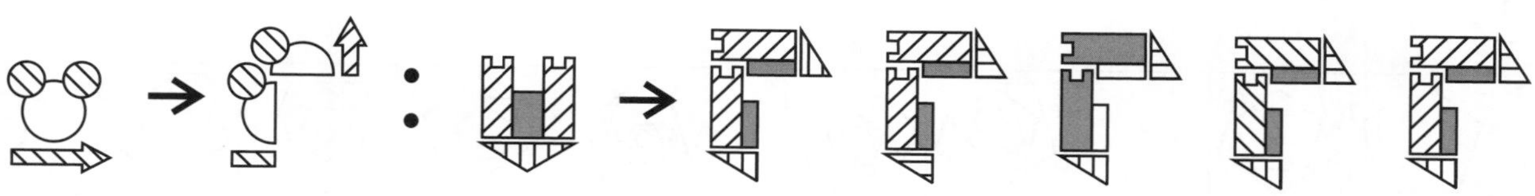

a b c d e

/ 10

Carry on to the next question → →

Section 5 — Complete the Series

Each of these questions has five squares on the left that are arranged in order.
One of the squares is missing. One of the squares on the right should go in its place.
Find which one of the five squares on the right should go in place of the empty square.

Example:

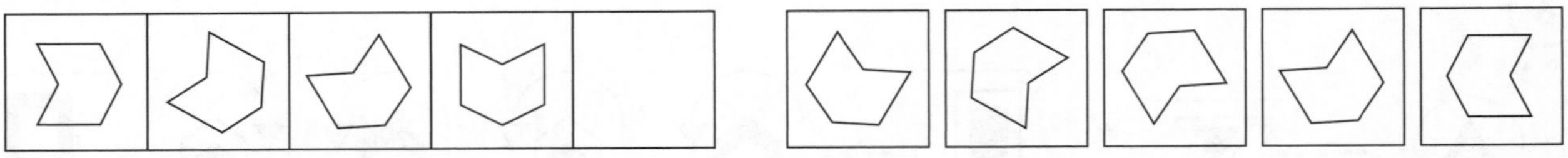

a b c d e

Answer: a

1

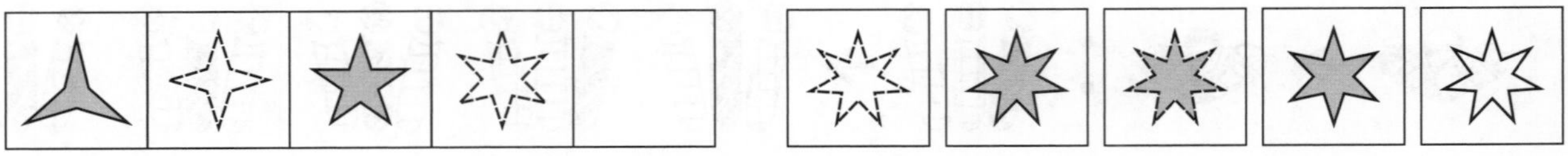

a b c d e

2

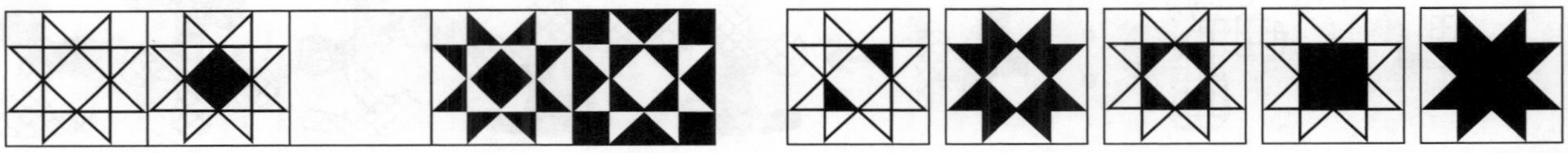

a b c d e

3

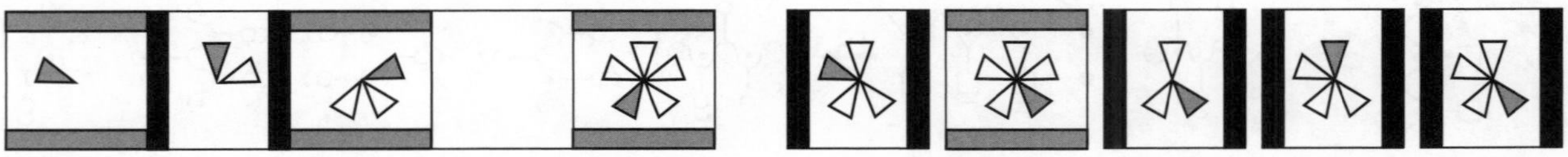

a b c d e

4

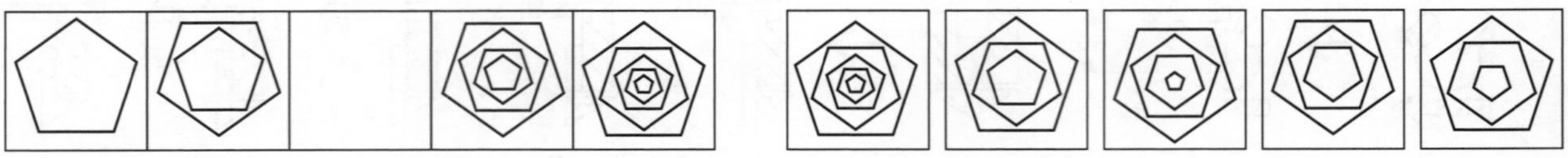

a b c d e

5

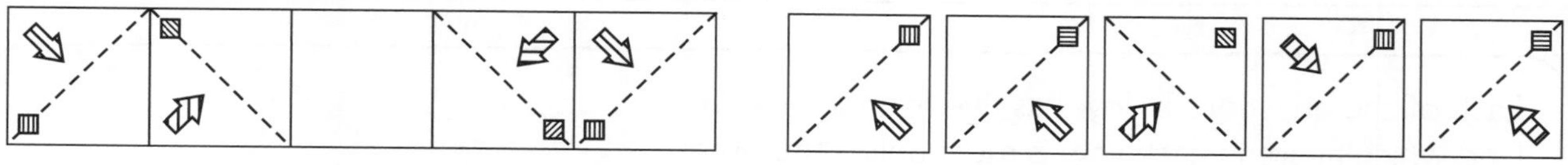

a b c d e

6

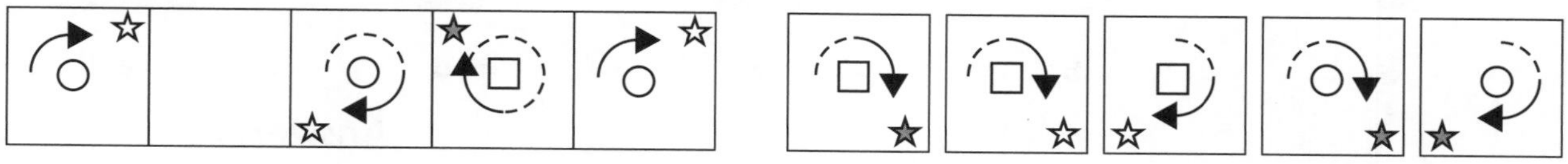

a b c d e

7

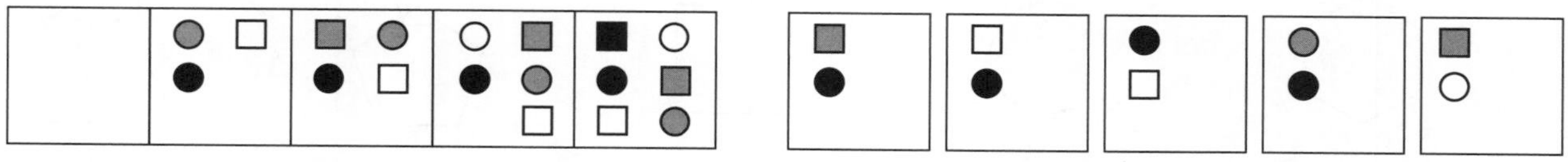

a b c d e

8

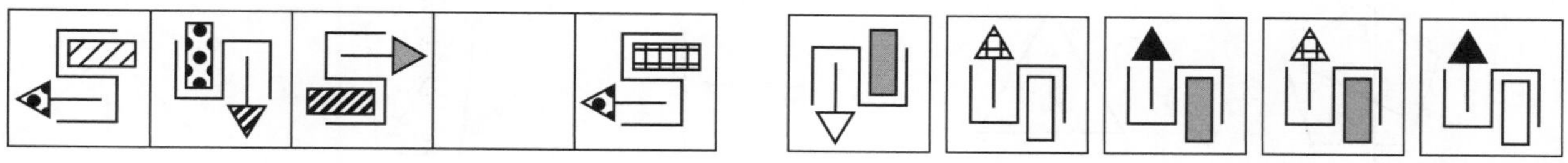

a b c d e

9

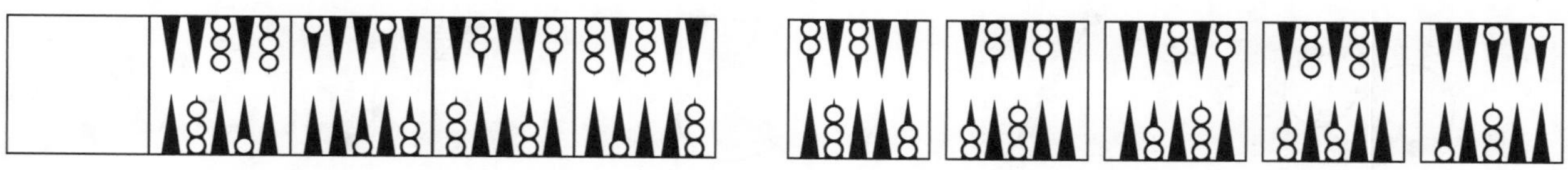

a b c d e

10

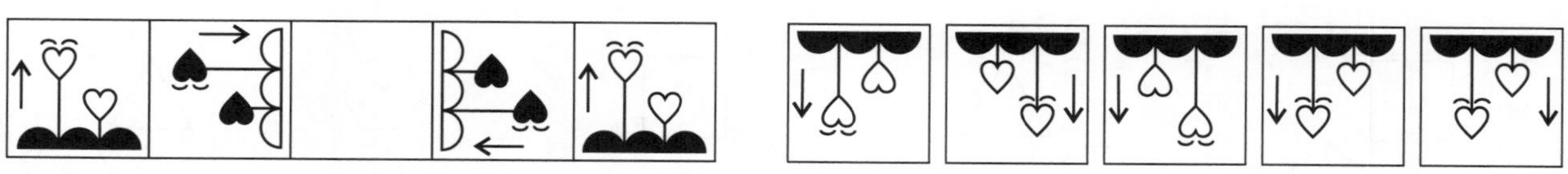

a b c d e

/ 10

Carry on to the next question → →

Section 6 — Odd One Out

Each of the questions below has five figures.
Find which figure in each row is most unlike the others.

Example:

a b c d e

Answer: b

1

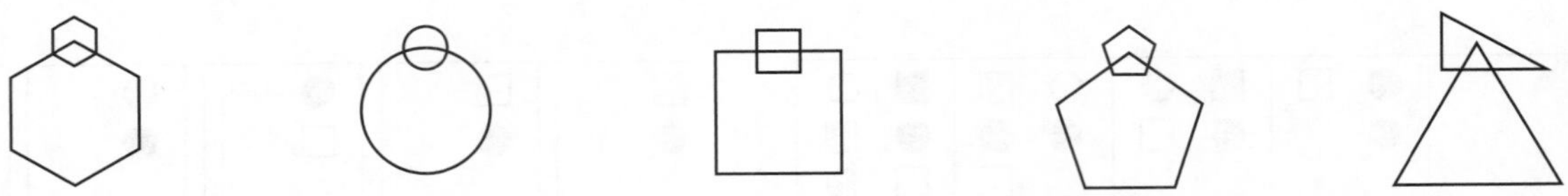

a b c d e

2

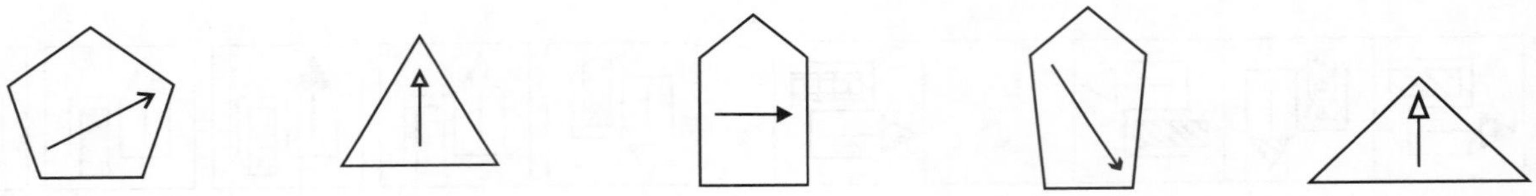

a b c d e

3

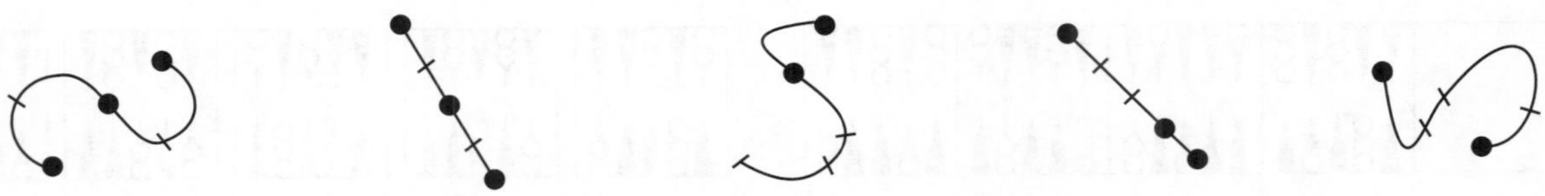

a b c d e

4

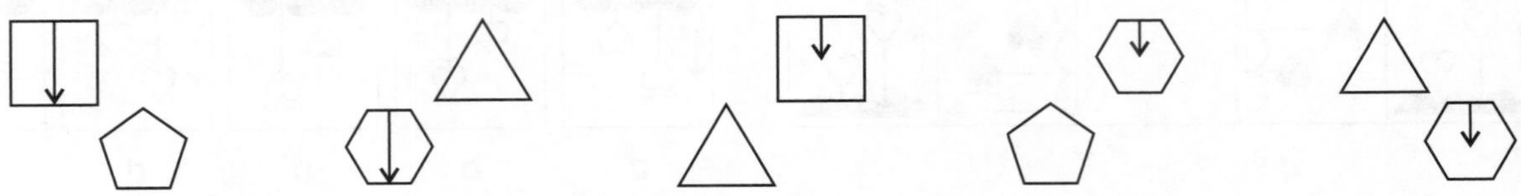

a b c d e

(5)

a b c d e

(6)

a b c d e

(7)

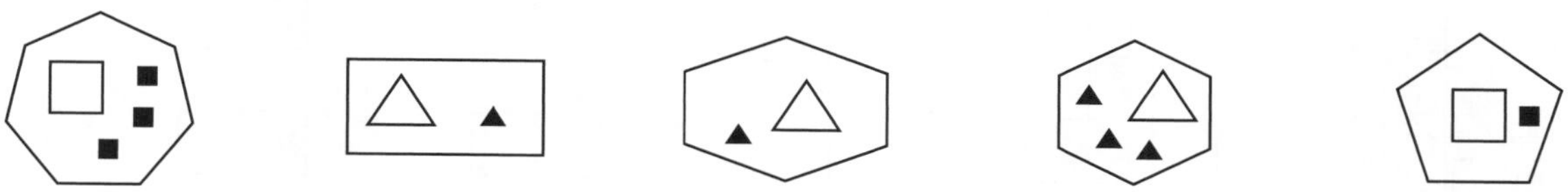

a b c d e

(8)

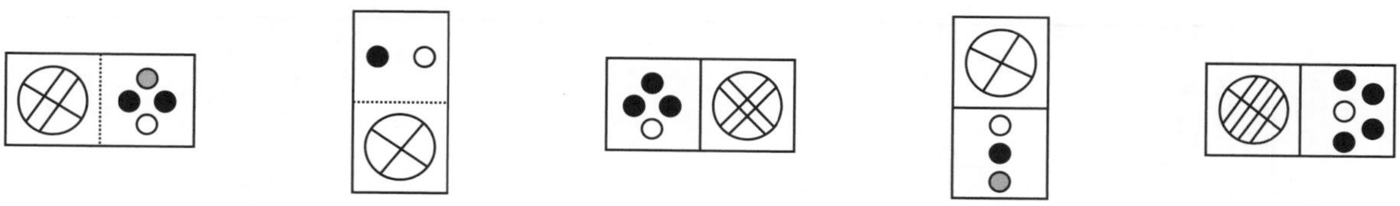

a b c d e

(9)

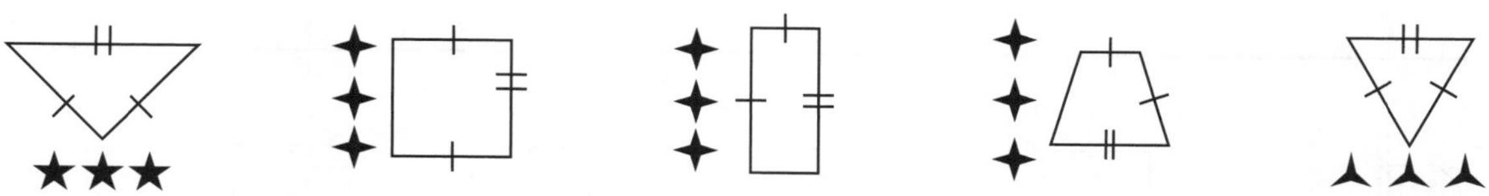

a b c d e

(10)

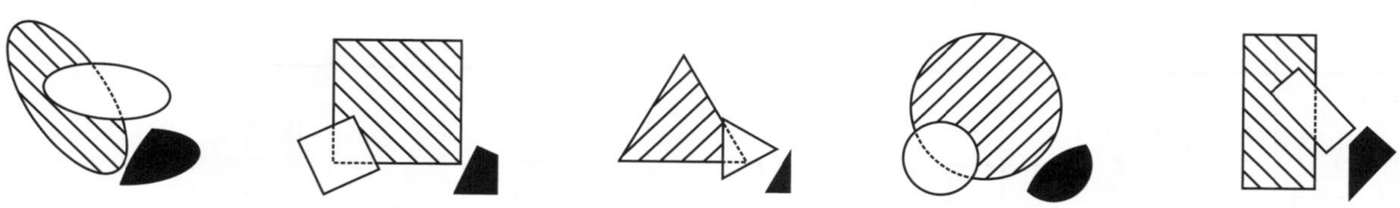

a b c d e

/ 10

Total / 56

End of Test

Assessment Test 6

You can print **multiple-choice answer sheets** for these questions from our website — go to cgpbooks.co.uk/11plus/answer-sheets or scan the QR code on the right. If you'd prefer to answer them in standard write-in format, just circle the letter underneath your answer. The test should take around 30 minutes.

Answer Sheets

You can ignore Assessment Test 6 if you're sitting the test in a region that does not test Spatial Reasoning. For more information on test content in different regions, please visit cgpbooks.co.uk/11plus.

Section 1 — 2D Views of 3D Shapes

Each of these questions has a 3D figure on the left, made out of cubes.
Work out which of the five options is a top-down 2D view of the 3D figure on the left.

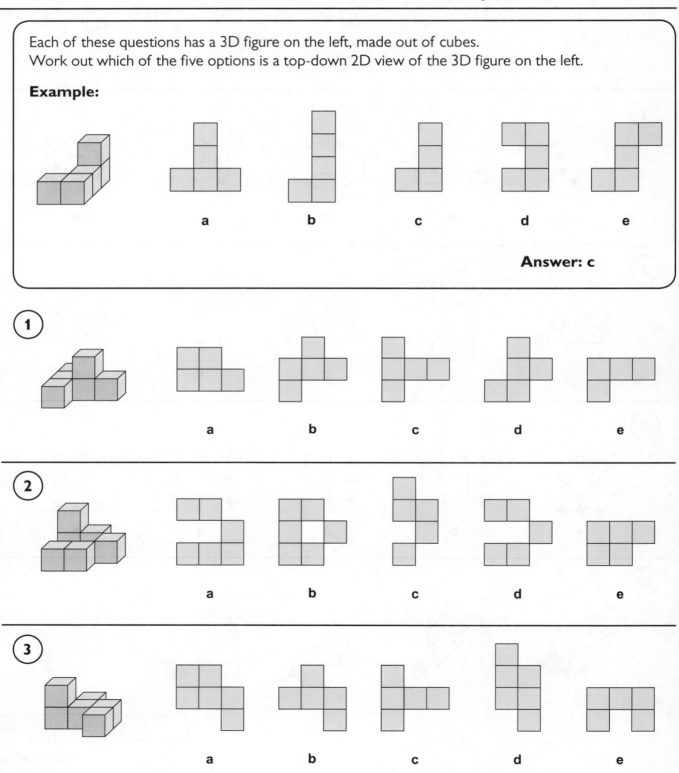

Example:

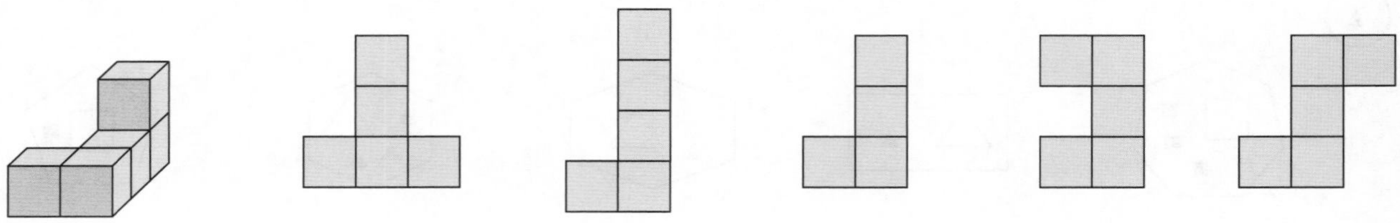

a b c d e

Answer: c

(1)

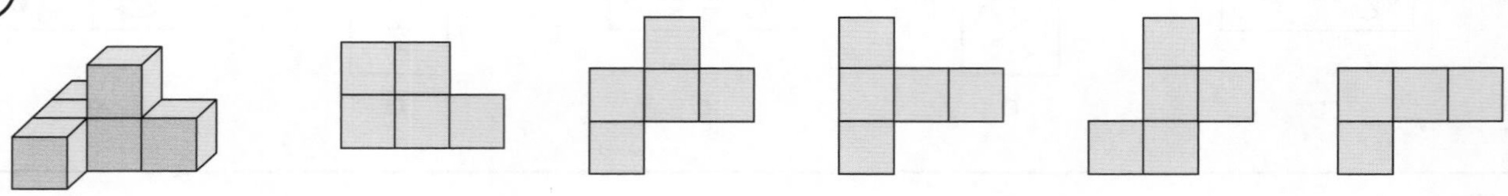

a b c d e

(2)

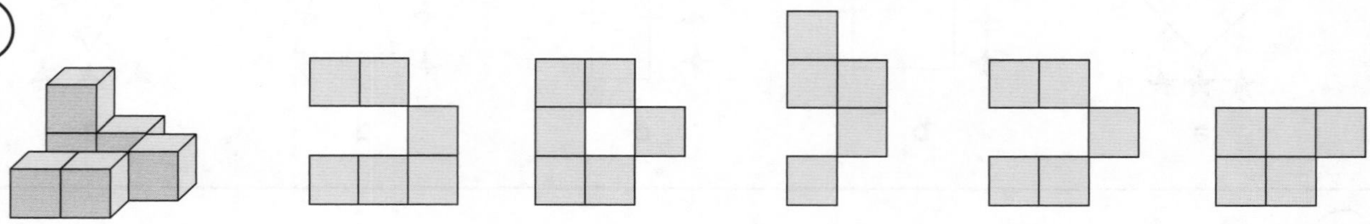

a b c d e

(3)

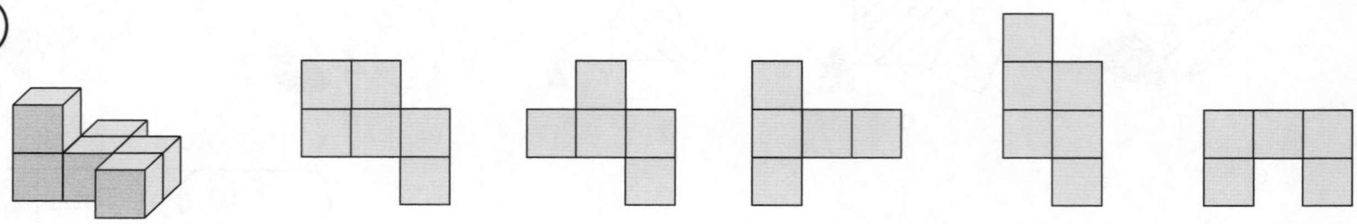

a b c d e

4

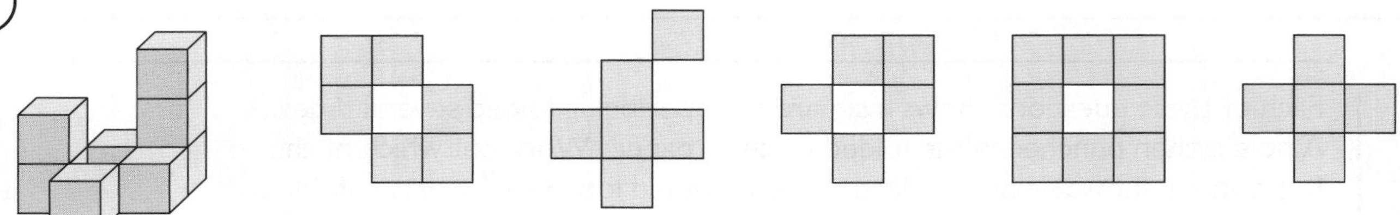

a b c d e

5

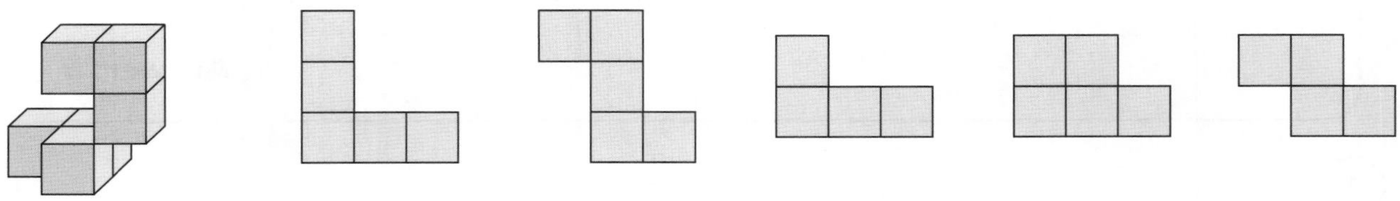

a b c d e

6

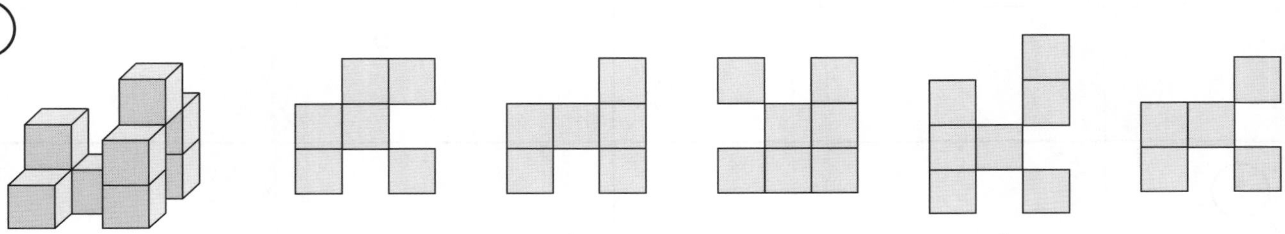

a b c d e

7

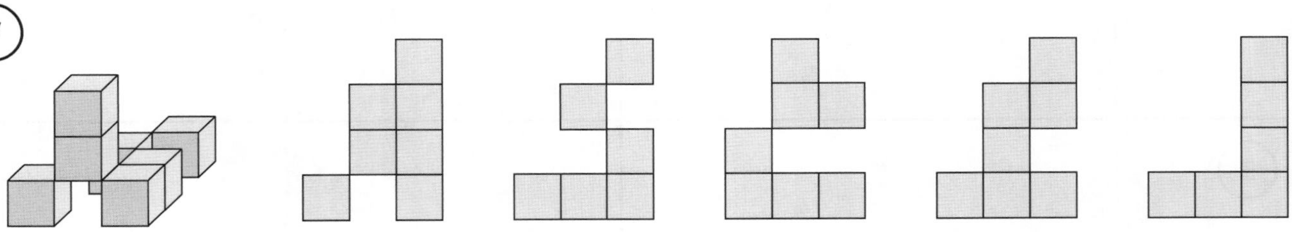

a b c d e

8

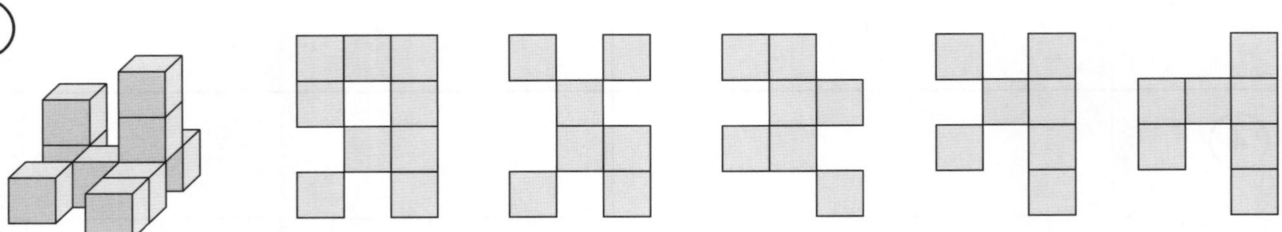

a b c d e

/ 8

Carry on to the next question →→

Section 2 — Fold and Punch

Each of these questions shows a square of paper being folded several times. A hole is then punched in the folded piece of paper. Work out which of the five options shows what the piece of paper would look like if it was unfolded.

Example:

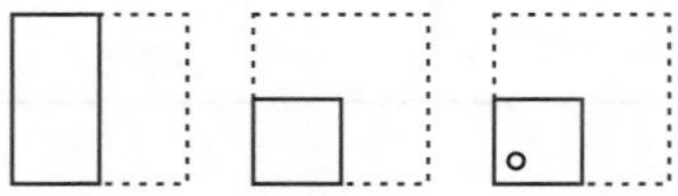

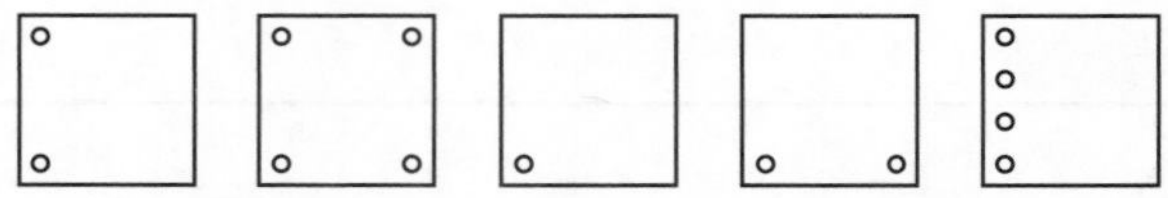

a b c d e

Answer: b

1

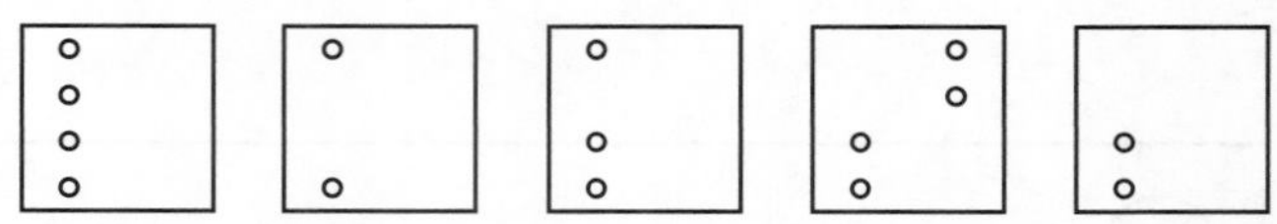

a b c d e

2

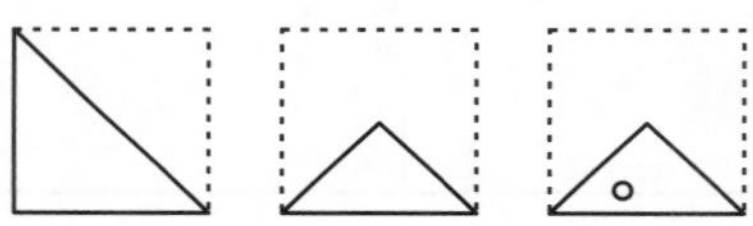

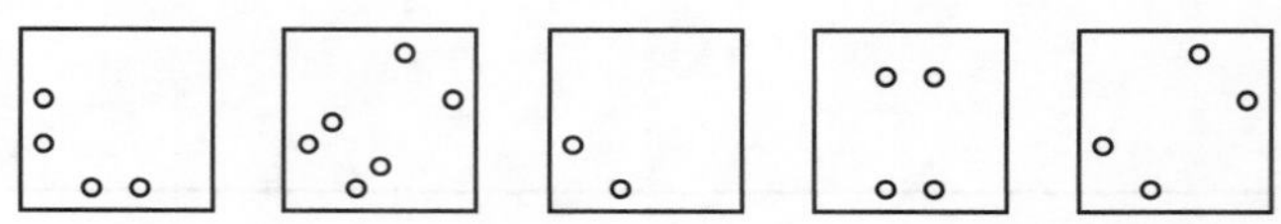

a b c d e

3

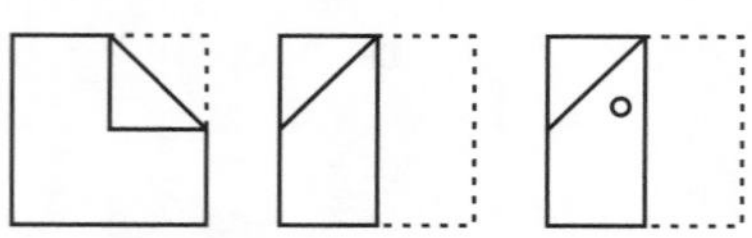

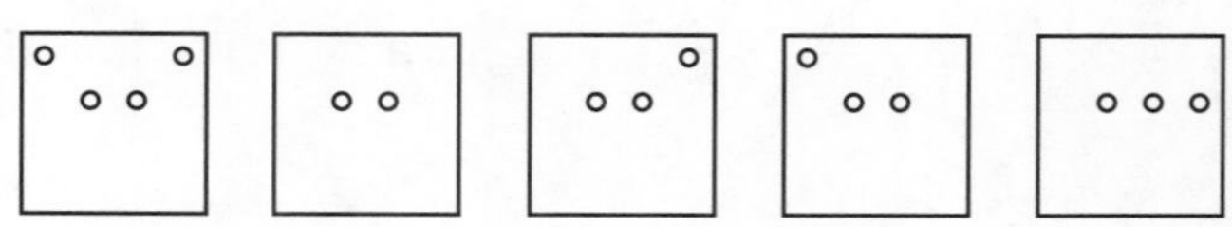

a b c d e

4

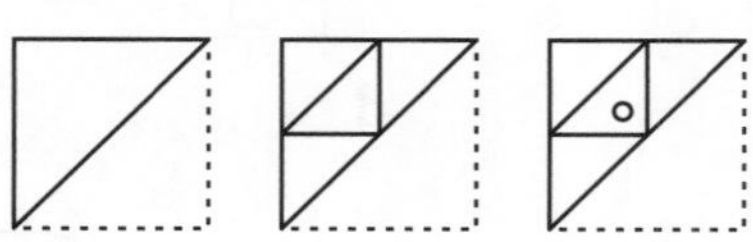

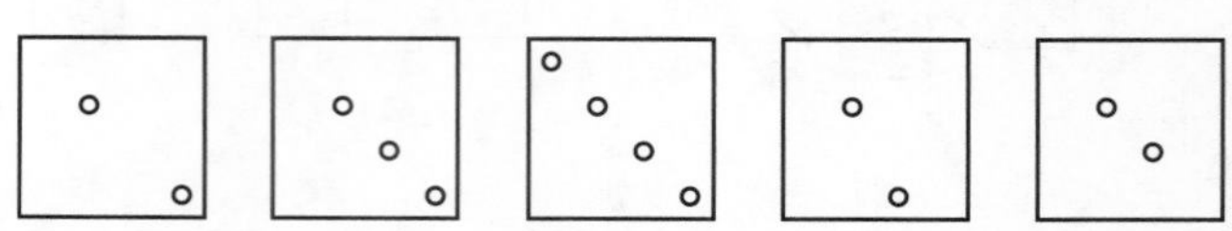

a b c d e

5

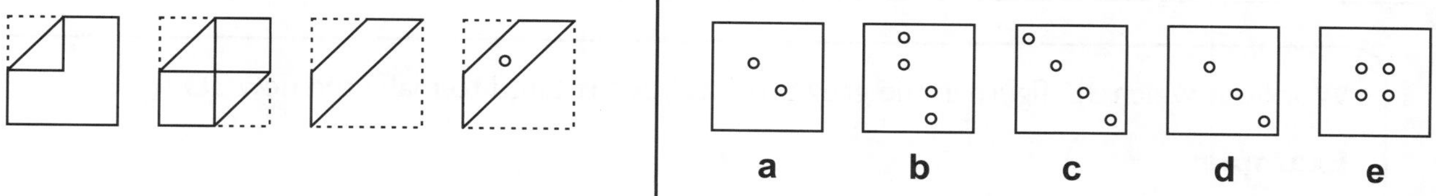

6

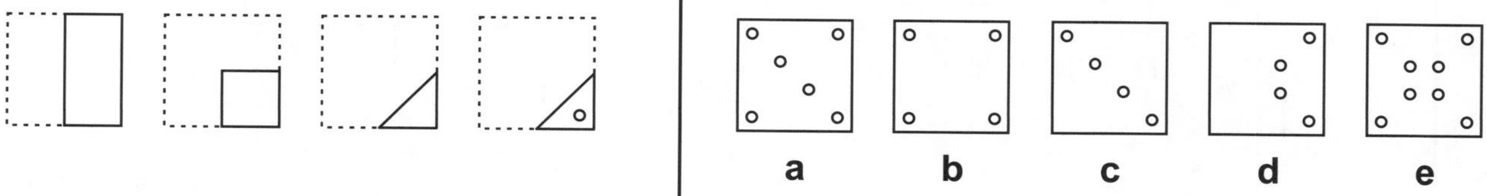

7

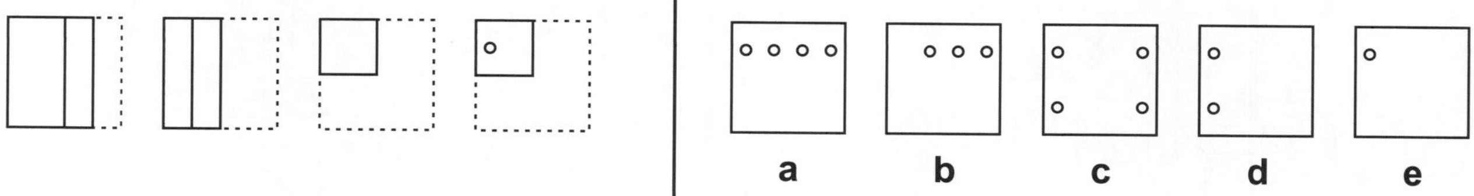

8

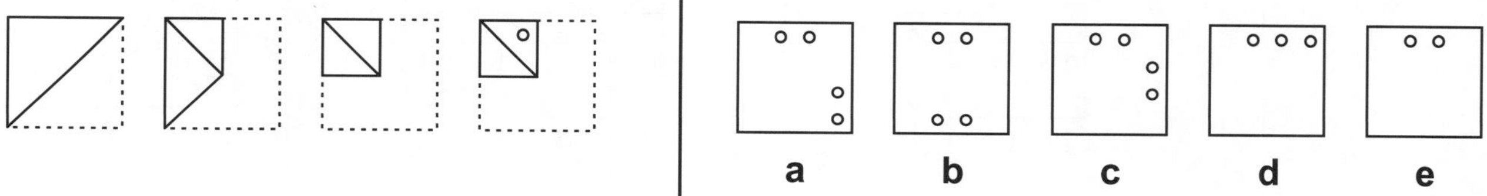

9

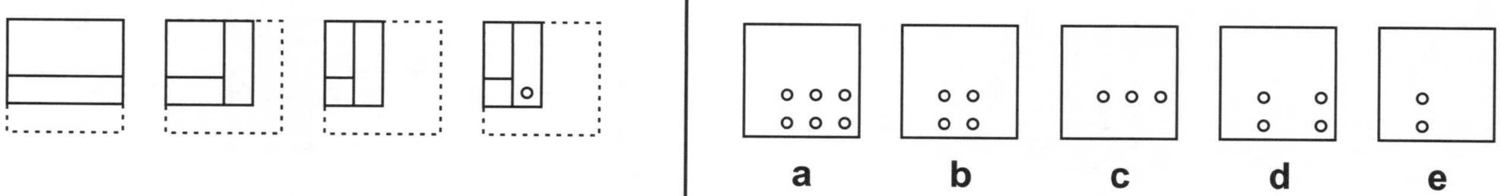

10

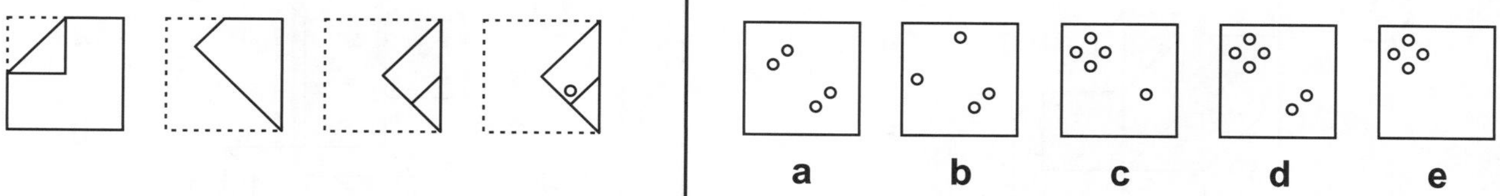

/ 10

Carry on to the next question → →

Section 3 — 3D Rotation

Work out which 3D figure in the grey box has been rotated to make the new 3D figure.

Example:

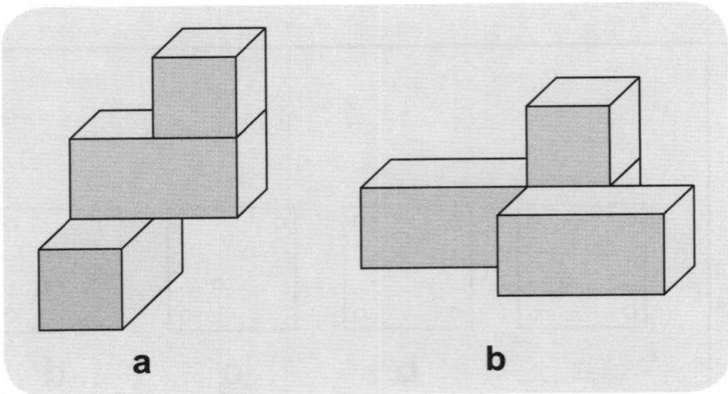

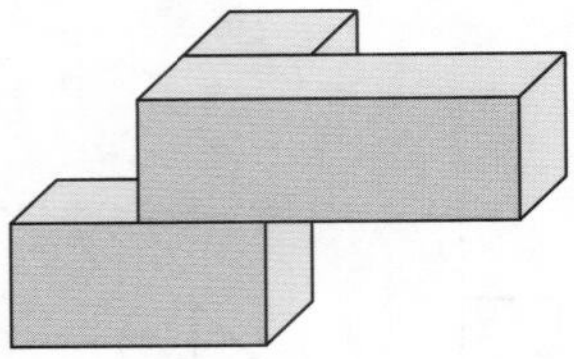

a

b

Answer: b

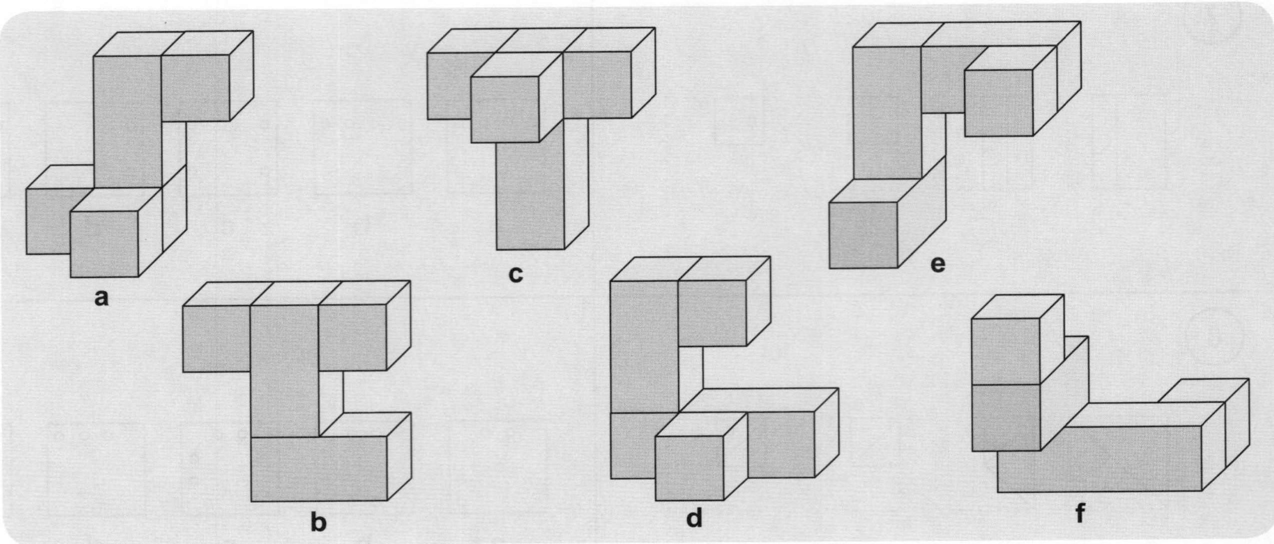

1

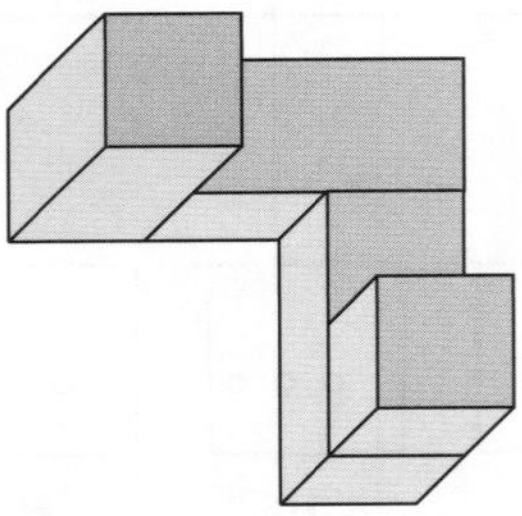

a d

b e

c f

2

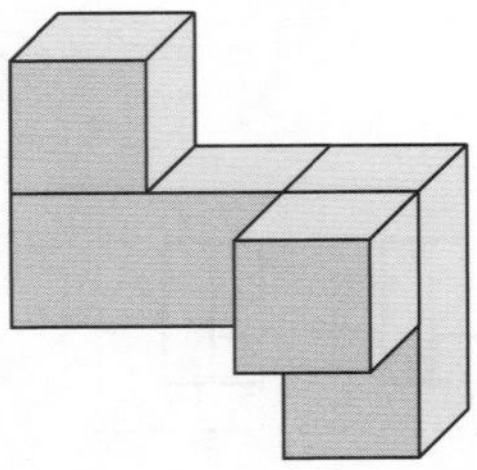

a d

b e

c f

3

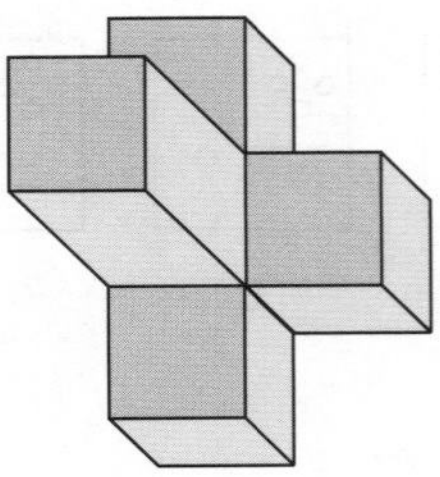

a d

b e

c f

4

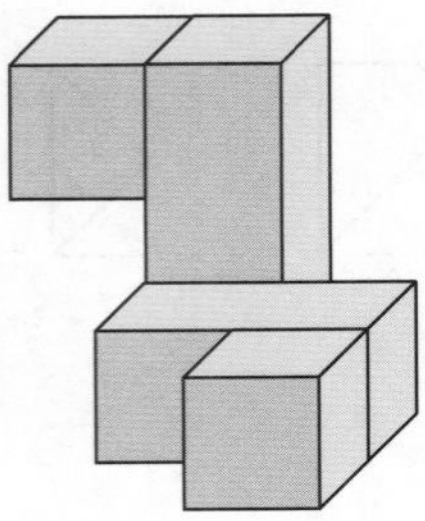

a d

b e

c f

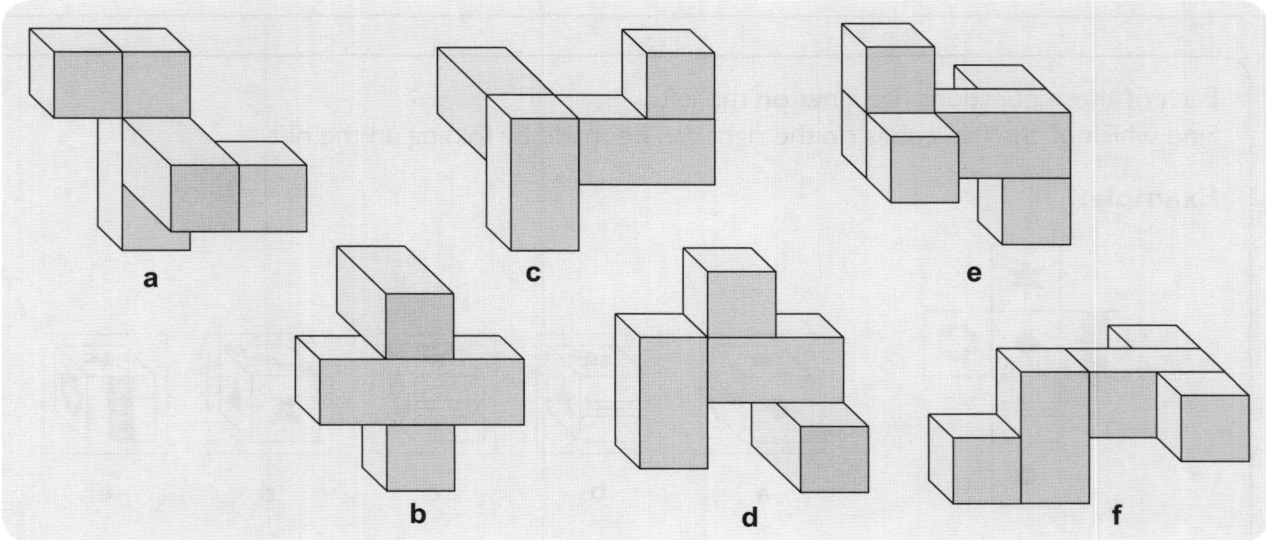

5 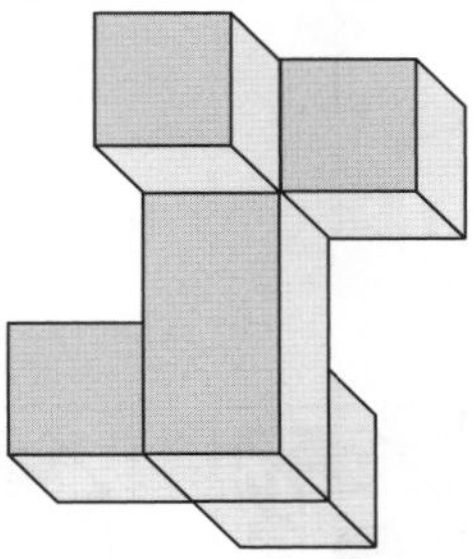

a d
b e
c f

6 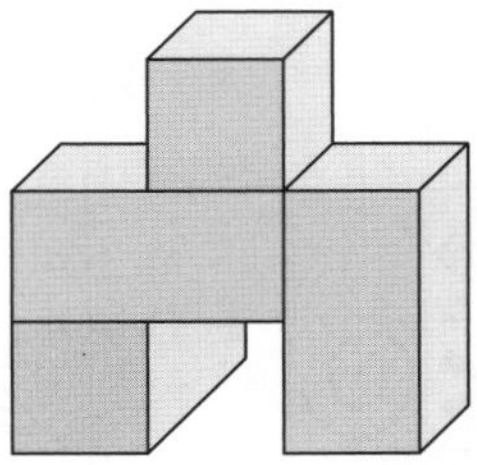

a d
b e
c f

7 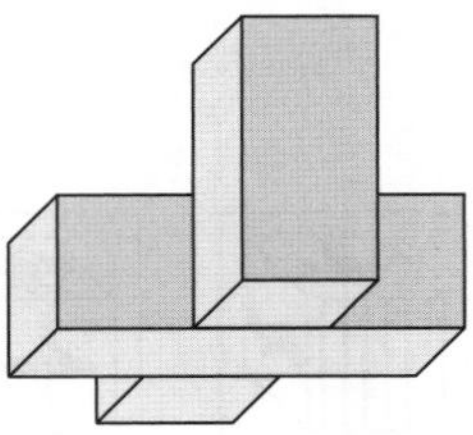

a d
b e
c f

8 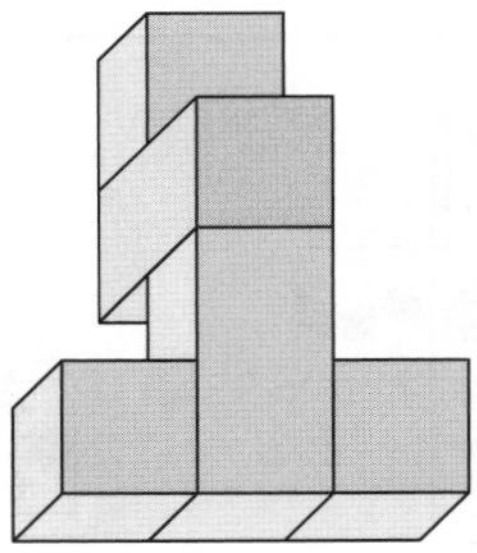

a d
b e
c f

9 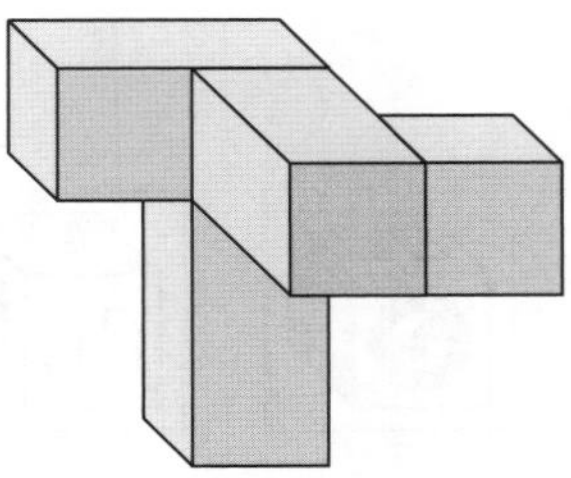

a d
b e
c f

10 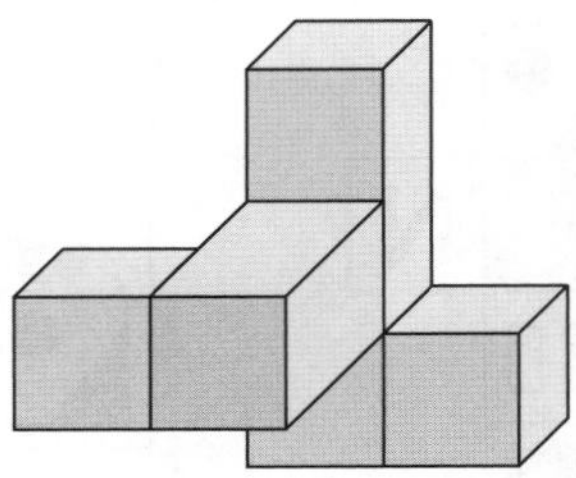

a d
b e
c f

/ 10

Carry on to the next question →→

Section 4 — Cubes and Nets

Each of these questions has a net on the left.
Find which of the five cubes on the right can be made by folding up the net.

Example:

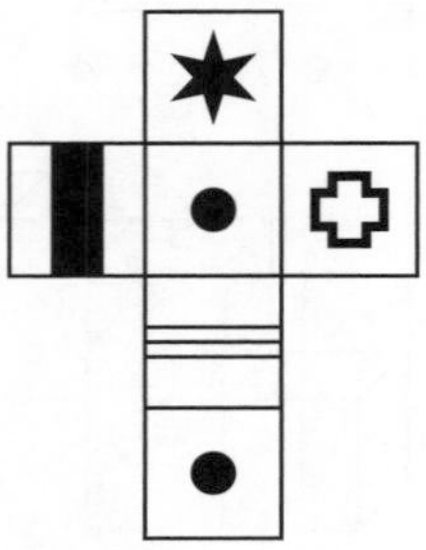

a b c d e

Answer: c

(1)

a b c d e

(2)

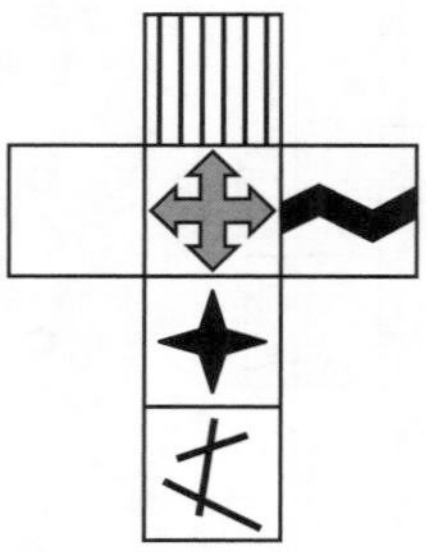

a b c d e

(3)

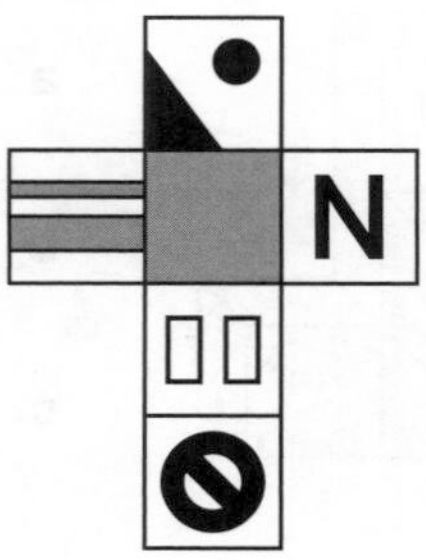

a b c d e

4

a b c d e

5

a b c d e

6

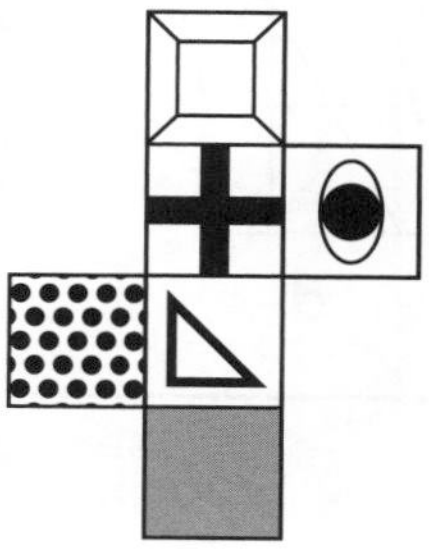
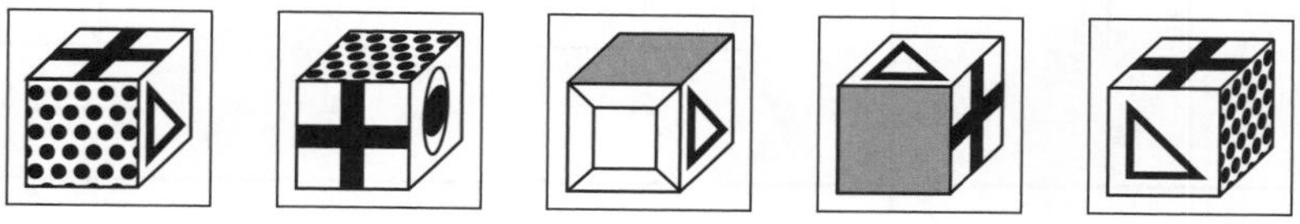

a b c d e

7

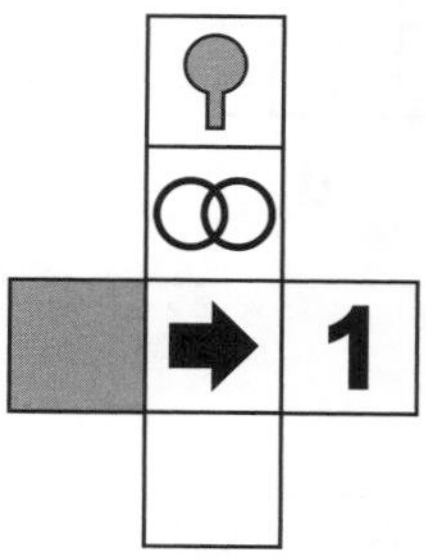

a b c d e

8

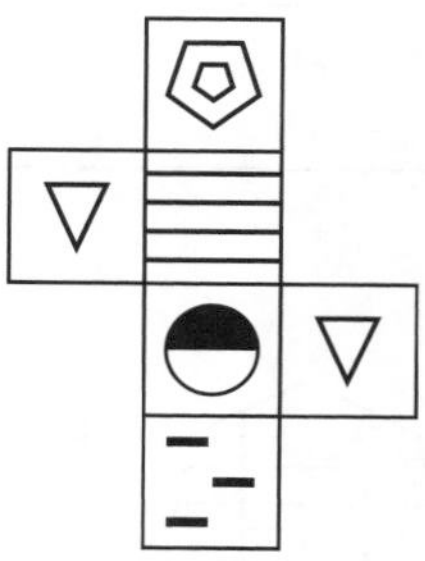

a b c d e

/ 8

Carry on to the next question → →

Section 5 — Hidden Shape

Each of these questions has a single shape on the left.
This shape can be found in one of the five figures on the right.
The shape must be the same size and orientation.
Find which of the five figures contains the shape.

Example:

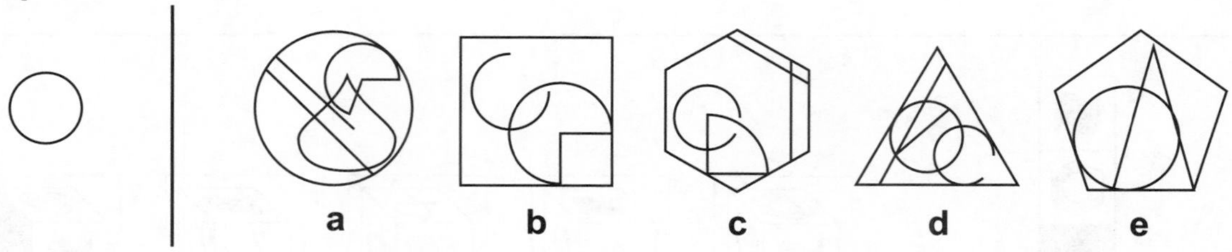

Answer: d

(1)

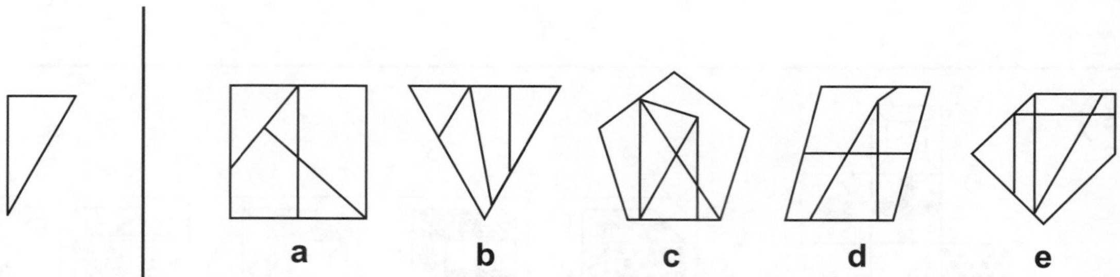

(2)

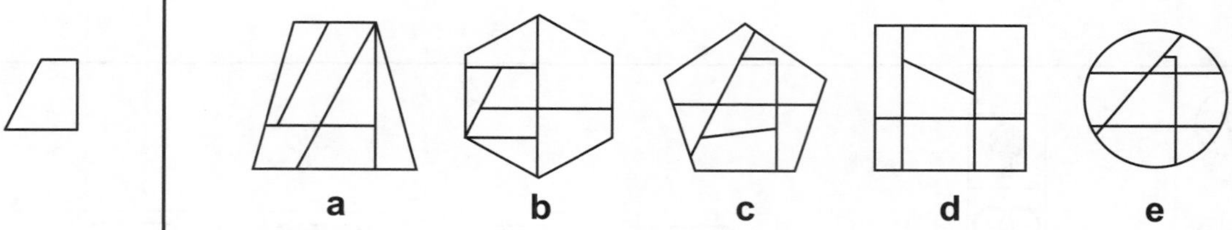

(3)

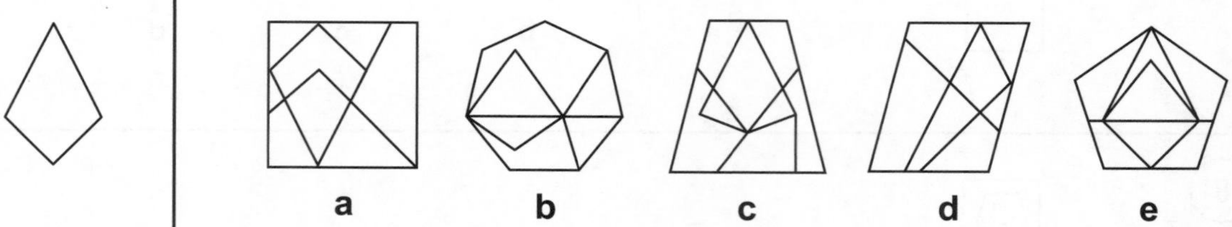

(4)

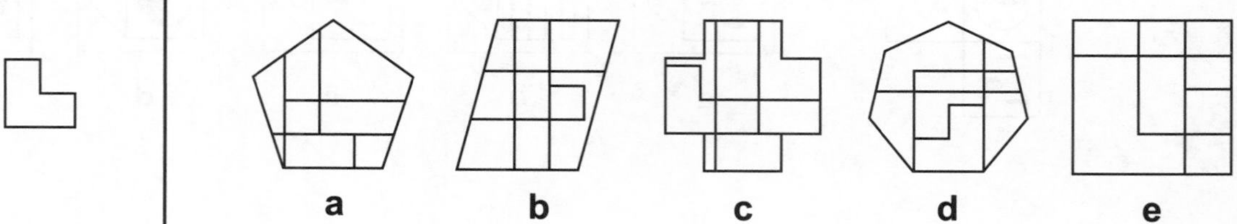

5

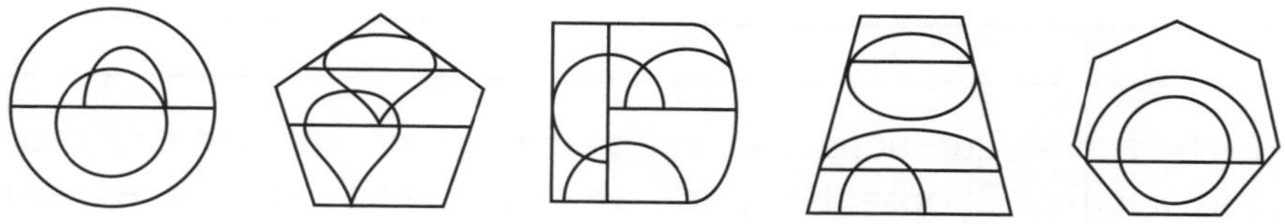

a b c d e

6

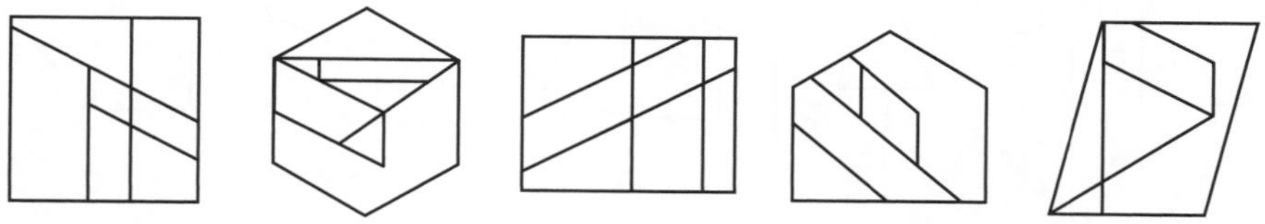

a b c d e

7

a b c d e

8

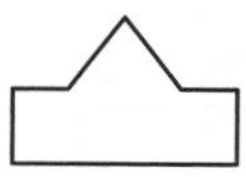

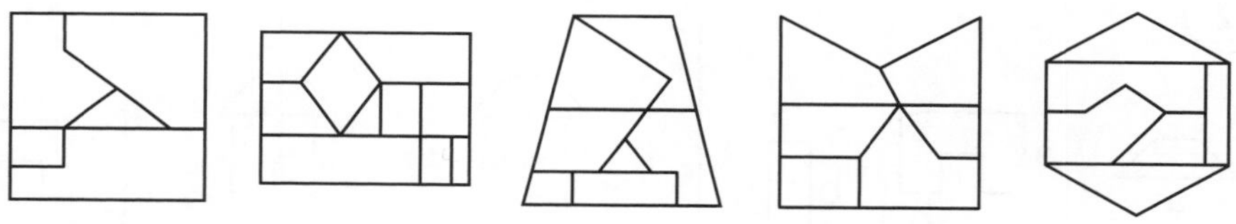

a b c d e

9

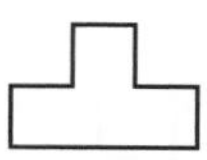

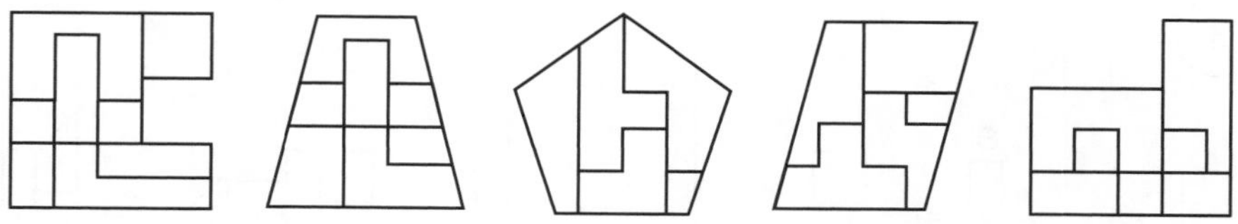

a b c d e

10

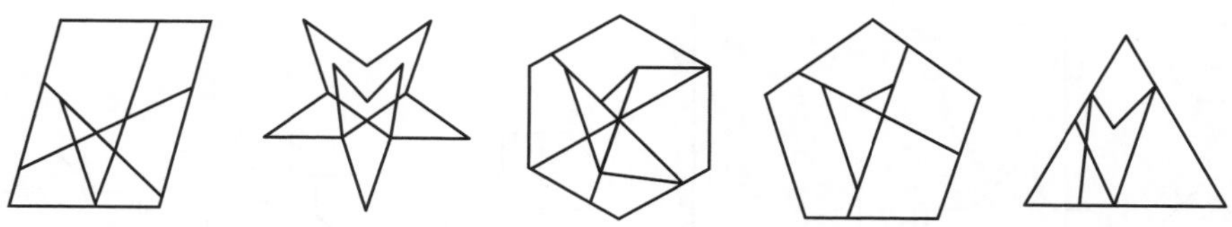

a b c d e

/ 10

Carry on to the next question → →

Section 6 — Connecting Shapes

Each of these questions has three shapes on the left. Some of their sides are labelled with a letter. Choose the option which shows how the shapes would look if they were joined together so that sides with the same letter are touching.

Example:

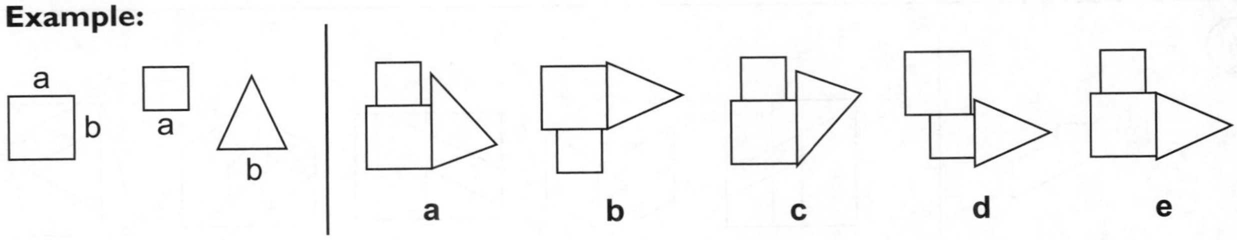

Answer: e

1

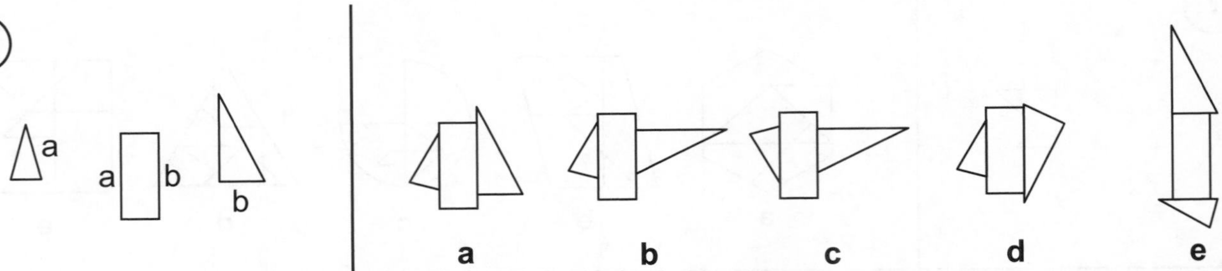

2

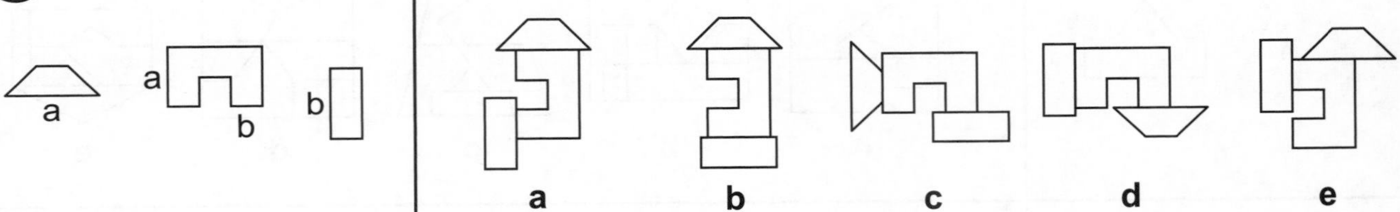

3

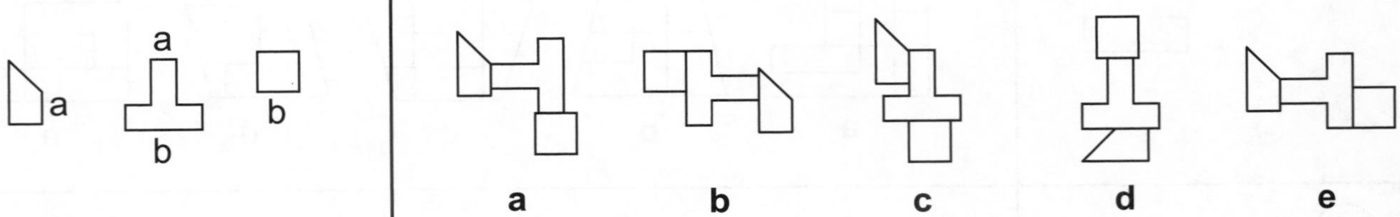

4

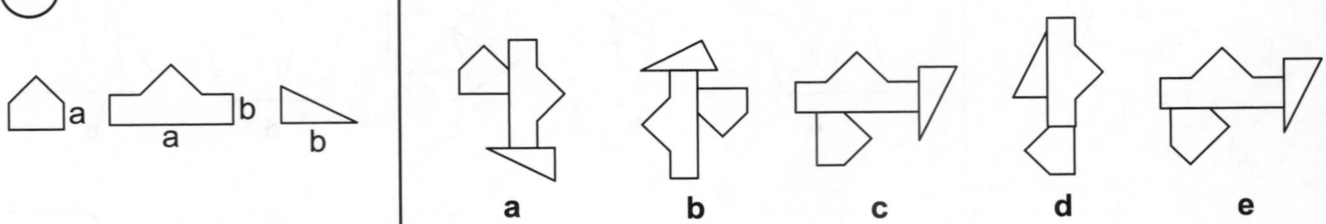

5

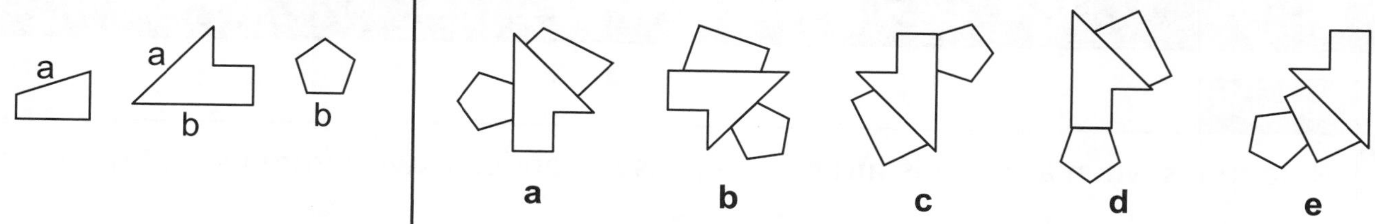

6

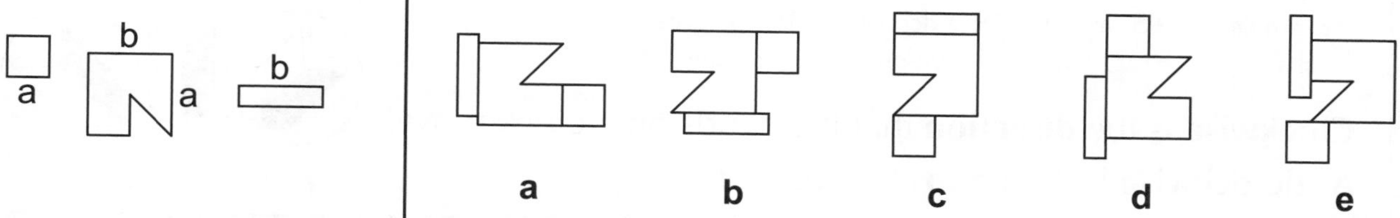

7

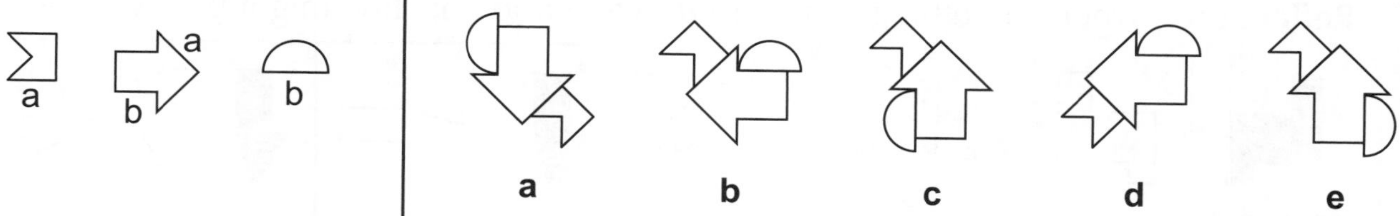

8

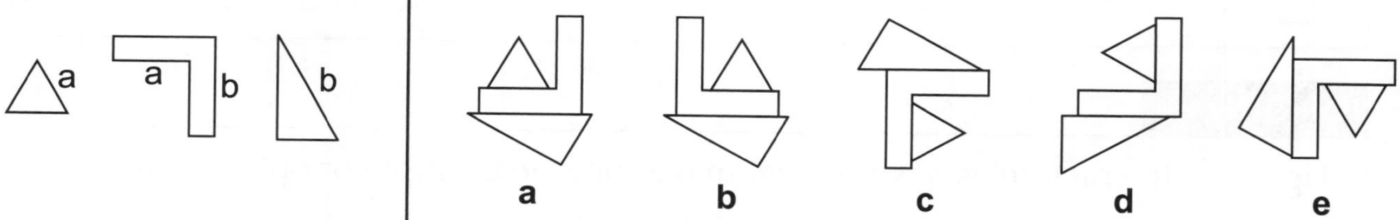

9

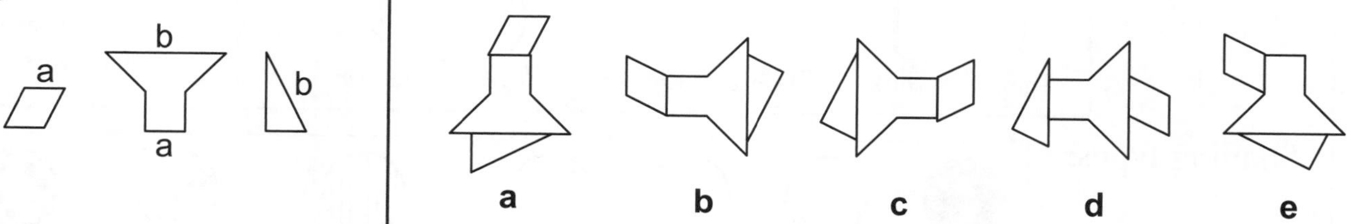

10

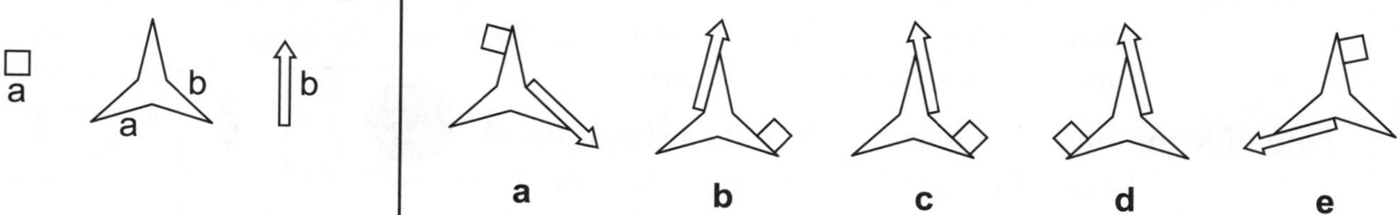

/ 10

Total / 56

End of Test

Glossary

Rotation

Rotation is when a shape is **turned** clockwise or anticlockwise from its starting point.

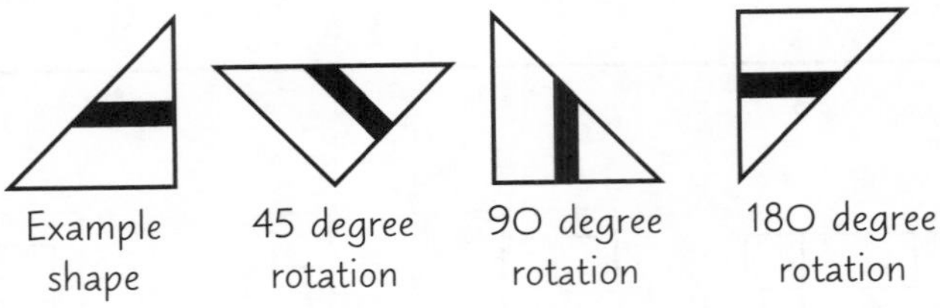

The left hand shape has been rotated 45 degrees anticlockwise.

The right hand shape has been rotated 45 degrees clockwise.

Clockwise is the **direction** that the hands on a clock move.
Anticlockwise is the **opposite direction**.

Reflection

Reflection is when something is **mirrored** over a line (this line might be invisible).

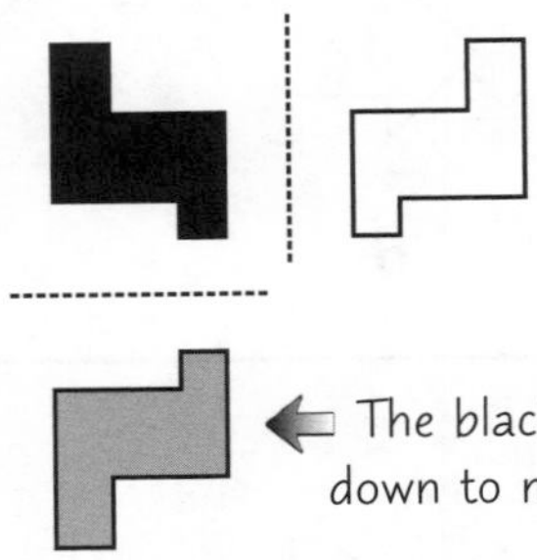

The black shape is reflected across to make the white shape.

The black shape is reflected down to make the grey shape.

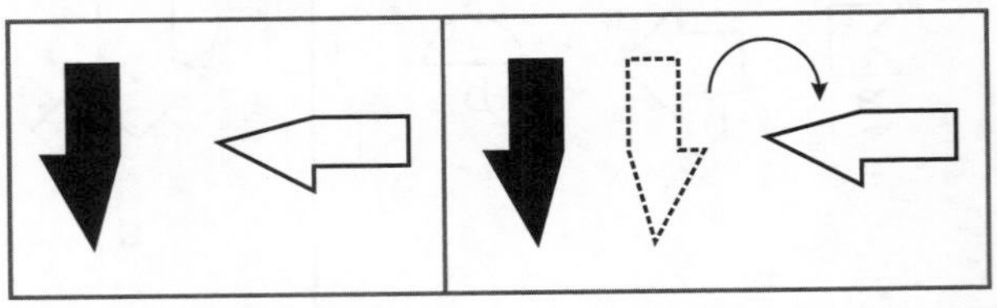

To get from the black shape to the white shape, first you need to reflect it across an invisible line (to make the dashed shape). Then you need to rotate it 90 degrees clockwise.

Other terms

Figure — the picture as a whole that makes up one example or option in a question.

Arrow-style Line — a line with a small shape at one end.

Line Types:

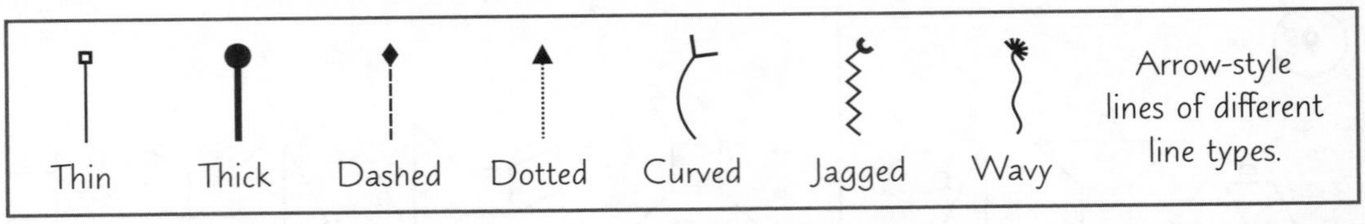

Shading Types:

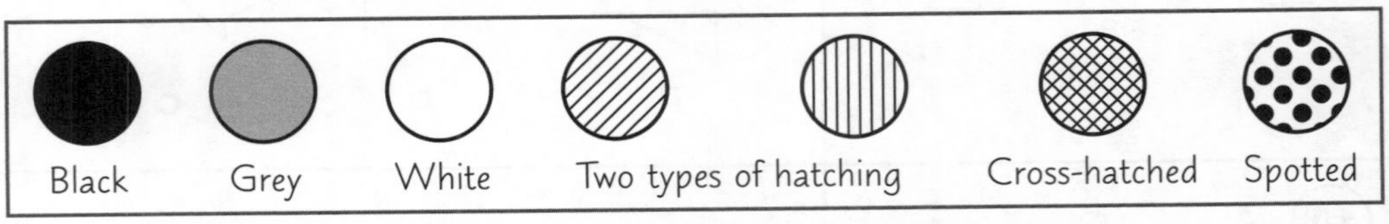

Layering — when a shape is in front of or behind another shape, or where two or more shapes overlap each other.

Layering — the circle is in front of the square. The right hand shape is a cut-out shape made from the overlap of the two shapes.

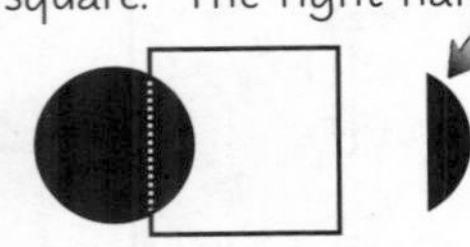

Line of Symmetry — a line which splits a shape into halves that are reflections of each other.

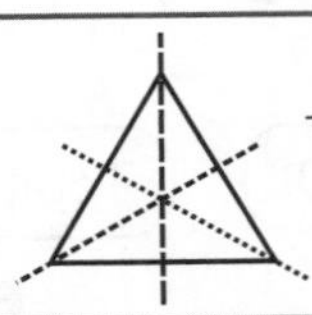

This triangle has three lines of symmetry.

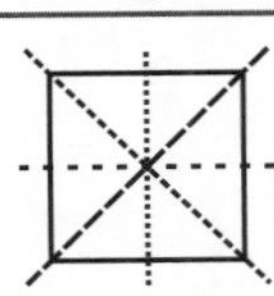

A square has four lines of symmetry.

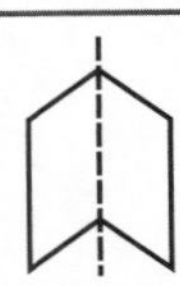

This shape has one line of symmetry.

Answers

Spotting Patterns

Page 2 — Shapes

Warm Up

1) a) 6 b) 7 c) 8 d) 8 e) 12 f) 7
2) a) 1 b) 0 c) 1 d) 1 e) 3 f) 2 g) 4

Odd One Out

3) B
All other figures have seven sides.
4) C
All other figures have two curved sides.
5) E
All other figures have a pentagon.

Page 3 — Counting

Warm Up

1) a) 9 b) 7 c) 9 d) 8 e) 5 f) 8 g) 6
2) Number of shapes with an odd number of dots: 6

Horizontal Code

3) B (FA)
F = large shape is divided into three sections,
G = large shape is divided into four sections.
A = large shape has four sides,
B = large shape has six sides.
4) E (YK)
X = two triangles, Y = one triangle.
J = two black dots, K = three black dots.
5) A (SY)
Q = shape made up of three separate lines, R = shape made up of two separate lines, S = shape made up of four separate lines.
X = three dots, Y = one dot, Z = two dots.

Pages 4-5 — Pointing

Warm Up

1) a) 2 b) 3 c) 4 d) 3 e) 2 f) 4 g) 2
2) a) yes b) no c) no d) no e) no f) yes g) yes
3) Most common direction: right
Type of shape: circle

Vertical Code

4) D (SR)
S = arrow pointing towards the shape,
T = arrow pointing away from the shape.
P = arrow on the left of the shape,
R = arrow on the right of the shape.
5) E (JY)
J = arrow goes over the top of the shape,
K = arrow goes under the shape.
X = arrow goes in a clockwise direction,
Y = arrow goes in an anticlockwise direction.
6) B (CG)
B = arrow pointing towards the circle,
C = arrow pointing towards the square.
F = arrow pointing at a grey shape, G = arrow pointing at a black shape, H = arrow pointing at a white shape.
7) C (JN)
J = black arrow pointing down, K = black arrow pointing up.
M = white arrow pointing right, N = white arrow pointing left.

Find the Figure Like the First Two

8) E
All figures have two arrows pointing down and one arrow pointing up.
9) B
In all figures, all inner lines must point exactly in the direction of the small black shape.
10) C
All figures must have two arrows going clockwise, and one arrow going anticlockwise.

Pages 6-7 — Shading and Line Types

Warm Up

1) Number of arrows hatched the same, ignoring rotation: 3
Number of arrows hatched the same, correcting for rotation: 3
2) Number of shapes with the same outline: 4 (second, fourth, sixth and ninth figures).
3) Most common shading: grey

Find the Figure Like the First Three

4) D
In all figures, there must be exactly one black and one grey dot.
5) C
All figures must be hatched in the same direction — diagonally down to the left.
6) A
The hatching of the innermost shape must be made from the hatchings of both the outer shapes added together.
7) E
In all figures, the shape with the fewest sides must have a dashed outline, and the shape with the most sides must have a solid outline.

Horizontal Code

8) B (LT)
L = hatching going diagonally down to the left, M = hatching going diagonally down to the right, N = vertical hatching.
R = dashed outline, S = solid outline, T = dotted outline.
9) E (FK)
F = one black section, G = no black sections.
J = three quarters of the shape is white,
K = one half of the shape is white.
10) C (BY)
B = thin solid outline, C = thick solid outline,
D = dashed outline.
X = inner line and outline are different line types,
Y = inner line and outline are the same line type.

Pages 8-9 — Order and Position

Warm Up

1) a) grey b) white c) black
d) white e) black
When the rightmost shape moves a place to the right, it then appears as the leftmost shape.
2) i) a) circle b) triangle c) star
d) circle e) square f) star
ii) a) grey b) grey c) black
d) grey e) white f) grey
3) a) circle b) star c) arrow
d) pentagon e) square

Odd One Out

4) D
In all other figures, the black shape is at the top.
5) B
In all other figures, from right to left, the shapes are in the order: four-sided shape, five-sided shape, six-sided shape.
6) B
In all other figures, there is a four-sided shape at the bottom.
7) A
In all other figures, the three shapes go in the order: circle, square, triangle, going clockwise round the large shape.

Complete the Series

8) C
In each series square, the grey square moves one place anticlockwise, between the middle of the series square's sides and the corners. The black square moves round the corners of the series square in a clockwise direction. The white square moves one place clockwise round the middle of the series square's sides.
9) A
In each series square the star loses a point. It moves clockwise round the four corners of the series square. The star alternates colour between black and white.
10) B
The shapes change in the order: three sides, four sides, five sides, four sides, and then three sides again. The dot moves one corner clockwise in each series square. There are four types of shading in the series. They move one shape anticlockwise in each series square, as if there were four shapes. But one shape is 'replaced' by the dot, which means one of the types of shading is missing in each series square.

Page 10 — Rotation

Warm Up

1) Number of identical shapes: 4
(second, third, fifth and seventh figures).
2) Number of clockwise rotations: 3
(third, fourth and sixth figures).

Find the Figure Like the First Two

3) C
In all figures, the hatching of the top shape is rotated 90 degrees to become the hatching of the bottom shape. Other than shading, the bottom shape must be an exact copy of the top shape, and must not be rotated.
4) D
All figures must be identical apart from rotation.
5) E
In all figures, the shape with the dashed outline must be a 90 degree rotation of the shape with the solid outline. The parts of the two shapes that do not overlap must be grey.

Page 11 — Reflection

Warm Up

1) a) reflection b) reflection c) rotation
d) reflection e) rotation f) rotation
2) a) no b) no c) yes d) yes e) no f) yes

Complete the Pair

3) C
The shape is reflected downwards.
4) D
The outer shape is reflected downwards, and the inner shape is reflected across.
5) C
The two small shapes reflect across and move to the other side of the large shape. The large shape stays the same and does not change shading.

Pages 12-13 — Layering

Warm Up

1) a) 4 b) 5 c) 6 d) 3 e) 6 f) 4 g) 4
2) a) 3 b) 2 c) 4 d) 2 e) 1 f) 3
3) a) S b) D c) S d) D e) S f) D

Complete the Pair

4) E
The three shapes go from being transparent to being solidly shaded white. The top shape moves to the front, and the bottom shape moves to the back.
5) B
The top and bottom shapes disappear. The inner shape made by the overlap between the top and middle shapes takes the shading of the old bottom shape. The inner shape made by the overlap between the bottom and middle shapes takes the shading of the old top shape.
6) C
The shape at the front moves to the back, and the shape at the back moves to the front.
7) E
The top and bottom shapes disappear. The middle shape and the two inner shapes, made by the overlapping outlines of the top, middle and bottom shapes, separate into three shapes. The large shape becomes black and rotates 90 degrees anticlockwise. The top small shape moves above the black shape. The bottom small shape moves below the black shape.

Vertical Code

8) A (TV)
S = inner shape has four sides, T = inner shape has three sides.
V = square has a partly dashed outline,
W = trapezium has a partly dashed outline.
9) A (GT)
F = grey shape is at the front, G = white shape is at the front,
H = black shape is at the front.
S = triangle is at the front, T = ellipse is at the front.
10) B (AY)
A = part-shaded circle is in between the other two circles,
B = part-shaded circle is at the front of the circles,
C = part-shaded circle is at the back of the circles.
X = the bottom square is in front of the top square,
Y = the top square is in front of the bottom square.

Spatial Reasoning

Pages 14-15 — Rotating 3D Shapes

Warm Up

1) a) 3 b) 2 c) 2 d) 3 e) 3 f) 1
2) Number of figures that are the same: 2
(the fourth and sixth figures)

3D Building Blocks

3) D
The right-hand block of set D rotates 90 degrees top-to-bottom and becomes the right-hand block of the figure on the left. The block on the left of set D moves to become the left-hand block of the figure.
4) A
The block at the top of set A rotates 90 degrees right-to-left and becomes the block in the middle of the figure on the left. The bottom block of the set rotates 90 degrees left-to-right and moves to the left of the figure. The middle block of the set becomes the back block of the figure.

5) D

The bottom right block of set D rotates 180 degrees in the plane of the page and becomes the back left block of the figure on the left. The block at the top of the set moves to become the middle right block at the back of the figure. The bottom left block of the set rotates 90 degrees in the plane of the page and moves to become the front middle block of the figure.

3D Rotation

6) B
Shape B rotates 180 degrees left-to-right.
7) C
Shape C rotates 90 degrees clockwise in the plane of the page. It then rotates 90 degrees left-to-right.
8) D
Shape D rotates 90 degrees anticlockwise in the plane of the page. It then rotates 90 degrees left-to-right.
9) A
Shape A rotates 90 degrees towards you, top-to-bottom. It then rotates 180 degrees left-to-right.

Pages 16-17 — 2D and 3D Shapes

Warm Up

1) a) yes b) no c) no d) yes e) yes f) no
2) The number of cubes that can be made: 3 (the second, third and fifth cubes)

2D Views of 3D Shapes

3) A
On the left-hand side of the figure there is a gap between the top and bottom blocks. This rules out options B and E. There are five blocks visible from above, which rules out options C and D.
4) C
There are two blocks visible at the bottom of the figure, which rules out option A. There are four blocks visible from above, which rules out options B and D. There are three blocks on the right-hand side of the figure, which rules out option E.
5) B
The block on the left-hand side of the figure is next to the middle block in the line of three blocks, which rules out option A. There is only one block visible on the left-hand side of the figure, which rules out option C. There are seven blocks visible from above, which rules out option D. There are blocks on four rows, which rules out option E.

Cubes and Nets

6) D
Option A is ruled out because the 8-pointed star and the white circle must be on opposite sides. Option B is ruled out because if the circle was on the top and the triangle was at the front, the face on the right would be the grey star. Option C is ruled out because the grey star and the black square must be on opposite sides. Option E is ruled out because there is no grey square on the net.
7) B
Option A is ruled out because if the triangle was on the top and the black square was at the front, the face on the right would be the circle. Option C is ruled out because the arrow could not be pointing at the circle. Option D is ruled out because there is no black arrow on the net. Option E is ruled out because the grey pentagon and the white circle must be on opposite sides.
8) E
Option A is ruled out because the two black arrows must be on opposite sides. Option B is ruled out because on the net there are no white and black arrows that point directly at each other. Option C is ruled out because the grey arrow should be pointing towards the white arrow. Option D is ruled out because the two grey arrows must be on opposite sides.

Pages 18-19 — Folding

Warm Up

1) Option: B
Options A, C and D are ruled out because the part of the figure that has been folded is the wrong shape.
2) a)

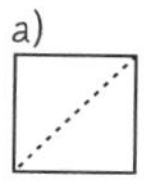

b)

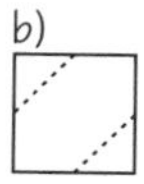

c)

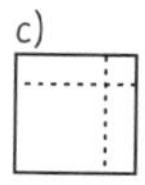

Fold Along the Line

3) C
Option A is ruled out because the fold line has moved. Option B is ruled out because the part of the figure that has been folded is the wrong shape. Option D is ruled out because the part of the figure originally above the fold line is the wrong shape. Option E is ruled out because the part of the figure originally above the fold line should still be visible.
4) E
Option A is ruled out because the part of the figure originally to the right of the fold line should still be visible. Options B and C are ruled out because the fold line has moved. Option D is ruled out because the part of the figure that has been folded is the wrong shape.
5) D
Option A is ruled out because the part of the figure that has been folded is the wrong shape. Option B is ruled out because the part of the figure originally below the fold line is the wrong shape. Options C and E are ruled out because the fold line has moved.

Fold and Punch

6) B

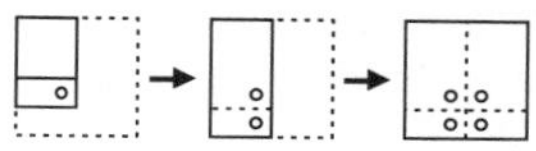

7) D

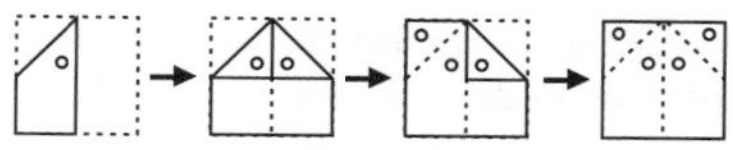

8) C

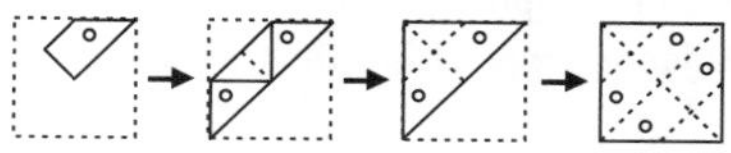

Page 20 — Hidden Shape

Warm Up

1) a) 3 b) 1
2) a)

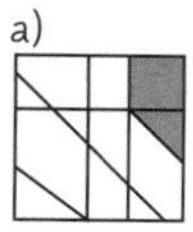

b)

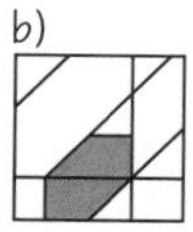

c)

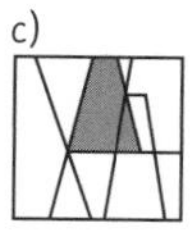

Hidden Shape

3) B

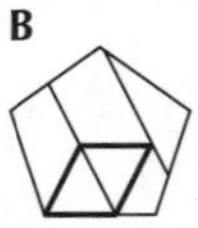

4) D

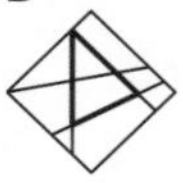

Page 21 — Connecting Shapes

Warm Up

1) a)

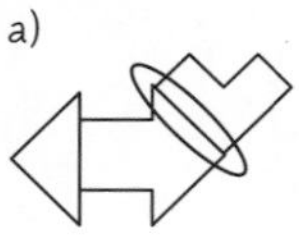

b)

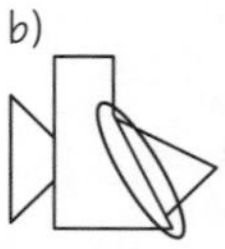

2) a)

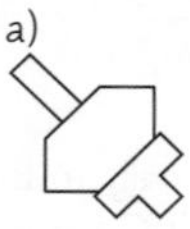

b)

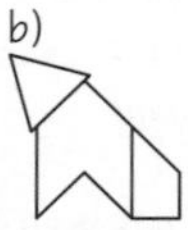

Connecting Shapes

3) E
Option A is ruled out because the triangle and the small L-shape are connected to the wrong sides of the large L-shape. Options B and D are ruled out because the wrong side of the small L-shape is connected to the large L-shape. Option C is ruled out because the wrong side of the triangle is connected to the large L-shape.

4) B
Option A is ruled out because the wrong side of the triangle is connected to the trapezium. Option C is ruled out because the pentagon is connected to the wrong side of the trapezium. Option D is ruled out because the triangle and the pentagon are connected to the wrong sides of the trapezium. Option E is ruled out because the wrong side of the pentagon is connected to the trapezium.

Pages 22-33 — Assessment Test 1

Section 1 — Find the Figure Like the First Two

1) B
All figures must be triangles with a flat side at the bottom.

2) C
All figures must have the same number of dots as inside lines.

3) D
All figures must have a black shape at the front.

4) B
All figures must have two shapes and an arrow pointing up.

5) B
All figures must have a dot directly next to the middle of the flat side of the large white shape.

6) B
All figures must have a large shape with the same small shape overlapping it on the left hand side.

7) E
All figures must have a large shape with five sides. There must be the same number of raindrops as the number of shapes with dashed outlines inside the five-sided shape.

8) D
All figures must have the same number of lines at the bottom as the number of dots at the top. There must be black and white dots at the top. All the vase shapes must be shaded black up to the same level.

9) B
All figures must have one less inner line than the number of sides of the shape.

10) E
In all figures, the shaded parts of the two inner shapes must equal one whole inner shape.

Section 2 — Complete the Series

1) E
The circle rotates 90 degrees clockwise in each series square.

2) C
The whole series square reflects across each time.

3) C
All of the circles move up one row in each series square. When they reach the top, they go back to the bottom in the next series square.

4) A
The cube turns one face in each series square. The front cube face becomes the left hand cube face, and a new cube face appears at the front.

5) A
In each series square, the grey square in the previous series square becomes white, and one of the black squares becomes grey.

6) E
The four-headed arrow shape rotates 45 degrees in each series square. The black dot moves anticlockwise round the corners of the series square. The two-headed arrow shape gets smaller in each series square.

7) B
The circle in the bottom left hand corner gets bigger, and the centre circle gets smaller in each series square. The two circles alternate colours between black and white. The star gets an extra point in each series square.

8) A
The hatching rotates 45 degrees anticlockwise in each series square. The raindrop rotates 90 degrees anticlockwise, and alternates between being white and transparent.

9) C
The two-headed arrow rotates 90 degrees in each series square. The line with the squares and the circles rotates 45 degrees clockwise each time. The circles swap colours in each series square.

10) A
The column with only two dots moves one place left in each series square. The white dot moves one place to the right.

Section 3 — Find the Figure Like the First Three

1) A
All figures must be shapes with a line going through them which shows a line of symmetry.

2) D
All figures must be made of two straight lines and two curved lines.

3) A
All figures must be identical apart from rotation.

4) C
All figures must be grey with one white quarter.

5) E
All figures must have a line which crosses both shapes.
6) D
In all figures, the number of sides of the overlapping shapes must add up to eleven (ignoring the inner shapes created by the overlaps).
7) A
In all figures, the shape with the smallest number of sides must have a dashed outline.
8) E
All figures must have the same number of small lines crossing the outline of the shape as the number of sides of the shape (including curved sides). There must be the same number of crosses as the number of curved lines.
9) A
All figures must have a large arrow shape with ten sides, with a four-sided black shape inside it.
10) E
In all figures, it must be possible to arrange the shapes into a square. There must be at least one grey and one white shape.

Section 4 — Odd One Out

1) D
All other figures have a black dot.
2) E
All other figures are hatched in the same direction.
3) B
All other figures are made of two identical shapes.
4) B
In all other figures, the two shapes are overlapping.
5) D
All other figures have an arrow pointing towards the grey semicircle.
6) A
All other figures have an arrowhead which is touching the outline of the right hand shape.
7) E
In all other figures, the two shapes cut out from the large shape are reflections of each other.
8) E
All other figures have one less shape in each row than in the row below.
9) C
All other figures have a small triangle inside the right hand side of the hourglass shape.
10) D
All other figures have one less dot than the number of curved sides of the shape immediately around the dots.

Section 5 — Vertical Code

1) C (PY)
P = solid outline, R = long-dashed outline,
S = short-dashed outline.
X = ellipse, Y = circle.
2) E (LR)
K = vertical rectangle, L = horizontal rectangle.
P = hatched rectangle, R = cross-hatched rectangle.
3) E (AY)
A = outside shape has the most sides,
B = inner shape has the most sides.
X = black inner shape, Y = white inner shape.
4) D (PZ)
P = inner triangle, R = inner circle , S = inner square.
X = arrow pointing down, Y = arrow pointing right,
Z = arrow pointing left.
5) E (GNX)
F = jagged inner line, G = straight inner line.
M = one black dot, N = two black dots.
X = six big rectangles, Y = five big rectangles.
6) B (JX)
G = central shape divided into three, H = divided into four,
J = divided into six, K = divided into two.
L = curved brackets, P = square brackets,
X = hexagonal brackets.
7) C (BV)
A, B, C and D = different rotations of the cross in the circle.
U = two black circles, V = one black circle,
W = three black circles.
8) B (BS)
A = grey square, B = white square.
P = bottom v-shape is on the right,
R = in the middle, S = on the left.

Section 6 — Complete the Grid

1) A
Working from top to bottom, the outer shape shrinks to fit inside the star.
2) C
Working from top to bottom, each shape moves one grid square left. The shape in the left hand grid square disappears, and a new shape appears in the right hand grid square.
3) A
Working from left to right, the two shapes swap places, sizes and shadings.
4) E
Working from left to right, the outer shape reflects across. The whole inner shape shrinks, and the shaded half splits into quarters. The shaded quarters move to the top and bottom of the inner shape.
5) C
Working from left to right, the contents of the grid square rotate 45 degrees clockwise.
6) E
Working from left to right, the line in the circle rotates 45 degrees anticlockwise. The rest of the arrow rotates 90 degrees clockwise.
7) C
Working from left to right, the grid square rotates 90 degrees anticlockwise.
8) E
Working from left to right, the number of corners in the arrow line increases by one in each grid square. The three different arrangements of the black and white shapes each only appears once in each row.

Pages 34-45 — Assessment Test 2

Section 1 — Odd One Out

1) E
In all other figures the inner and outer shapes are the same shape.
2) D
In all other figures, the shapes go clockwise in the order: circle, square, triangle. (D goes in an anticlockwise direction.)
3) C
In all other figures the two shapes are identical apart from rotation.

4) D
In all other figures, the line inside the rectangle has the same shading as the shapes inside the other rectangle.
5) B
In all other figures the arrow goes in an anticlockwise direction.
6) D
In all other figures the small line crosses over the same corner (the top corner) of the triangle.
7) B
In all other figures the shape with the fewest sides is white.
8) D
All other figures have the same number of lines as black hexagons.
9) C
In all other figures the square is in the top half and the diamond shape is in the bottom half.
10) A
All other figures have a large shape divided into two triangles and a four-sided shape.

Section 2 — Complete the Grid

1) E
Working from left to right, the bottom shape reflects across. The two shapes swap shadings.
2) B
Working from right to left, the entire figure reflects across. After reflection, the arrow rotates 180 degrees.
3) D
Working from left to right, one dot is added in each grid square. The three different positions of the quarter circle (top left, top right and bottom right) only appear once in each row and column.
4) D
Working from left to right, each of the three shapes moves backwards one place and gets bigger. The order of the shadings (from front to back) stays the same for all grid squares along each row.
5) A
Working from left to right, the large shape rotates 90 degrees anticlockwise. The two arrows rotate 90 degrees clockwise.
6) B
Working from left to right, each grid square rotates 90 degrees clockwise. The shading of the small square alternates between black and white.
7) D
Working from top to bottom, the hatched shape rotates 90 degrees anticlockwise in each grid square. The hatching does not rotate. The grey shape gets narrower. The small white shape moves up in each grid square.
8) A
Working from left to right, each grid square rotates 90 degrees clockwise. The different types of shading of the big and small circle (black, grey and white) appear only once in each row and column.

Section 3 — Vertical Code

1) B (NY)
M = white shape, N = black shape.
X = circle, Y= ellipse.
2) B (LY)
L = figure has a dashed line, M = figure has a dotted line.
X = two black segments, Y = three black segments.
3) B (MF)
L = white centre circle, M = hatched centre circle.
F = one hatched shape, G = two hatched shapes,
H = no hatched shapes.
4) B (RWD)
R = triangle pointing up, S = triangle pointing right,
T = triangle pointing down.
V = triangle has a line behind it, W = triangle has no line behind it.
C = straight inner shape, D = wavy inner shape.
5) A (VK)
V = black raindrop on the right, W = black raindrop on the left.
K = horizontal inside line, L = inside line going diagonally down to the right, M = inside line going diagonally down to the left.
6) C (SWY)
R = jagged line, S = wavy line, T = square-toothed line.
V = dots below the thin line, W = dots above the thin line.
Y = thick bottom line, Z = no thick bottom line.
7) C (BDG)
A = inner shapes are different, B = inner shapes are the same.
C = black left outer star, D = white left outer star.
F = black left inner shape, G = white left inner shape.
8) A (SWX)
R = one dashed spiral, S = no dashed spirals,
T = two dashed spirals.
V = the spirals face the same way,
W = the spirals face in different ways.
X = different spiral shapes, Y = the same spiral shapes.

Section 4 — Complete the Series

1) A
In each series square, an extra triangle is added diagonally below the triangle(s) in the previous series square. The colour of each triangle alternates between black and white.
2) D
The two black triangles reflect across in each series square. The arrow's shading alternates between white and grey.
3) B
The large hexagon and the square reflect across in each series square. The circle moves half a side anticlockwise round the square (alternately between the square's sides and corners).
4) D
In each series square there is an extra triangle.
5) C
In each series square, the white circle segments rotate 45 degrees anticlockwise around the black dot. The black and grey shapes move half a side clockwise and reflect along their longest side, so that the longest side is always flat against the edge of the series square.
6) A
In each series square, the three solid lines that are attached to each other rotate together 90 degrees anticlockwise. The dotted line rotates 90 degrees clockwise around the centre of the series square. The shield shape alternates between being the right way up with hatching going diagonally down to the left, and being upside down with horizontal hatching.
7) A
The figure rotates 90 degrees anticlockwise in each series square. Each shading moves one place towards the thinner end of the figure in each series square.
8) D
In each series square, the box shape alternates between two positions. The first position has the front rectangle with its long side along the bottom, with the arrow on the right hand side and vertical lines on the left. The second position has the front rectangle with its short side along the bottom, with the arrow on the bottom half and horizontal lines at the top. A new line is added in each series square. The arrow rotates 45 degrees clockwise in each series square.
9) E
In each series square, the star shape loses one point, and another point becomes black. The hatching of the inner shape rotates 45 degrees anticlockwise in each series square.
10) D
In each series square, the small black shape that the arrows point away from swaps places with the small black shape outside the circle. After the two shapes swap, the arrows swap directions. The new shape outside the circle moves one corner anticlockwise round the series square.

Section 5 — Complete the Pair

1) E
The two shapes swap outline types.
2) B
All the black sections become white and all the white sections become black.
3) C
The two shapes swap places.
An extra side is added to the big shape.
4) D
The top and bottom parts of the figure swap shadings.
The bottom inner shape rotates 180 degrees.
5) B
A reflection of the figure is added behind the original figure, above it and to the right.
6) D
The top two shapes get smaller and become the bottom two shapes. The bottom two shapes get bigger and become the top two shapes. Both the inner shapes rotate 180 degrees.
7) A
The short arrow rotates 45 degrees anticlockwise.
The other arrows rotate 90 degrees anticlockwise.
8) D
The two black triangles move up behind the large shape.
The three dots rotate 90 degrees around the middle dot.
9) D
The outer top shape moves down and grows to become the outermost shape. The bottom shape moves up and takes the place of the old outer top shape, around the inner top shape.
10) C
All the hearts move round one section anticlockwise.
All the other shapes move round one section clockwise.

Section 6 — Find the Figure Like the First Three

1) B
All figures must be identical apart from rotation.
2) C
All figures must have three black hearts.
3) D
All figures must have five inner shapes. There must be three inner shapes on one side of the dividing line, and two inner shapes on the other side.
4) D
All figures must have the same number of legs on both sides, and all feet must point outwards.
5) C
In all figures, the large shape must be a horizontally stretched version of the inner shape. The small shape must be the same height as the large shape.
6) D
All figures must have three overlapping rectangles.
7) B
All figures must have a hatched shape with one less side than the number of sides of the white shape.
8) D
All figures must have the same number of black shapes as the number of sides of one of the black shapes.
9) B
All figures must have the same number of small shapes at the bottom (in the stalk) as each of the shapes at the top (the petals) has sides (including curved sides).
10) D
All figures must have an arrow and a four-sided shape with a cross in it. The arrow must be the shape made by three sides of the shape with the cross.

Pages 46-57 — Assessment Test 3

Section 1 — Find the Figure Like the First Three

1) E
All figures must have three black circles and at least one hatched circle.
2) B
All figures must be identical apart from rotation.
3) D
All figures must have four shapes which are the same apart from size. The shapes must all be centred on the same point.
4) C
All figures must be half black and half white.
5) C
All figures must have two arrows inside the shape and one outside the shape. All arrows must point in the direction that the shape's curved side bulges.
6) D
Ignoring the shapes created by overlaps, all figures must have three white shapes which each have the same number of sides. Each shape must overlap another shape, and one shape in each figure must have a single side which curves inwards.
7) B
All figures must have exactly one shield shape.
8) E
All figures must have three small shapes. Two of the small shapes must have the same shape, but one must be black. The other small shape must be the shape of half of the big shape, only smaller.
9) A
In all figures, the star must be at the front of its set of shapes, and the hexagon must be at the back of its set of shapes.
10) C
In all figures, there must be a four-sided shape, a five-sided shape and a six-sided shape (ignoring overlaps).

Section 2 — Complete the Grid

1) A
Working from top to bottom, the top grid square is reflected downwards to make the bottom grid square. The white circles become black.
2) C
Working from left to right, a thick line is added in the middle of each grid square. The small shape moves one place clockwise round the corners of each grid square. The different types of small shape (triangle, square and pentagon) only appear once in each row and column.
3) B
Working from left to right, two extra sides are added to the large shape. Two extra lines are added to the bottom of the large shape. Working from top to bottom, the arrow reflects across.
4) A
Each type of corner shading (one corner, two corners, three corners) only appears once in each row and column. The corners always appear in the same positions for each type of corner shading. Each type of shape (semicircle, circle and square) only appears once in each row and column. The size of each shape (small, medium and big) is the same along each row.
5) C
In each row, a new shape is added to the shape in the left hand grid square to make the right hand grid square — with all overlapping lines between the two shapes showing. The overlapping shapes in the right hand grid square rotate 90 degrees anticlockwise to make the shape in the middle grid square. After rotation, the overlapping shapes lose their overlapping lines.

6) D
Working from left to right, the cross rotates 45 degrees clockwise in each series square. The small shape stays in the same corner of the cross as it rotates, but the shape itself doesn't rotate. The different colours of the small shape (black, grey and white) only appear once in each row and column.

7) A
There are black triangles in every corner of the central grid square, and in every corner that touches it. In each row, the shape in the right hand grid square is made up of the shading of the square from the left hand grid square, added to the outline of the main shape from the middle grid square.

8) B
Each type of main shape (triangle, rectangle and circle) only appears once in each row and column. There is only one grey shape in each row and column, which is paired with an arrow-style line with a white shape on the end. All the other main shapes are white and have black arrow-style lines with them. In each row, all the arrows are positioned in the same way in the grid square, and point in the same direction. Each column has its own shape of 'arrowhead'. Each arrow-style line has two parallel lines crossing it in one of three places — near the arrowhead, in the middle, or at the end away from the arrowhead. The lines cross the arrow-style line once in each of these three places in each row.

Section 3 — Horizontal Code

1) D (BZ)
A = white shapes, B = hatched shapes.
Y = triangles, Z = squares.

2) A (CG)
C = grey heart, D = white heart.
F = circle outer shape, G = square outer shape.

3) E (SM)
Q = three black dots, R = no black dots,
S = two black dots, T = one black dot.
M = arrow pointing to the right, N = arrow pointing to the left.

4) A (GE)
G = arrow going anticlockwise, H = arrow going clockwise.
D = two black dots, E = three white squares.

5) B (GR)
G = six-sided top shape, H = four-sided top shape.
P = one grey shape, R = two grey shapes.

6) D (XC)
W = two curved lines and one short straight line at the end of the triangle, X = four curved lines,
Y = two curved lines and one long straight line.
B = stars on the left, C = stars on both sides,
D = stars on the right.

7) E (LS)
L = two black shapes, M = one black shape.
S = cross shape, T = cross shape rotated to become an X shape.

8) E (JR)
H = vertical lightning shape,
J = the lightning shape goes diagonally down to the right,
K = the lightning shape goes diagonally down to the left.
R = square is bottom right, S = square is bottom left,
T = square is top right.

Section 4 — Complete the Pair

1) D
The figure shrinks and the two shapes swap colours.

2) C
The big shape reflects across. The small shapes become white, and a third small white shape is added.

3) E
The whole figure rotates 180 degrees. The arrowhead at the end of the arrow with the black rectangle changes to match the other end of the arrow.

4) C
The figure rotates 90 degrees anticlockwise (hatching included). The outline of the large arrow becomes dashed.

5) D
The number of sides of the outer shape increases by one. The number of sides of the inner shape decreases by one. The two shapes swap shadings with each other.

6) A
The pair of vertical lines gets shorter and rotates 90 degrees. The shape at the bottom rotates 90 degrees clockwise and moves to the right hand side of the shield shape. The hatching lines in the two small shapes turn into spots.

7) C
The long white shape gains an extra grey stripe below its other two stripes. The grey ellipse at the bottom becomes a black rectangle. Another line is added above the raindrop at the top.

8) A
The spiral shape gains a side. The top small shape becomes grey, and gains a side (so it has the same number of sides as the new spiral shape). The small squares turn into circles. The whole figure then reflects across.

9) C
The number of dots minus one becomes the number of sides of the big shape. One of the dots moves to the middle of the new shape, and the others move to the new shape's corners. The number of sides of the old big shape becomes the number of outside lines. The dots and the big shape swap colours.

10) A
The middle shape rotates 90 degrees anticlockwise and gets bigger to become the outermost shape. The old top shapes rotate together 90 degrees anticlockwise and move down to become the left inner shape. The old bottom shapes rotate together 90 degrees anticlockwise and move upwards to become the right inner shape. In the new figure, the two right hand inner shapes swap places and sizes with each other.

Section 5 — Odd One Out

1) D
All other figures have white circles instead of a white ellipse.

2) E
In all other figures, the number of lines drawn from the edge of the ellipse to the centre of the dashed shape is the same as the number of sides of the dashed shape.

3) D
In all other figures, there is one shape with a solid outline and one shape with a dashed outline.

4) A
All other figures are made up of the outline of three shapes, divided in half. (The two halves of each of the shapes are shaded differently from each other.)

5) B
All other figures are identical apart from rotation.

6) D
In all other figures, the dashed line goes between points that are one quarter of the shape's perimeter apart. (Lines drawn from both of these points to the centre of the shape would outline a quarter of the shape).

7) C
All other figures have an outer line next to the longest side of the big shape.
8) E
In all other figures, the two arrows at the end of the line point in different directions.
9) C
In all other figures, the thick black line is a larger version of the outline of the grey shape, with a single side missing.
10) E
In all other figures, only where the two shapes with the same number of sides overlap is shaded black.

Section 6 — Find the Figure Like the First Two

1) B
All figures must have two white shapes that are the same apart from size.
2) B
All figures must have a grey heart, a black semicircle, two white ellipses and two black triangles. The two triangles must partly overlap the two ellipses.
3) A
All figures must have the same number of straight lines as the number of points on each star.
4) B
Each figure must have an outer shape with one more side than the inner shape.
5) E
All figures must have the same number of short straight lines crossing the S shape as the number of black shapes.
6) E
All figures must have the same number of dots as the number of curved lines inside the circle.
7) D
All figures must have the same sized stars. All stars must have five points, with one star overlapping the sides of the large shape.
8) A
All figures must have three shapes that all have four sides. There must be one of each type of shading (white, black, grey and hatched — the hatching must go diagonally down to the left) in each figure.
9) C
All figures must have a large black outer shape, which is reflected downwards and shrunk to become the white shape in front of it. Within this white shape must be three versions of another shape, one black, one grey and one white, with the black shape the smallest.
10) C
In all figures, the inner shapes must add up to one whole circle. All figures must have two small lines crossing the outline of the large shape.

Pages 58-69 — Assessment Test 4

Section 1 — Complete the Series

1) E
Each series square gains an extra heart shape. The hearts alternate between being the right way up and upside down. The black section of the circle shrinks in a clockwise pattern.
2) B
In each series square, the circle and the triangle rotate together 45 degrees clockwise. After rotation the triangle rotates 180 degrees on its own, and alternates between the inside and outside of the circle's perimeter.
3) A
In each series square, the three different background types of shading (black, grey and white) move down one rectangle. The arrow alternates between pointing up and pointing down.
4) B
In each series square, the two black rectangles become grey, and two new rectangles become black.
5) B
In each series square, the outer shape rotates 90 degrees anticlockwise. The inner shape rotates 90 degrees clockwise each time. The hatching of the inner shape always goes diagonally down to the left, and alternates between the two halves.
6) C
Each series square rotates 90 degrees anticlockwise (including shadings). The two complete ellipses swap shadings in each series square. (This means that when the small ellipse is hatched, its hatching goes diagonally down to the left, and when the large ellipse is hatched, its hatching goes diagonally down to the right).
7) C
In each series square, there are three central shapes that are identical apart from size and shading. One of the central shapes is shaded black. The black shading of the central shapes moves outwards one shape in each series square. An extra side is added to the central shapes in each series square. The corner shapes alternate between being vertical and being diagonal. The grey shading moves one place anticlockwise round the corner shapes.
8) A
In each series square, all of the shadings move up one flag (which means they all move to the other side of the flag pole). After the shadings move, the whole figure is reflected across. (This means there are always two black flags on the right, and one on the left.)
9) B
The entire figure rotates 90 degrees anticlockwise around the centre of each series square. An extra row of triangles is added each time. In each series square, the black triangle moves one row diagonally towards the new row.
10) A
The series square rotates 90 degrees clockwise each time, and a new hexagon is added.

Section 2 — Complete the Pair

1) C
The entire figure is reflected downwards and all the colours swap.
2) B
The entire figure rotates 45 degrees anticlockwise, and the arrow changes from black to grey.
3) D
The left hand shape and the middle shape swap places.
4) B
The hatched shape reflects across and shrinks, but the hatched shading stays the same. The top and bottom shapes swap colours.
5) B
The shape that the arrows make changes to become the same shape as one of the inner shapes. The two inner shapes take the same shape as the old outer shape made by the arrows. The arrows go from pointing clockwise to anticlockwise. The two new inner shapes have the same sizes and positions as the old inner shapes.
6) A
The entire figure rotates 180 degrees.
7) D
Each shading moves one place to the right (including the shading of the flagpole).

8) C
The central white shape grows bigger and becomes the outermost shape. The central black shape stays in the same place but turns white. The top arrowhead shape moves down and the bottom arrowhead shape moves up so that they are against the sides of the new middle white shape. The dots move onto the new middle white shape — the old top dot goes to the bottom, and the old bottom dot goes to the top.
9) E
The entire figure is reflected downwards. The different parts of the shield shape all separate. The top and bottom parts of the shield swap colours with each other.
10) C
The hearts move one corner anticlockwise round the big diamond shape. The stars and circles reflect across the middle of the diamond shape.

Section 3 — Find the Figure Like the First Three

1) B
All figures must be square.
2) B
All figures must contain a U shape.
3) D
All figures must have two shapes on the left of the arrow and one shape on the right of the arrow.
4) E
All figures must be identical apart from rotation.
5) E
The semicircle in each figure must be divided into a black and a white section by a straight line that runs from the middle of the flat side to a point on the curved side. The four-pointed star must be directly above the black section of the semicircle.
6) D
In all figures, the two lines at the top must touch the outline of the large shape directly above the right-angled corners at the base of the large shape. The two lines must be the same length.
7) D
All figures must have five dots in total. The number of brush shapes inside the large shape must be the same as the number of dots outside the large shape.
8) D
Even-sided shapes must be hatched diagonally down to the left. Odd-sided shapes must be hatched diagonally down to the right. (Rule-based questions like this one are rare, but they can come up in the test.)
9) E
In all figures, the outer shape must have one more side than the inner shape. There must be three fewer diamond shapes than the number of sides of the inner shape.
10) A
All figures must be made of one line which crosses over itself three times.

Section 4 — Horizontal Code

1) B (AM)
A = upwards pointing triangles,
B = downwards pointing triangles.
M = two triangles, N = one triangle.
2) E (BE)
A = the horizontal line goes below the shapes,
B = the horizontal line goes above the shapes,
C = the horizontal line goes through the shapes.
D = the middle shape is bigger,
E = all the shapes are the same size.
3) D (PX)
P = hexagon, Q = circle, R = square.
X = hatched shading, Y = white shading.
4) A (SQ)
Correcting for rotation so that the ends of the W shape point upwards, R = circle on the left hand side of the W shape,
S = circle on the right hand side of the W shape,
T = circle in the middle of the W shape.
P = solid W shape, Q = dashed W shape.
5) C (AG)
A = four lines in total, B = three lines, C = two lines.
G and H = rotation of shield shape.
6) D (JR)
H = small rectangle towards the left of the tall rectangle,
J = small rectangle towards the right of the tall rectangle,
K = small rectangle in the middle of the tall rectangle.
P = small rectangle at the bottom of the tall rectangle,
Q = small rectangle at the top of the tall rectangle,
R = small rectangle halfway up the tall rectangle.
7) C (AN)
A = two lines at the bottom, B = four lines at the bottom,
C = three lines at the bottom.
L = the inner ellipse going diagonally down to the left,
M = horizontal inner ellipse, N = the inner ellipse going diagonally down to the right, O = vertical inner ellipse.
8) B (HV)
F = arrow made of five separate lines, G = arrow made of four separate lines, H = arrow made of six separate lines.
U = arrow in the middle, V = arrow at the top,
W = arrow at the bottom.

Section 5 — Find the Figure Like the First Two

1) A
All figures must have four small shapes that are the same type of shape as the large shape. One of the small shapes must be shaded in the same colour as the large shape, the other three must be white.
2) E
All figures must have an X shape in the circle rather than a cross (diagonal not horizontal lines). The figure must have two black circles over points at which the X shape meets the circle.
3) E
In all figures, the arrows must go in a clockwise direction.
4) A
All figures must have the same number of inner lines as the number of sides of the small shape at the top.
5) D
All figures must have the top square at the very front.
6) B
All figures must have two inner shapes — one must be hatched, the other must be black. The hatched shape must have one more side than the black shape.
7) A
All figures must have a grey shape and a white shape. The inner shape must have one more side than the number of dashed lines. The dashed lines must only cross over the raindrop's outline once.
8) B
All figures must have two sets of the same two shapes but in different sizes. The outer shape in the top set of shapes must be a 45 degree rotation of the outer shape in the bottom set of shapes. The inner shape in the top set of shapes must be a 180 degree rotation of the inner shape in the bottom set of shapes. The inner shape in the top set of shapes must have the same shading as the outer shape in the bottom set of shapes. The outer shape in the top set of shapes must have the same shading as the inner shape in the bottom set of shapes.

9) A
In all figures, the big shape must have one more side than there are circles. There must be two circles which are hatched diagonally down to the right.
10) C
In all figures the lines must go from the corner of one shape to the corner of another. The shapes at opposite ends of each line must be the same colour.

Section 6 — Vertical Code

1) C (BG)
A = anticlockwise arrow, B = clockwise arrow.
D = square, F = cross, G = circle.
2) A (GHK)
F = three-headed arrow on left, G = four-headed arrow on left.
H = black right hand shape, J = black left hand shape.
K = a black three-headed arrow, L = a black four-headed arrow.
3) E (BD)
A = the two shapes are different,
B = the two shapes are the same.
C = the second shape is hatched diagonally down to the left,
D = the second shape is hatched horizontally,
E = the second shape is hatched diagonally down to the right.
4) D (HZ)
G = a grey cross, H = a white cross, J = a black cross.
X = the top half of the quarter of the shield divided horizontally is white, Y = the top half of the quarter of the shield divided horizontally is hatched, Z = the top half of the quarter of the shield divided horizontally is black.
5) E (XQ)
X = three objects in total (including vertical lines),
Y = five objects in total, Z = four objects in total.
P = three-pointed stars, Q = four-pointed stars.
6) E (EKW)
D = inner straight line and inner circle have the same line type,
E = inner straight line and inner circle have different line types.
K, L, M and N = different hexagon rotations.
U = diagonal inner line, V = horizontal inner line,
W = vertical inner line.
7) A (BPH)
A = hatched triangle, B = hatched circle, C = hatched square.
P = the square is on the left hand side,
Q = the triangle is on the left hand side.
G = triangle at the front, H = circle at the front,
J = square at the front.
8) A (CQ)
C = the triangles are rotated differently from each other,
D = the triangles have the same rotation as each other.
P = the figure doesn't have a line of symmetry,
Q = the figure has a line of symmetry.

Pages 70-81 — Assessment Test 5

Section 1 — Complete the Grid

1) C
Working from left to right, the large shape gets shorter and rotates 45 degrees clockwise. The dot moves to the centre of the new shape.
2) C
Working from left to right, the grid square rotates 90 degrees anticlockwise. The white shape and the hatched shape swap places.
3) E
Working from left to right, the hatching of the large shape rotates 45 degrees clockwise. The diagonal shape which appears to pierce the hatched shape rotates 180 degrees, so that the part in front moves from the bottom left to the top right, and the part behind moves from the top right to the bottom left.
4) B
In each row, the shape in the middle grid square is the smaller of the shapes from the right hand grid square, rotated 45 degrees anticlockwise, with the shading from the large shape in the right hand square. (The big shape in the right hand grid square is the shape from the left hand grid square, rotated 90 degrees anticlockwise, with the shading of the shape from the middle grid square).
5) C
Working from left to right, the hatched shape from the first grid square moves to the bottom right corner of the right hand grid square. The hatched shape in the middle grid square reflects across and becomes white. It moves to the top left corner of the right hand grid square.
6) A
Each type of arrow-style line (circle, triangle and square) and its matching shields only appear once in each row and column, and always in the same arrangement. Working from left to right, the arrow and the shields rotate 90 degrees clockwise in each grid square.
7) A
Working from left to right, all of the shapes move one place clockwise round the four corners. The hatched shape gains an extra side in each grid square. Working from right to left, both of the black and white shapes are halved in each grid square. The black and white shapes always lose the opposite half to each other (e.g. the white shape loses its top half and the black shape loses its bottom half; the white shape loses its left hand half and the black shape loses its right hand half).
8) D
Working from left to right, each grid square rotates 180 degrees. The shading of the inner circle becomes the shading of the big circle in the next grid square. The shading of the big circle becomes the shading of the separate circle in the next grid square. The shading of the separate circle becomes the shading of the inner circle in the next grid square.

Section 2 — Find the Figure Like the First Two

1) E
All figures must have three black and three white circles.
2) C
All figures must have five sides.
3) A
The outer shape in all figures must be identical apart from rotation. In each figure, the inner shapes must be the same apart from shading.
4) B
In all figures, the large shape must be the same shape as the top half of one of the inner shapes. Each outer shape must have a different shading from the inner shape directly above it.
5) D
In all figures, the number of sides of the large shape is the same as the number of small shapes and the number of separate lines added together.
6) D
Ignoring shading, all figures must have two lines of symmetry. The two shapes in each figure must have different shadings.
7) E
In all figures, the parts of the inner shapes shaded black must add up to a total of one whole inner shape. The top inner shape in all figures must be on the left hand side.

8) C
In all figures, there must be three overlapping shapes and one separate shape. Each of the overlapping shapes should only have one side more or less than the shape(s) it is overlapping. The separate shape must have the most sides.
9) D
In all figures, the arrow must point at the middle of the three small shapes. The three small shapes must all be the same type of shape. The line next to the big grey shape must have a gap in it.
10) D
All figures must have an X shape on the outline of the large shape, directly below the left hand circle. In all figures, the small circles must be joined by straight lines going from the centre of one circle to the centre of another circle.

Section 3 — Horizontal Code

1) B (BG)
A = big shape is a semicircle, B = big shape is a cross.
F = triangle inside shape, G = circle inside shape,
H = a square inside shape.
2) E (TR)
S = the figure is horizontal, T = the figure is vertical.
P = the triangles have different shadings,
R = the triangles have the same shadings.
3) A (GK)
G = straight line, H = a wavy line.
J = black circles, K = white circles.
4) C (CG)
C = the base is a circle, D = the base is a trapezium,
E = the base is a rectangle.
G = vertical hatching, H = horizontal hatching.
5) A (PX)
M = black top circle, N = grey top circle, P = white top circle.
X = dashed outside line, Y = solid outside line.
6) E (AY)
A = lines on the left of the spiral, B = lines underneath the spiral,
C = lines on the right of the spiral.
X = two small lines, Y = three small lines.
7) D (KT)
H = small black shapes above the rectangle,
J = small black shapes below the rectangle,
K = small black shapes to the left of the rectangle.
R = short-dashed line over the top,
S = long-dashed line over the top, T = solid line over the top.
8) E (BH)
A = solid outline square, B = dashed outline square.
Correcting for rotation so that the thick, angled line is at the top of the figure, F = the small shape is positioned in the bottom left corner, G = the small shape is positioned in the bottom right corner,
H = the small shape is positioned in the top right corner.

Section 4 — Complete the Pair

1) B
The whole figure is rotated 180 degrees. The two small shapes swap shadings with the large shape.
2) B
The whole figure rotates 90 degrees clockwise. The large shape and the stripe going across it swap shadings. The star changes from white to grey and loses a point.
3) B
The outer shape reflects across. The inner shapes swap positions and are cut in half along a central vertical line. The left half of the inner shapes disappears. (You can only work out that the outer shape has been reflected rather than rotated by looking at how the inner shapes have changed in each of the answer options).
4) D
The left hand shape swaps layers with the top shape.
The right hand shape swaps layers with the bottom shape.
5) E
All the separate long lines move closer to the centre of the figure. The shape around the star gets smaller and moves to the left of the new figure. It takes the shading from the old rectangle, which disappears. A second shape identical to this shape is added to the right of the new figure. The star moves up to the top of the new figure.
6) A
The whole figure rotates 180 degrees. The solid straight line becomes dashed. The two large shapes swap colours.
7) C
The shadings of all the small shapes move one place to the left.
The shadings of all the large shapes move one place to the right.
8) A
The figure rotates 90 degrees clockwise and gets bigger.
All of the straight lines become curved. The different shadings of the two sides of the shape swap over.
9) B
The whole figure rotates 90 degrees anticlockwise. The jagged line becomes wavy. The squares with straight lines next to them become circles with curved lines. The middle circle and its curved line stay in place, but the other two circles and curved lines move across to the other side of the wavy line. A dot is removed, and the two remaining dots move to the other side of the wavy line, inside the two indents closest to the centre of the wavy line.
10) E
The whole figure is divided in half down a central vertical line. The right hand side of the figure is rotated 90 degrees anticlockwise and is moved to the top of the figure. The hatching of the right hand half of the bottom shape rotates together with the figure. The hatching of the top right shape does not rotate — it stays the same.

Section 5 — Complete the Series

1) B
The series alternates between a grey star with a solid outline, and a white star with a dashed outline. An extra point is added to the star in each series square.
2) C
The colour of the middle shape alternates between black and white. Each time the middle shape becomes black an extra row of black shading starts to move outwards one set of shapes. The black shading then continues to move out one row of shapes in each series square.
3) E
In each series square the triangles move round one position clockwise (the fifth series square shows that there are five possible positions for the triangles). In each series square a new white triangle is added in the next available position (going clockwise, starting from the grey triangle). The series squares alternate between having horizontal grey stripes and vertical black stripes.
4) B
The series square rotates 180 degrees each time. After rotation, a smaller pentagon is added, flat side down, inside the other pentagons.
5) E
Ignoring hatching, the dashed line and the arrow rotate 90 degrees anticlockwise around the centre of each series square. The square moves clockwise round the four corners of the series square. Ignoring other rotations, the hatching of the arrow rotates 45 degrees clockwise and the hatching of the square rotates 45 degrees anticlockwise.

6) A
In each series square the arrow rotates 90 degrees clockwise around the central shape. The arrow leaves a dashed trail behind it where it has already been. When the arrow gets back to its starting point, the series starts again. The middle shape alternates between a circle and a square. The star alternates between white and grey, and moves clockwise round the four corners of the series square.

7) B
The black dot stays in the same place in all series squares. A new shape is added in the top left of each series square. All the rest of the shapes move round one place clockwise.

8) D
The entire figure rotates 90 degrees anticlockwise in each series square. The shading of the arrow becomes the shading of the rectangle in the next series square. (You can work out the shading of the arrow by looking at the shading of the rectangle in the next series square.)

9) B
In each series square, each set of circles moves along one triangle to the right, and the number of circles in a set changes in the order: one, two, three, one, two, three.

10) B
Apart from the arrow, the series square rotates 90 degrees anticlockwise. After rotation, the hearts, together with the two straight lines, swap places. The hearts and the semicircles swap shadings. Independent of the 90 degree rotation, the two hearts alternate between pointing up and down. The arrow rotates separately 90 degrees clockwise around the centre of the series square.

Section 6 — Odd One Out

1) E
In all other figures, the small shape is a smaller version of the big shape.

2) C
In all other figures, the arrow is pointing at a corner.

3) C
In all other figures, there is a black circle at both ends of the line.

4) A
In all other figures, the arrow is in the shape with the most sides.

5) B
In all other figures, the square has the same shading as the top middle circle.

6) E
All other figures have a large shape made up of four lines.

7) C
In all other figures, the number of small black shapes added to the number of sides of the small white shape is the same as the number of sides of the large shape.

8) C
In all other figures, the number of black dots is the same as the number of lines going through the circle diagonally down to the left. (The other dots and the lines going diagonally down to the right are unimportant).

9) A
In all other figures, the number of points on a single star is the same as the number of sides of the large shape.

10) D
In all other figures, the black shape is a sideways reflection of the shape made by the overlap of the white and the hatched shape. (The black shape in D is a rotation of the shape.)

Pages 82-93 — Assessment Test 6

Section 1 — 2D Views of 3D Shapes

1) C
There are three blocks on the left-hand side of the figure, which rules out options A, B, D and E.

2) D
There are only five blocks visible from above, which rules out options A and B. The block on the right does not have any blocks next to its sides, which rules out options C and E.

3) B
There are only five blocks visible from above, which rules out options A and D. There is only one block visible on the left-hand side, which rules out options C and E.

4) C
There are only five blocks visible from above, which rules out options A, B and D. There are two blocks visible on the right-hand side, which rules out option E.

5) E
There are only four blocks visible from above, which rules out options A, B and D There are only two blocks visible at the front, which rules out option C.

6) B
There are six blocks visible from above, which rules out options C, D and E. There are three blocks visible on the right-hand side, which rules out option A.

7) B
There are only six blocks visible from above, which rules out options A, C and D. There are only three blocks visible on the right-hand side, which rules out option E.

8) D
There are only seven blocks visible from above, which rules out option A. There are four blocks visible on the right-hand side, which rules out options B and C. There are two blocks visible at the back, which rules out option E.

Section 2 — Fold and Punch

1) A

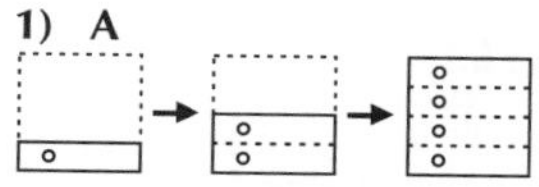

2) E

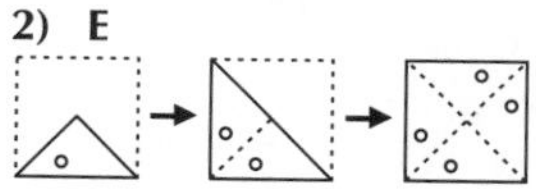

3) C

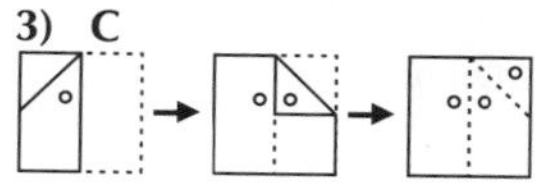

4) B

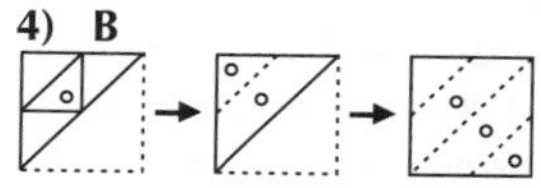

5) C

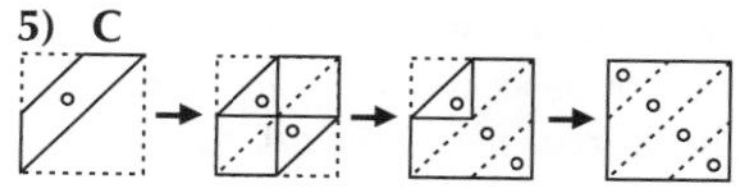

6) E

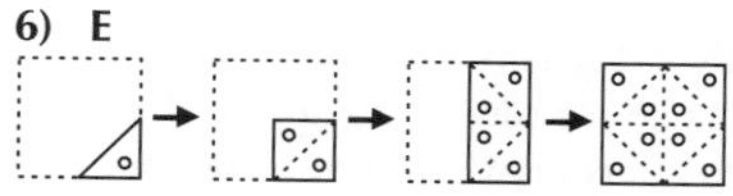

7) D

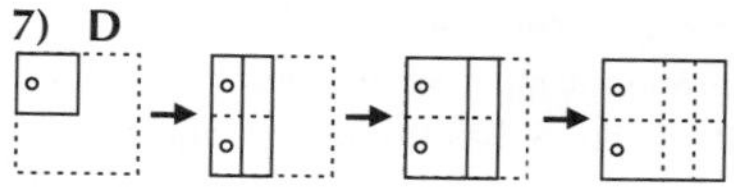

8) C

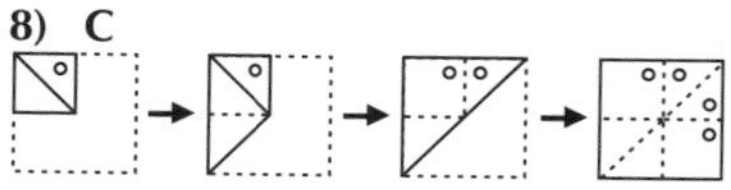

9) A

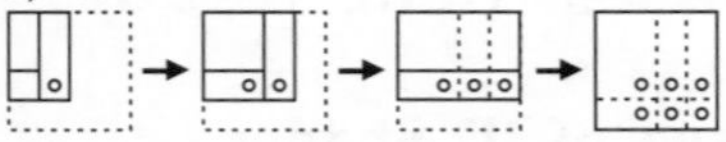

10) D

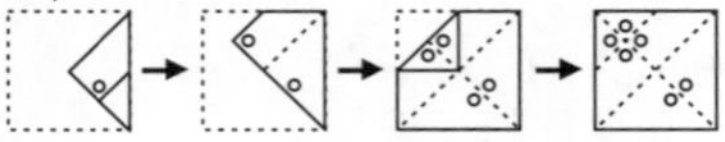

Section 3 — 3D Rotation

1) E
Shape E has been rotated 90 degrees clockwise in the plane of the page.

2) A
Shape A has been rotated 90 degrees anticlockwise in the plane of the page.

3) C
Shape C has been rotated 90 degrees away from you, top-to-bottom. It has then been rotated 90 degrees clockwise in the plane of the page.

4) F
Shape F has been rotated 90 degrees anticlockwise in the plane of the page. It has then been rotated 90 degrees left-to-right.

5) E
Shape E has been rotated 90 degrees clockwise in the plane of the page.

6) D
Shape D has been rotated 180 degrees left-to-right.

7) B
Shape B has been rotated 90 degrees towards you, top-to-bottom.

8) F
Shape F has been rotated 90 degrees towards you, top-to-bottom. It has then been rotated 90 degrees clockwise in the plane of the page.

9) C
Shape C has been rotated 90 degrees away from you, top-to-bottom. It has then been rotated 90 degrees right-to-left.

10) A
Shape A has been rotated 180 degrees in the plane of the page.

Section 4 — Cubes and Nets

1) D
Option A is ruled out because the cube face with the spiral and the cube face with the black dot must be on opposite sides. Option B is ruled out because the cube face with the star and the black cube face must be on opposite sides. Option C is ruled out because the net doesn't have two identical faces. Option E is ruled out because there is no black pentagon on the net.

2) A
Option B is ruled out because the cube face with the three thin lines and the cube face with the four-way arrow must be on opposite sides. Option C is ruled out because the white cube face and the cube face with the black zig-zag must be on opposite sides. Option D is ruled out because the cube face with the thin lines and the cube face with the star must be on opposite sides. Option E is ruled out because there is no black rectangle on the net.

3) A
Option B is ruled out because the net doesn't have two identical faces. Option C is ruled out because the cube face with the letter N and the cube face with the grey bars must be on opposite sides. Option D is ruled out because the grey cube face and the cube face with the circle with a line through it must be on opposite sides. Option E is ruled out because the letter N has the wrong rotation.

4) E
Option A is ruled out because the face with the ellipse is never above the 'top' of the grey mushroom shape. Option B is ruled out because the black triangle should be opposite either the face with the letter E or the grey mushroom shape, so these three faces cannot be seen together. Option C is ruled out because the grey mushroom shape has the wrong rotation. Option D is ruled out because the ellipse and the hatched face must be on opposite sides.

5) B
Option A is ruled out because the face with the heart and the face with the hexagon and circle must be on opposite sides. Option C is ruled out because the net doesn't have two identical faces. Option D is ruled out because the cube face with the three circles and the cube face with the loop must be on opposite sides. Option E is ruled out because the face with the curved black shape and the black face must be on opposite sides.

6) A
Option B is ruled out because the dotted cube face and the cube face with the eye shape must be on opposite sides. Option C is ruled out because the cube face with the triangle and the cube face with the square in the middle must be on opposite sides. Option D is ruled out because the grey cube face and the cube face with the cross must be on opposite sides. Option E is ruled out because if the face with the triangle is on the front and the face with the cross is on the top, then the face with the eye shape should be on the right.

7) B
Options A and C are ruled out because the grey cube face and the cube face with the number 1 must be on opposite sides. Option D is ruled out because the 'handle' of the racquet shape must point towards the cube face with the overlapping circles. Option E is ruled out because if the white face is on the front and the number 1 is on the top, then the black arrow would be on the left.

8) E
Option A is ruled out because the face with the three short black lines does not appear twice on the net. Option B is ruled out because the face with the triangle has the wrong rotation. Option C is ruled out because the face with the circle and the face with the two pentagons should be on opposite sides. Option D is ruled out because the white half of the circle must be closest to the cube face with three short lines.

Section 5 — Hidden Shape

1) E

2) B

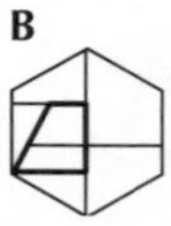

3) E

4) A

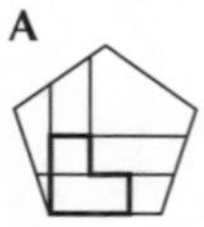

5) C

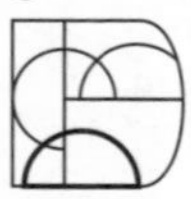

6) B

7) A

8) B

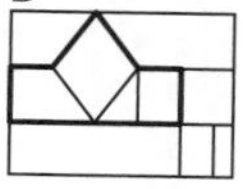

9) E

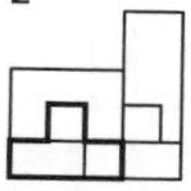

10) C

Section 6 — Connecting Shapes

1) B
Options A and D are ruled out because the wrong side of the larger triangle is connected to the rectangle. Option C is ruled out because the wrong side of the small triangle is connected to the rectangle. Option E is ruled out because both triangles are connected to the wrong sides of the rectangle.

2) A
Options B and E are ruled out because the rectangle is connected to the wrong side of the C-shape. Option C is ruled out because the wrong side of the trapezium is connected to the C-shape. Option D is ruled out because the rectangle and the trapezium are connected to the wrong sides of the C-shape.

3) E
Option A is ruled out because the square is connected to the wrong side of the T-shape. Option B is ruled out because the wrong side of the trapezium is connected to the T-shape. Option C is ruled out because the trapezium is connected to the wrong side of the T-shape. Option D is ruled out because the square and the trapezium are connected to the wrong sides of the T-shape.

4) A
Option B is ruled out because the wrong side of the triangle is connected to the large shape. Options C and E are ruled out because the wrong side of the five-sided shape is connected to the large shape. Option D is ruled out because the five-sided shape and the triangle are connected to the wrong sides of the large shape.

5) C
Option A is ruled out because the wrong side of the trapezium is connected to the arrow shape. Option B is ruled out because the trapezium and the pentagon are connected to the wrong sides of the arrow shape. Option D is ruled out because the pentagon is connected to the wrong side of the arrow shape. Option E is ruled out because the pentagon should be connected to the arrow shape.

6) D
Option A is ruled out because the square is connected to the wrong side of the large shape. Option B is ruled out because the square and the rectangle are connected to the wrong sides of the large shape. Options C and E are ruled out because the rectangle is connected to the wrong side of the large shape.

7) E
Options A and D are ruled out because the wrong side of the five-sided shape is connected to the arrow. Option B is ruled out because the five-sided shape is connected to the wrong side of the arrow. Option C is ruled out because the semi-circle is connected to the wrong side of the arrow.

8) C
Option A is ruled out because the small triangle is connected to the wrong side of the L-shape. Option B is ruled out because the large triangle is connected to the wrong side of the L-shape. Option D is ruled out because the wrong side of the large triangle is connected to the L-shape. Option E is ruled out because both triangles are connected to the wrong sides of the L-shape.

9) B
Option A is ruled out because the wrong side of the triangle is connected to the large shape. Option C is ruled out because the wrong side of the parallelogram is connected to the large shape. Option D is ruled out because the triangle and the parallelogram are connected to the wrong sides of the large shape. Option E is ruled out because the parallelogram is connected to the wrong side of the large shape.

10) B
Options A and C are ruled out because the arrow is connected to the wrong side of the star shape. Option D is ruled out because the square and the arrow are connected to the wrong sides of the star shape. Option E is ruled out because the square is connected to the wrong side of the star shape.

Progress Chart

Use this chart to keep track of your scores for the Assessment Tests.

You can do each test more than once — download extra answer sheets from cgpbooks.co.uk/11plus/answer-sheets or scan the QR code on the right.

Answer Sheets

	First Go	Second Go	Third Go
Test 1	Date: Score:	Date: Score:	Date: Score:
Test 2	Date: Score:	Date: Score:	Date: Score:
Test 3	Date: Score:	Date: Score:	Date: Score:
Test 4	Date: Score:	Date: Score:	Date: Score:
Test 5	Date: Score:	Date: Score:	Date: Score:
Test 6	Date: Score:	Date: Score:	Date: Score:

Look back at your scores once you've done all the Assessment Tests.
Each test is out of 56 marks.

Work out which kind of mark you scored most often:

0-33 marks — Go back to basics and work on your question technique.

34-47 marks — You're nearly there — go back over the questions you found tricky.

48-56 marks — You're a Non-Verbal Reasoning star.